JESUS IS JEWISH

By

TYRONE NICHOLS

Copyright © 2023

All Rights Reserved

No part of this publication may be reproduced, stored in a retrieval system, or transmitted in any form or by any means, electronic, mechanical, photocopying, recording or otherwise without prior permission of the publisher or in accordance with the provisions of the Copyright, Designs and Patents Act 1988.

ISBN: 978-1960116567

Dedication

In honor of those who have influenced my journey toward deeper understanding and appreciation of my faith, I offer my heartfelt gratitude.

In loving memory of Pastor Ray Bentley, who profoundly influenced me with his steadfast faith and resolve in exploring the Jewishness of Jesus Christ and expressing his compassion for all. My deepest gratitude.

To Boaz Michael, whose vision and steadfast leadership of the First Fruits of Zion ministry served as a constant source of inspiration to me. Your dedication to reconciling disciples with God's prophetic promises to Israel have contributed greatly to my own personal growth and spiritual journey.

To D. Thomas Lancaster, whose fearless commitment to teaching and writing about the Jewishness of Jesus impacted my life in immeasurable ways. Your passion and devotion to this important subject ignited a flame in my heart that will forever burn bright.

To Rey Luque, through your incredible ability, you revealed the connection between the teachings of the Talmud and Chassidic sages to the words, life, and teaching of Yeshua of Nazareth. Your insights helped me see the Messiah with new eyes and deepened my appreciation for the richness and depth of our heritage.

To my parents Rle and Fern Nichols, whose lives are shining examples of faithfulness and devotion to Jesus. Your firm commitment to his call is a beacon of hope and inspiration to us all. Through your loyalty to the King and to one another, you held our family together and showed us the true meaning of love. You passed down to us a legacy of faith and showed us the power of prayer. Thank you for your incredible example.

To my cherished son J.T. Nichols, who values truth and freedom with a spirit of unwavering determination. May you continue to seek after HaShem and walk boldly in his ways as a disciple of Yeshua of Nazareth. Hold fast to wisdom as she will be your best friend. Your love and light shine brightly in this world. You are a gift beyond measure.

To my beloved wife Patti Nichols, my partner in every sense of the word on this journey through life. Your unwavering support and willingness to tackle tough and complex issues with courage and strength have been a true blessing. I am eternally grateful for your love, companionship, and steadfast commitment to our shared faith.

Acknowledgment

I am humbled and grateful for the invaluable contributions of those who have helped shape and refine this book. Your dedication and commitment to this project inspire me.

To Ruth Sabin, who believed in the potential of this book from the very beginning and devoted countless hours to editing and refining each sentence. Your keen eye and encouraging support have helped me find my voice and tell my story with clarity and grace. I cannot thank you enough.

Mary Pat Huxley, God brought you into this project when I needed you most. Your exceptional expertise, amazing editing skills, sharp intellect, and profound understanding of the subject matter were nothing short of a miracle. Without your invaluable contributions, I wouldn't have made it to the finish line. I cannot thank you enough!

To my beloved wife Patti Nichols, whose late nights of editing, insightful discussions and careful attention to detail have been indispensable to the development of this book. Your consistent support, encouragement and love are evident on every page. Your contributions have made this book what it is today, and I am forever grateful.

To every author, academician, pastor, and rabbi whose words and convictions upon which I have drawn in this book, I offer my deepest appreciation. Your courage to share your insights and knowledge with the world paved the way for my own understanding and deeper relationship with God. I am humbled and grateful for the invaluable contributions you have made to my life and to the lives of countless others impacted by your wisdom and faithfulness.

May God bless each of you richly and reward you in this life and the life to come.

About the Author

Meet Tyrone Nichols, a dedicated scholar deeply invested in the historical fact that Jesus is Jewish. Undergirded by his Master of Divinity from The King's University, Tyrone's extensive research and teachings position him as a distinguished authority on theology, particularly regarding the Jewish foundations of Christianity.

In his book, Jesus is Jewish, Ty delves into the often-overlooked identity of Jesus Christ, an identity obscured and masked by various historical, cultural, and theological narratives through millennia. Drawing on ancient manuscripts, historical contexts, and an incisive understanding of the cultural tapestry of the time, Tyrone offers readers a unique lens to rediscover Jesus. His expertise illuminates Jesus's Jewish heritage, and through his guidance, readers discern the interwoven threads of history, tradition, and faith that come together to reveal Yeshua of Nazareth.

Ty's diverse background encompasses not only academic pursuits but also high school and collegiate coaching, writing, and public speaking engagements. This rich tapestry of experiences fine-tunes his capabilities as a compelling communicator.

Beyond his written works, Tyrone extends his exploration of Scriptures through a home fellowship, welcoming other truth-seekers. His talent for meaningful conversation is further reflected in his blog and podcast, "Poignant Perspective" (tynichols.substack.com), where he offers discerning viewpoints on various topics including America, faith, finance, and the Bible.

Journey with Tyrone as he delves into the Jewish roots of Christianity and shares a captivating cultural narrative. As he guides you, his warmth and authority combine to make readers feel as though they are embarking on a personal voyage with a well-versed confidant, eager to shed light on the undeniable truth that Jesus is Jewish.

Table of Contents

Dedication iii

Acknowledgment v

About the Author vii

Introduction 1

Chapter 1 The Power of Paradigms 7

Chapter 2 Setting the Foundation 15

Chapter 3 God Does Not Lie, Right? 23

Chapter 4 The Covenants 38

Chapter 5 The Covenants - Part Two 55

Chapter 6 The Parting of the Ways - Part 1 What Really Happened? 71

Chapter 7 The Parting of the Ways - Part 2 What Really Happened? 85

Chapter 8 The Parting of the Ways - Part 3 What Really Happened? 101

Chapter 9 The Parting of the Ways - Part 4 What Really Happened? 120

Chapter 10 When Matthew Used the Word "Church," What Did He Mean? 131

Chapter 11 The Apostle Paul or Rabbi Shaul? Part 1 146

Chapter 12 The Apostle Paul or Rabbi Shaul? Part 2 174

Chapter 13 Jesus Is Jewish 208

Chapter 14 Why It Matters – Dismantling Replacement Theology 247

Chapter 15 Why It Matters – Course Correction 262

Chapter 16 Why It Matters – Restoring Israel to Her Rightful Place 280

Appendix A 300

Appendix B 301

Appendix C 303

Appendix D 308

Bibliography 311

Books 311

PDF 319

DVD 321

End Notes 322

JESUS IS JEWISH

Introduction

Before 2008, nothing in my evangelical Christian life seemed out of order. I loved going to church, attending Bible studies and life groups, journaled in my prayer diary, and strove to be more like Jesus by loving God and people. This didn't mean that my life was perfect. I wasn't free from trials, battled sin like every other believer in God, worked on my marriage, as most people do. I, too, "toiled under the sun."

At the time, if you asked me to describe my Christian faith, my answer would have been something like: "I believe that Jesus is the savior of the world, he died on the cross for my sins, he rose from the dead three days later and he now sits at the right hand of God in the heavens, waiting for a command from his Father to return to the earth to set up his millennial kingdom. I need a savior because every human has sinned (we cannot help that we are born with a sinful nature, according to Calvin) [1] and that sin separates me from God. Instead of dying for my sins, which would be the just penalty as prescribed by God, Jesus took my place on the cross and paid the price for me. The Bible says, "For God so loved the world that He sent His only begotten Son, that whosoever should believe on Him shall not perish but have everlasting life." (John 3:16) In other words, I believed in Jesus, prayed the salvation prayer,[2] and followed him as best I could. I was constantly comforted that I would one day see him face-to-face and live in the afterlife, forever, with him.

This, in a very simplified and truthful way, was my theology. I was "saved." Jesus was the answer and the focal point of my Christian life. My sins were paid for...all of them. On Billy Graham's website, one of the most famous evangelical Christians of all time, we find the following: "One of the Bible's greatest truths is that Christ died to take away all our sins, not just part of them, but all of them: past, present, and future."[3]

This understanding of Scripture allowed me to relax when it came to putting pressure on myself to live a good life. A little sin here, a little sin there (even a big one now and then), ultimately didn't matter that much because a) I had prayed the prayer and b) Christ died for all my sins...even the ones I hadn't committed yet. Don't get me wrong: I wanted to be like Jesus because I loved him and was loyal to him, especially considering all that he had done for me. Who wouldn't be loyal to the man who literally sacrificed his life for you? As much as I could, without pressure, I tried to live a good life, not because it saved me, but out of love and fidelity to Jesus. However, I always knew in the back of my mind that if I did sin, I would be okay. My ticket on the train to heaven had been punched!

JESUS IS JEWISH

My world turned upside-down in 2008 when the stock market crashed. At the time, I invested in the stock market and real estate, spoke, and taught around the country on the merits of technical analysis. I did well for myself...until all of it vanished. The economic turmoil that descended on the globe like a plague in September 2008 crushed me. I lost investments, friends, house, employment...almost everything. As reality began to sink in, I clearly remember one morning not being able to get out of bed. Fear, shock, depression, anxiety, stress, and panic pressed upon me so hard that I could not get up. If it were not for my wife's encouraging words and comfort, I don't know what would have happened to me. I was in a dark, dark place.

My wife and I had saved up enough to live for about a year, but if things didn't change, we would run completely out of money. Up until this point in my life, I was the kind of guy who acted first and prayed second, hoping that God would bless my endeavors. (In other words, I would make plans to be successful, and after I began to execute my plan, I would pray about it.) This was not a great recipe for success.

However, this time was different. I told Patti that I wasn't going to do a thing to look for work. I wasn't going to make a phone call, ask a friend, network, or reach out for help until I literally "heard" from God. I was tired of playing the "game" of Christianity and needed to hear a bona fide voice from Heaven. I needed to know God was real, and that He not only saves people in the Bible but also saves people like me. To give Him what I considered to be the maximum amount of room to maneuver in my life and to clear out any psychological clutter that might be blocking His message, I determined to hike the hills of Poway, California, each day, memorize scripture, and wait for the audible voice of God. Thankfully Patti was supportive, so that's exactly what I did.

I fell in love with my daily routine: I'd get up in the morning, read my Bible with a nice warm cup of coffee, have a little breakfast, put on my hiking boots, grab my little "memorize Scripture book," and head into the back hills for hours on end. I prayed, talked, cried, and laughed with God. In the back of my mind, I knew our bank account dwindled and I could see that soon, we'd be broke. I held to my conviction to wait for His leading, His voice, or a clear sign from Heaven, despite being able to see the proverbial financial cliff.

After several months of this, I came across a Scripture verse that stopped me in my tracks. It read, "Stand at the crossroads and look; ask for the ancient paths, ask where the good way is, and walk in it, and then you will find rest for your souls." (Jeremiah 6:16)

Rest for my soul.

JESUS IS JEWISH

That's exactly what I wanted! I felt as if God gave me my first order of business, my first directive, but it puzzled me. I repeated to myself: Stand and look, ask for the ancient paths, ask where the good way is and walk in it. Hmmm. I asked out loud, "The ancient path? Isn't Christianity ancient? Isn't Jesus the good way? Aren't I already walking in it?" It's difficult to explain the impression that came over me when I asked those questions, so let me just recount it as best I can: He answered with a smiling "No."

This was not the answer I anticipated. For the next several weeks, I chewed and chewed on this verse. I turned it upside down, inside out, investigated and considered it from every angle imaginable. On one of my afternoon hikes, as I digested what it means to walk on a path more ancient than Christianity, I experienced another...impression. I call them impressions because I honestly don't know what else to call them.

Ahead of me on the trail, Jesus cooked a fish over a fire. Not literally, of course, but I could see him. I knew it was Jesus. He motioned for me to come to sit with him. Gently, I heard him say, "I'd like to introduce myself to you."

"I know who you are. You are Jesus, my King," my voice quivered.

TYRONE NICHOLS

"Yes," he said, "I am your King, and you know me as Jesus, but I'd like to introduce you to who I really am." He smiled.

"I don't understand," my voice low.

"My name is Yeshua."

JESUS IS JEWISH

Chapter 1

The Power of Paradigms

Interpreting the Bible is a difficult task. We bring our past, our preconceived notions, our already-formed theology, our cultural blind spots, our social standing, our gender, our political views, and many other influences into our interpretation of the Bible. This doesn't imply that the meaning of the text depends on its reader; on the contrary, the author's intended meaning remains constant. The meaning of the text does depend on many factors, one of which is the theological paradigm of the reader that can influence interpretation. How a reader understands the text can differ greatly from person to person.

I didn't realize this in general, and about myself in particular. I'd never studied the idea or considered the notion that I might be "missing" or "misreading" the Bible based on my theological paradigm.

Historian Thomas Kuhn gave the term its modern-day meaning when he wrote his 1962 book *The Structure of Scientific Revolutions*. He describes paradigms as "universally recognized scientific achievements that, for a time, provide model problems and solutions for a community of practitioners."[4] In other words, paradigms define learning models, and the academic world relies on them.

According to Dictionary.com, a paradigm is "a framework containing the basic assumptions, ways of thinking, and methodology that members of a scientific community (or any community) commonly accept." We're all born into a paradigm, a way of seeing the world through various cultural, religious (or lack thereof), social, gender, and political lenses.

Look at the following pictures. Your brain will naturally see one picture while another picture is "hidden," in the sense that you don't see it right away. This can help show a paradigm you already have. The two pictures, or views, are there; you'll usually see only one until you "adjust" your paradigm. Remember to record which image you see first, then record your answers.

JESUS IS JEWISH

TYRONE NICHOLS

JESUS IS JEWISH

1) Do you see an old woman or young one?
2) Do you see a young woman or a saxophone player?
3) Do you see a young woman's face or flowers?
4) Do you see a face or the word "liar"?
5) Do you see a candlestick or two people facing each other?

Either answer is correct in this exercise. I use it to point out that your brain "sees" what it does based on your most accessible paradigm. To see the "hidden picture," you must focus intently on it. You must tell your brain to set aside your current picture or "paradigm" so you can see the other. For some, seeing both pictures is simple; for others, it's difficult. If seeing both pictures is hard, you must want to see them. If you are comfortable with only seeing one image and have no desire to see the other, you won't.

How does this exercise help us? If you come from a Christian background like I have, seeing Jesus as Yeshua-the-Torah-Observant-Jew from Nazareth is hard. The Torah-observant Jew is 100% portrayed within the pages of the New Testament, yet you need diligence and hard work to see him.

You may ask, "Why does it matter? Why do I need to see Jesus as a Jew?" In answer to that, let me quote author and film writer Bernard Starr, who did extensive research on Jesus. In his article "Some People Still Don't Know That Jesus Is Jewish," he writes, "When I tell people that I've written extensively about the 'Jewish Jesus,' they frequently say, 'but everyone knows that Jesus was Jewish.' It would seem so. But dig deeper and you will find what I discovered in interviewing Christians and Jews: Most people mean that Jesus used to be Jewish."[5] To see that Jesus not only was, but is, Jewish, we must be willing to examine a new paradigm, to look intently at the picture presented to us in the Bible to see the Jewish, Torah-observant man from Nazareth.

JESUS IS JEWISH

"So, Jesus was a Jew, and I'm going to read the rest of your book to find that out. Fine, but he still started Christianity, right?"

That question highlights your paradigm. A myriad of reasons exists as to why you might think that Jesus abandoned being a Jew and started a new religion called Christianity. We'll look at many of these reasons in the following pages; however, none of them are biblical. The Scriptures never tell us that Jesus came to start a new religion, or that he met in a church, or that he even started the church. He didn't initiate a Catholic papal system or leave marching orders for the institution called "Universal Christianity." Jesus wasn't a Christian. The above statements may cause your eyebrows to rise. It may cause cognitive dissonance, "the state of having inconsistent thoughts, beliefs, or attitudes, a mental discomfort that comes from holding onto two or more conflicting attitudes or beliefs."[6] Another definition to assist your understanding comes from Psychology Today, which reads, "The theory of cognitive dissonance helps explain the lengths to which people sometimes go to account for thoughts, words, and behaviors that seem to clash."[7]

I consider myself a disciple of Jesus. Yet, I worship and follow him inside of an institutional framework he never established.

How did that happen?

TYRONE NICHOLS

In the rest of this book, I take you on a journey to figure this out, explain how I resolved my own cognitive dissonance and show you how the concealed became revealed.

Jesus is Jewish.

JESUS IS JEWISH

Chapter 2

Setting the Foundation

Resolving cognitive dissonance can become straightforward if you take an honest look at *why* you believe what you believe.

Two foundational precepts live within Christendom; the first – God doesn't lie and the second – He doesn't change. I hold to these beliefs, as do most practicing Christians. Numbers 23:19 tells us that "God is not human, that he should lie, not a human being, that He should change His mind. Does He speak and not act? Does He not promise and fulfill?"

Simple. God doesn't lie. He doesn't change.

We can take His promises to the bank. They are "as good as gold," you might say, guaranteed and backed by Heaven's full weight and authority. All of God's promises, no matter what they are and no matter to whom they are given, will happen as stated.

God gave promises to Abraham and told him that these would be *everlasting* for him and his descendants. Most of Universal Christendom teaches that these promises no longer apply to Abraham and his descendants but are now only for those in the Church.[8]

TYRONE NICHOLS

I couldn't understand why God would go back on His promises to Abraham and give them to the "Church." I reasoned that if the Church had it right and God went back on His word to Abraham, what would keep Him from going back on His word to me as a member of the Church and believer in Jesus?

Let's start our exploratory journey with the covenant promises God made with Abraham. Genesis 17:7 reads, "I am establishing my covenant between me and you, along with your descendants after you, *generation after generation, as an everlasting covenant, to be God for you and your descendants after you.*" Last time I checked, "everlasting" meant everlasting. To whom were the promises made? "To you (Abraham) and to your descendants (offspring) after you." If a person had Abraham as his or her biological ancestor, these promises apply that person, too.

My question became, "Why isn't God's promise to Abraham still in effect today?" I'd been taught that this promise no longer applied to Abraham's descendants and now only applied to the Church (as in those who believe in Jesus). "If it were not in effect and had been given over to the Church, why did God break His promise? Did God lie to Abraham? Did God change His mind?"

That's cognitive dissonance for me.

JESUS IS JEWISH

If you're like me and want questions like this and others answered, you've found the right book.

I know brave souls who look for the truth, who want to know exactly what the Bible says and follow it to the best of their ability. If you're hungry for deep truth, and if you're willing to put theological tenants and dogmas on the table and evaluate beliefs and doctrines in detail regardless of where it might lead, then you're in the right place. I welcome you to come on this journey with me.

Fair warning; this exploration of truth isn't easy. Seeing the "hidden picture" takes time. You will be challenged, pushed, and confronted. If you stay with me, you will see the Bible and Jesus in ways you never dreamed possible. He will become more real to you than ever. The narrative of the Bible will sing from Genesis to Revelation with consistent anthem and resonating harmonies like you've never heard. God's symphony of truth will sound like the orchestra of heaven.

"I'm in! So where do we start?"

Great!

First, you and I need to be willing to re-examine our current paradigms. You may not know what yours is yet. Willingness is all you need at this point. A heart attitude that says, "Whatever I believe that I find to be untrue, I will examine carefully and decide along my journey what to act upon" is enough for now.

Second, I will give you initial ideas to help uncover your theological paradigm – yes, you have one! – and its parameters.

Third, *anachronism* is a word with which you need to familiarize yourself. It denotes something that is out of place in terms of chronology and out of synchrony with time. In recent decades, academic scholarship turned its attention to re-thinking the vocabulary we use in our study and teaching of Scripture. In her work *Mandatory Retirement: Ideas in the Study of Christian Origins Whose Time Has Come to Go,* Paula Fredriksen writes, "…terms serve scholars of ancient Christianity both as kind of academic shorthand and as interpretive concepts. They lead us down a path of anachronism and abstraction,[9] ultimately obscuring the lives and concerns of the ancient people whom we seek to understand."[10]

Anachronistic biblical scholarship infects the theology of Western Christianity and has done so for almost two millennia. Only in recent years has the world of theological academia begun to identify and remove this infection from the body of Western biblical hermeneutics. (Note: Hermeneutics is the theory and methodology of interpretation.)

JESUS IS JEWISH

Anachronistic biblical scholarship took modern-day terms and laid them over first-century words and concepts. This practice hid the text's original meaning and kept it veiled from the 21st-century reader.

For example, Jesus tells Peter in Matthew 16:19, "I will give you the keys to the kingdom of heaven; whatever you bind on earth will be bound in heaven, and whatever you loose on earth, will be loosed in heaven." There are various interpretations of this verse in Universal Christendom, depending on the denomination.

For instance, charismatic Christians understand the power to bind and loose as the power to bind evil spirits.[11] The Catholic Church teaches that this verse means "whomever you exclude from your communion, will be excluded from communion with God; whomever you receive anew into your communion, God will welcome back into His. Reconciliation with the church is inseparable from reconciliation with God."[12]

One problem arises with these and many other Universal Christian explanations. They're not true. They're derived from the practice of anachronistic biblical scholarship.

"What did Jesus mean?"

To "bind" and to "loose" are common rabbinic terms used in

the religious literature of that era. To "bind" means to forbid, and to "loose" means to permit:

> When the rabbis needed to decide an issue of *Halachah* (Jewish law), they argued whether to "bind" (asar, אסר) or to "loose" (hittir, התיר) a particular act or deed. To "bind" means to forbid; to "loose" means to permit…The Torah vested the power to bind (forbid) and loose (permit) in the Sanhedrin, the priesthood, and judges over Israel.[13]

Jesus gave Peter the power to "bind" or "loose" issues of *halachah* (Jewish law) for his newly forming assembly within Judaism. *That's the meaning.* Peter led the nascent movement of Jesus followers through some very difficult situations.[14] Jesus's proclamation empowered Peter to "bind" (forbid) and "loose" (permit) within the community of Jesus, which connected to greater Israel at that time. Jesus gave him the "keys to the Kingdom" to be able to lead and legally rule on matters of Torah and life for the newly forming group of Jesus followers.

Contemporary interpretations imposed on "bind" and "loose" in Biblical texts constitutes anachronistic scholarship and applies a present-day lens on the authority given to Peter to preside over legal matters of the Torah. I discovered throughout my research that most Bible versions and numerous Christian

JESUS IS JEWISH

commentaries contain these anachronistic distortions. Such distortions skew a person's theological perspective and can lead to misinformation, division, and confusion.

I came to an obvious conclusion. To discover the Jewish Jesus and understand the Bible in its own context, I needed to reach back in time and do my best to discover a reading of the biblical text that reflected the authors' thinking *in their setting and in their time.* Let's call this their *semantic framework*. I needed to orient my sematic framework to match theirs, which is an "Ancient Near Eastern, Mediterranean, Hebraic structure. In this space, perception is reconfigured, vision 're-visioned,' and whatever is focused on within that space is seen and understood in the landscape we have entered and which encloses us."[15]

Our tool belt full of 21st-century terms and ideas, which carry with them concepts and notions that are only relevant in our "futuristic" structure relative to the first century, must be left in the present day. We must replace this 21st-century toolbelt with devices and instruments that would serve a first-century builder constructing a first-century semantic framework.

I hope that doesn't sound easy.

It's not. It takes a lot of work.

TYRONE NICHOLS

That is where we bravely head. To the best of our ability, we'll build an understanding that allows us to see the world and Scripture from a first century Jewish paradigm.

As we do this, you will begin to see the "hidden picture" that was always there, always true, yet veiled due to a paradigm and worldview you didn't even know you had.

I didn't.

JESUS IS JEWISH

Chapter 3
God Does Not Lie, Right?

Let's resolve our cognitive dissonance around God's promise to Abraham because it's important. After reading Genesis 17:7, three questions stared back at me from my study journal:

Is God's promise to Abraham still in effect?

If so, why?

If not, did God lie to Abraham?

Understanding God's relationship with Abraham is vital to unlocking the rest of the Bible's story. At the time, I didn't know that these answers would become foundational to my journey but, without equivocation, they are.

In history, seven dynasties of Egypt's Old Kingdom had come and gone before Abraham. By his day, circa 2700 B.C.E., people considered the Epic of Gilgamesh as ancient lore. Human history wrote thousands of courageous tales and witnessed countless heroes and villains. It saw the fall of Adam and Eve, worldwide evil, the flood, the rebirth of humanity, and the tower of Babel.

From this history and within a polytheistic culture, Abraham found the One True God. Amazing.

In Genesis Chapter 12, God made promises with Abraham which were elaborated further in Genesis 15. God asked Abraham to count the stars and promised him descendants as numerous as the stars. Abraham's faith in God's promise was counted as righteousness. In Genesis 17, we learn about the duration of God's promise. Verses 7 and 8 state:

> And I will establish My covenant between Me and you and your seed after you in their generations for an *everlasting* covenant, to be a God unto you and to your seed after you.

> And I will give unto you and to your seed after you the land wherein you are a stranger, all the land of Canaan, for an *everlasting* possession; and I will be their God. [Italics mine]

Here we have the first mention that God's promises to Abraham are everlasting. Circumcision is the sign of the everlasting covenant between God, Abraham, and his descendants. We read in verses 11 – 13:

> And you shall circumcise the flesh of your foreskin, and it shall be a token of the covenant between Me

JESUS IS JEWISH

and you. And he that is eight days old shall be circumcised among you, every man-child in your generations, he that is born in the house or bought with money from any stranger who is not of your seed. He that is born in your house, and he that is bought with your money must be circumcised, and My covenant shall be in your flesh for an *everlasting* covenant. [Italics mine]

The *everlasting* covenant between God and Abraham is in the flesh of every male in the house of Abraham (both at that time and his future progeny), as well as any stranger who lives among his descendants, as a constant reminder of the *everlasting* nature of this relationship.

The prophet Isaiah confirmed these forever promises. He wrote in Chapter 49 of his book in verse 9, "You (Israel) whom I have taken from the ends of the earth and called from its remotest parts and said to you, 'You (Israel) are My servant, I have chosen you *and not rejected you.*'" [Italics mine] God is quite clear that even in Israel's rebellion, He has not rejected them. Therefore, they remain His people to this day.

"Where did the idea come from that the members of the Church are now the people of God, rather than the Jews?"

TYRONE NICHOLS

Good question.

Many throughout Christendom's history argued that Israel's catastrophes witness against her. They claim she forfeited her right to be the covenantal chosen people of God. They use her inability or unwillingness to consistently and properly follow the stipulations outlined in the covenant between God and Israel at Mt. Sinai as a reason for God's rejection of them. The coup de gras in this declaration states that because the Jews killed the Messiah (Jesus), they forever lost their status as God's partners. Christendom asserts that God abandoned Israel and decided to create for Himself a new people group of covenant partners...the Christians, or the Church.

Theologians name this idea "Replacement Theology" or "supersessionism," meaning that the Church replaced, or superseded, Judaism. The question for us is, "Are they right?" If passages in the Bible exist that show God going back on his word to Abraham, or maybe a prophecy or two that predict the emergence of a new people of God, then the supersessionist camp might have a point. This dogmatic understanding of Scripture has a problem; such a premise can't be found anywhere in the Old Testament or anywhere in the New Testament.

Even the *possibility* of God rejecting His people isn't written in the covenant agreement between Israel and God or the covenant

JESUS IS JEWISH

promises between God and Abraham. The Bible doesn't contain a proclamation by God that says, "If you (Israel) do not follow my laws, I will replace you with a new group of people and cast you aside."

What *do* we find?

Throughout the Bible, God only guarantees Israel punishment for lack of obedience, followed by promises of redemption, rescue, and hope, even if she decides to be unfaithful.[16]

Let's for a moment assume that Replacement Theology is correct, and that God has replaced Israel with the "church." If so, then the everlasting promises He made to Abraham are *not everlasting*, making God a liar.

"Not good."

I agree. Not good.

We need to figure out how Universal Christendom came up with the idea that God abandoned Israel. That's the only way we will be able to resolve our cognitive dissonance regarding God's promise to Abraham.

After all, God doesn't lie, right?

TYRONE NICHOLS

An interesting point to consider about God and His relationship with Abraham and his descendants is this: in the Old Testament God is most often referred to as the God of Abraham, Isaac, and Jacob. The primary relationship throughout the entire Bible in which God chose to reveal Himself is with Israel. He also *identifies* Himself by this same title. In Genesis 50:24, Joseph reminds his sons that God will bring them out of Egypt and into the land God swore to give to Abraham, Isaac, and Jacob. In Exodus 3:6, God identifies Himself as "the God of Abraham, Isaac and Jacob." He later tells Moses to tell the people of Israel that He is "The God of Abraham, Isaac, and Jacob." (Exodus 3:15-16)

Although it should be obvious that God wanted and continues to require recognition as the covenant-keeping God of Abraham and his descendants, somehow, it's not obvious to people who hold to a Replacement Theology paradigm. Jesus in the New Testament also identifies God as the God of Abraham, Isaac, and Jacob. In Matthew 22:32, Jesus quotes the Father from Exodus, "I am the God of Abraham, and the God of Isaac, and the God of Jacob. God is not the God of the dead, but of the living." (See also see Mark 12:26, Luke 13:28, Luke 20:37, Acts 3:13 and Acts 7:32.) Even a cursory study of this title throughout Scripture confirms that this is how God desires to be identified.

Yet, God isn't acknowledged in such a way in Christian

JESUS IS JEWISH

creeds. The first time I realized that Christian creeds fail this acknowledgment, I said to myself, "No way!" I decided it best to double-check.

I found that every major ancient Christian creed, from the Apostles' Creed to the Nicene Creed, from the Chalcedonian Creed to the Athanasian Creed, God is not even once referred to as the God of Abraham, Isaac, and Jacob. And not even the God of Abraham! I thought, "Surely this mistake was corrected by modern Protestant churches like mine."

Nope.

Here is a link to the American Baptist statement of belief page: https://www.abaptist.org/beliefs. Can you find any reference to God using this title? Here is another link to the Apostles' Creed, used by the Westminster Presbyterian Church: http://wpcbryan.org/what-we-believe/apostles- creed/.

Do you see it? Here is a final link to the Lutheran use of the Three Ecumenical Creeds: http://els.org/beliefs/the-three-ecumenical-creeds- 2/. Again, God is not recognized as the God of Abraham, Isaac, and Jacob.

"How can this be?"

TYRONE NICHOLS

Now that, my fellow journeyman, is another great question. It's the question that led me to pursue my Master of Divinity at The King's University with an emphasis on Messianic Judaism. The idea astonished me that through all of Christendom's history, not one major denomination *ever* identified God in their credal statements as the God of Abraham, Isaac, and Jacob.

Before I tell you what I found out, I must introduce you to a term, "canonical narrative," that theologians use. "A canonical narrative is an interpretive instrument that provides a framework for reading the Christian Bible as a theological narrative unity...it reflects a fundamental decision about how the Bible 'hangs together' as a whole."[17]

Whether you realize it or not, you understand the Bible according to your *pre-programmed canonical narrative* (similar to your pre-programmed worldview paradigm). In truth, differences between a Christian canonical narrative and a biblical canonical narrative do exist. Once you grasp the ideas I present in this book, your pre-programmed Universal Christian narrative becomes clearer as I present the "hidden picture" of our biblical canonical narrative.

I know that last statement may offend some of you. "What do you mean? My Christian narrative is a biblical narrative!" I

JESUS IS JEWISH

understand what you mean, as I felt the same way and bristled in indignation as well. But hang in there with me as we explore this concept and I think you will understand what I mean.

The Old Testament is the first and most explicit theological witness we have that describes God. It depicts God in terms of *His relationship with Israel*. For nearly two thousand years, Christians emphasized the Bible's witness to God – in Jesus – with such fervor that the Old Testament's unique witness became muted at best and ignored at worst. One of the most startling things I realized is how little the OT says about God apart from his relationship with Israel. The Hebrew Scriptures begin with the creation story but quickly focus on the lives of Israel's patriarchal families: Abraham and Sarah; Isaac and Rebecca; and Jacob, Rachel and Leah. From there, the scope of the OT widens to the relationship between God and a people group called Israel.[18]

The standard Christian canonical narrative, according to Kendall Soulen, is "structurally supersessionist [substitutes the Church for Israel] because it unifies the Christian canon in a manner that renders the Hebrew Scriptures largely indecisive for [i.e., excluded from] shaping conclusions about how God's purposes engage creation in universal and enduring ways."[19]

He further writes that "the Christian narrative neglects the

Hebrew Scriptures, with the exception of Genesis 1-3, and then leaps immediately to the Apostolic Witness (New Testament) interpreted as God's deliverance of humankind from the fall through Jesus Christ...thus outflanking the greater part of the Hebrew Scriptures and, above all, their witness to God's history with the people of Israel."[20]

Soulen, in his groundbreaking work *The God of Israel in Christian Theology*, argues that much, if not all, of the Christian canonical narrative goes something like the following: Creation, the Fall, Redemption (Jesus) and Heaven. While true, this narrative leaves out God's covenantal relationship with Israel. Abraham and his descendants move to the distant background of the Christian narrative, whereas the narrative of the Bible states that Israel is the protagonist throughout the Bible, including both the Old and New Testaments. This biblical narrative is: Creation, Fall, Noah and the Flood, Abraham, Sinai, the history of God and his relationship with Israel, the prophets of Israel, Jesus of Israel ministers to Israel, salvation comes from Israel, Crucifixion and Resurrection, the Acts of the earliest apostles of Jesus, letters of encouragement and exhortation and John's Revelation.

The reason for this obvious omission of Israel from the Universal Christian storyline began with an idea circulated in the mid-second century by many of our church fathers. Justin Martyr,

JESUS IS JEWISH

author of *Dialogue with Trypho*, taught that the word "Israel" in the Tanakh (the Old Testament) doesn't refer to the Jewish people but to the Church (circa 150 C.E.). He wrote, "For the true spiritual Israel, and descendants of Judah, Jacob, Isaac, and Abraham... are we who have been led to God through this crucified Christ." He continued, "God blesses these people [i.e., Christians] and calls them Israel, and declares them to be His inheritance." Soon after, Clement of Alexandria (circa 150-215) reasoned that since Israel "denied the Lord," they had "forfeited the place of the true Israel." Tertullian (circa 155-230) added, "Israel has been divorced" by God. And Origen (circa 185-254) asserted that the people of Israel were "abandoned because of their sins."[21]

The fact that none of these ideas can be found in the Bible confused me. According to the church fathers above (Justin Martyr, Clement of Alexandria, Tertullian and Origen), "the entire Old Testament can be explained as a concealed version of the New, and the New Testament is the key to unlocking the inner meaning of the persons, practices, and events of the Old. Without this key, the meaning of the Old Testament would remain locked. St. Augustine summed this up in his famous saying, 'The new is concealed in the old; the old is revealed in the new.'"[22]

The church fathers' line of reasoning, again referred to as Replacement Theology or supersessionism, became the standard

Christian canonical narrative and stifled the Old Testament, its message hidden. The Old Testament simply "anticipated" the New Testament. This reduced or eliminated the role of the Old Testament as a distinct witness to God and His intimate relationship with Israel, even though Israel is the very people group with whom He has chosen to be identified! Thus, we are left with a single witness to God in terms of the person, words, and works of Jesus.[23] "As a result, God's identity as the God of Israel and God's history with the Jewish people becomes largely indecisive for the Christian conception of God."[24]

So where does this leave us? Most of us read the Bible as if the only purpose of the Old Testament is to point to Jesus. Please do not misunderstand me, that's one of the jobs of the Old Testament. In particular, *these writings remain as the only body of writings that identify the proper Messiah*. However, that's not the only purpose or even the main purpose for the Old Testament. The Old Testament acquaints us with the Creator God, who chooses to identify Himself with a particular people group; the Jews.

As we develop a biblical canonical narrative, one that identifies God as He chooses to be identified and recognizes God as he wishes to be recognized, we must hold to the foundational truth that God does not lie and therefore remains the God of Abraham, Isaac, and Jacob. Forever.

JESUS IS JEWISH

Daniel Gruber, in His book *Copernicus and the Jews*, organizes a fantastic reference list that includes one of the most amazing facts about the God of the Bible, which is "how He, the infinite Creator of all, identifies Himself with particular finite individuals."[25] In the chapter entitled "God Who?" Gruber walks through passage after passage, from Genesis to Revelation, gives many examples of how God identifies with Abraham and his descendants. Gruber's reference list is in Appendix C of this book. I strongly suggest you take a moment to read it now. I encourage you to "hang in there" and read to the end. You'll be enlightened and helped as you develop a new biblical canonical narrative paradigm for yourself.

Please don't skip over this exercise. This truth should become a foundational precept for you. We need it to build a proper narrative of our first-century, Hebraic, Jewish, Middle Eastern paradigm.

God, the Scriptures, and Jesus all identify the Creator of the universe as the God of Abraham, Isaac, and Jacob. On this point, we can't waver. If God wants to be identified this way, then it's how we should identify Him. It's the way that God choses to be known.[26]

Jeremiah 10:16 says, "The Portion of Jacob is not like these, for He is the Maker of all things, and Israel is the tribe of His inheritance. The LORD of hosts is His name."

Who is the Lord's inheritance? The tribe of Israel.

When was the last time you heard that in church? Or maybe you heard it, but your pastor meant the tribe of Israel is now called the church? In the Bible, the tribe of Israel is exactly that, the tribe of Israel.

The words of Jesus, his disciples' words, and Scripture are all anchored in the everlasting covenant agreement between God and Abraham. This is the only way to understand Scripture so that God remains consistent in His word and can't be called a liar.

> Yet we are Your people,
>
> the children of Your covenant,
>
> the children of Abraham,
>
> Your beloved, to whom
>
> You made a promise on Mount Moriah;
>
> the offspring of Isaac his only one
>
> who was bound on the altar;
>
> the congregation of Jacob
>
> Your firstborn son

JESUS IS JEWISH

whom – because of the love with which

You loved him

and the joy with which You rejoiced in him –

You called Yisrael and Yeshurun.[27]

You may be wondering why Universal Christianity doesn't refer to God as the God of Abraham, Isaac, and Jacob despite believing in Him as such. It's a valid question to consider.

One of the reasons we abandoned proper acknowledgment of God and His people is that we misunderstand God's *covenantal agreements* outlined for us in the Old Testament. Let's examine these covenants to help resolve the cognitive dissonance caused by our current paradigm.

My friend, we need to dive into history.

Chapter 4
The Covenants

Before we settle into the study of the covenants, a little history is in order.

When you think of a covenant, you probably think of words like "contract" or "promise." Although these words may point us in the right direction, they come up short of communicating the meaning of "covenant" in the Bible.

The Hebrew word for covenant is *berit* and finds its semantic roots in ancient Middle Eastern culture. Gary Herion and George Mendenhall in *The Anchor Yale Bible Dictionary* define the term *berit* in the following manner: "A covenant is an agreement enacted between two parties in which one or both make promises under oath to perform or refrain from certain actions stipulated in advance."[28] The most general opinion is that *berit* is derived from the Hebrew root word *barah* which means "to cut."[29] Thus, when two parties enter a covenantal arrangement, it is said they are "cutting a covenant."

In ancient times, sometimes parties cut an animal (or multiple animals) into two parts and then walked between the parts to enter and seal the covenant. The walk of the two parties between

JESUS IS JEWISH

the halved animal(s) symbolized deep commitment and religious significance. The parties communicated to one another in a very graphic way that if either of them violated any item in the covenant, that as this animal had been cut in two, so it shall be done to the one who broke even the smallest agreed stipulation in the covenant.

Biblical covenants had deep similarities to ancient Near Eastern suzerainty treaty models made between the suzerain (often a great king), this king's vassal, a subordinate person or a dependent nation or state. People formed these treaties in a very specific manner. They started with a preamble, added some historical prologue, outlined stipulations, identified consequences of either faithfulness or unfaithfulness, recorded witnesses, highlighted the length of the covenant, detailed where to store the covenant, and how often public reading of the covenant occurred to ensure its renewal from generation to generation.[30]

Ancient Near Eastern covenants also included a covenant meal. Examples of this can be seen in the biblical narrative on multiple occasions. For instance, "So Abraham took sheep and oxen and gave them to Abimelech, and the two men made a covenant."[31]

God entered nine major covenants with man. They are as follows:

1. The Noahic Covenant: Genesis 8, 9
2. The Abrahamic Covenant: Genesis 12, 15, 17
3. God's Covenant with Isaac: Genesis 26
4. God's Covenant with Jacob: Genesis 28
5. God's Covenant with Israel at Mt. Sinai: Exodus 19, 20
6. God's Covenant with Aaron: Numbers 18
7. God's Covenant with Pinchas: Numbers 25
8. God's Covenant with King David: 2 Samuel 7
9. The New Covenant with the house of Israel and the house of Judah: Jeremiah 31

In this chapter, we focus on two of these covenants, the Abrahamic and the Mosaic or Sinai Covenants. In the following chapter, we study the Davidic and the New Covenant and give some closing thoughts regarding covenants in general.

During the first several thousand years of human existence, people lived without the Jews. Then, out of all the souls of humanity on earth at the time, God found one man with whom to enter a covenant relationship. His name was Abram. (From this point forward, I will use the name Abram until we reach the point in the biblical text where God changes his name to Abraham.) He lived in Chaldea, an ancient city that thrived near the Euphrates River, which most archeologists believe to be in modern-day southern Iraq.

JESUS IS JEWISH

According to the text, Abram had a mystical encounter with God. Genesis 11 introduced Abram, along with his father, Terah and his two brothers, Nahor and Haran. In Chapter 12 of Genesis, God introduced Himself to Abram and instructed him to leave his father's land and embark on an adventure to a faraway land. In this vision, God promised Abram that he would become a great nation; God would bless him and make his name great. He also promised Abram that those who blessed him would be blessed, and those who cursed him would be cursed. Somehow, all the nations of the earth would be blessed through him.[32] Based on the promises outlined in the vision, Abram set out on the journey with his wife Sarai, his nephew Lot, their possessions and all the people they had assembled while in Haran.

Abram's journey became difficult. He took a detour through Egypt due to a famine. While there, Pharaoh took Abram's beautiful wife Sarai for himself. Then God afflicted Pharaoh and his household with a plague so that he would not defile Sarai. A close call! Abram and Sarai left Egypt and journeyed on to the promised land. Lot and Abram agreed to part ways. Lot and his group settled in the Jordan Valley and Abram's group proceeded to the land of Canaan.

All didn't go as planned. Soldiers captured Lot and his family during a war often referred to as "The Four Kings vs. the Five

Kings." A warrior from the battlefield escaped to deliver the news to Abram. He gathered 318 men from his household and set off at night on a clandestine mission to rescue Lot, defeated Lot's captors, rescued Lot and his household, and on the return trip to Canaan, met the King of Salem, Melchizedek.

Melchizedek is one of the most mysterious and fascinating characters in the Old Testament. The Bible records that he was "…a priest of God Most High…"[33] Melchizedek blessed Abram, and Abram gave the king a tenth of everything he acquired in the battle. This incredible exchange is worth deeper study, but it is beyond the scope of this book.

The war of the kings, Lot's rescue, and the exchange with Melchizedek bring us to Chapter 15 of Genesis, where God initiated a covenant with Abram, often referred to as the "Covenant Between the Parts." In this chapter, we find a record of the covenant ratification and the covenant ceremony itself.

Let's review the covenant provisions and promises outlined in Genesis 12:1-3:

1) God will make Abram a great nation.
2) God will bless Abram.
3) God will make Abram's name great.
4) God will make Abram a blessing to other people.

JESUS IS JEWISH

5) God will bless all those who bless Abram.
6) God will curse all those who curse Abram.
7) God will bless all the families on the earth through Abram.

Did Abram have any obligation in this covenant agreement? Yes. He placed his trust in God always. We read in verse 6 of Chapter 15, "Abram *believed* the LORD, and He *reckoned* it to him as righteousness." [Italics mine] Because Abram believed, God considered Abram a faithful covenant partner. In that culture and time, belief had more to do with "doing" or following through with actions on one's belief. A correct biblical understanding of faith is much more than a mental assent to a credal statement; true faith is belief *plus* action. True faith manifests itself in faithfulness. God confirms this idea later in Genesis 26:3-5 when He tells Isaac, "I will establish the oath which I swore to your father Abraham...*because* Abraham obeyed Me and kept My charge, My commandments, My statutes, and My laws." [Italics mine] True faith manifests as obedience, and Abraham is the archetype for all those who wish to practice an authentic faith. Jesus said, "If you love me, you will *keep my commandments*." [Italics mine][34]

Was there a sign involved in the Covenant Between the Parts with Abram and God? Yes. We find the sign in Genesis 17 when God expanded upon the foundational covenant as outlined in Chapter 15 and increased the blessings originally given to Abram.

Let's walk through Chapter 17 in closer detail to see exactly what God promised to do and what He gave as the sign of the covenant.

God told Abram to walk before Him blamelessly and for this, God would multiply him greatly. In verse 4, just in case there was any doubt, God reiterated that He made this covenant with Abram to make Abram the father of many nations. The sign of this specific promise; God changed Abram's name to Abraham, which means "father of many." Every time we refer to Abraham, we are saying the name as a reminder of the sign that God's covenant is cut with him! God's covenant is with Abraham…no one else, no other entity, and no other people group.

We read terms like "exceedingly fruitful," "nations will come from you," and "kings shall come from you," which expanded and enlarged the original promises in Chapter 12. In verse 7, we come to the passage that much of Universal Christendom misinterprets and applies to itself rather than to the plain and obvious meaning of the text. We read, "I will establish my covenant between Me and you, and your offspring after you throughout their generations, *for an everlasting covenant*, to be God to you and your offspring after you." [Italics mine]

Can it be any clearer that God's covenant is with Abraham and his offspring?

JESUS IS JEWISH

No.

Every time a Jewish baby boy is circumcised on the eighth day after birth, it is an affirmation, a reminder, an emblem that God's covenant with Abraham remains in effect. It is *everlasting*. We read, "Every male among you shall be circumcised. You shall be circumcised in the flesh of your foreskins, and it shall signify the covenant between Me and you. He who is eight days old among you shall be circumcised..."[35]

Revealing the concealed identity of Jesus's Jewishness can be compared to putting a jigsaw puzzle together, where the four corner pieces to the puzzle represent: 1) Rightly understanding that God's covenant promises are *everlasting*; 2) The promises are specifically given to *Abraham and his physical descendants*; 3) Abraham's name change signifies that he will be the father of many nations and kings; and 4) circumcising the male child on his eighth day is a sign of the everlasting nature of this covenant. These jigsaw corner piece must be there, else the puzzle is impossible to put together. With "the corners" correctly identified early in the puzzle-building process, the edges, the foundations, and the borders of the puzzle can all be determined.

In Genesis 22, we find Abraham's tenth trial: "The *Akeidah* – the binding of Isaac on the altar."[36] Both Jewish and Christian traditions offer various explanations as to why God would ask Abraham to sacrifice his only son, the son of the promise. We won't take an in-depth look into this story and the paradox it presents, that's not the purpose of this book. Ours is to evaluate the results of Abraham's faithful obedience and the legacy his obedience has left for those of faith in the One God.

The Lord responded to Abraham's unwavering fidelity by expanding upon the covenant blessings found in Chapters 15 and 17. Verse 17 of Chapter 22 says that God will "surely" bless him by "greatly multiplying his seed as the stars of the heaven and as the sand of the seashore," a promise already given in Chapter 15. He also added to this promise military prowess by stating, "...they will inherit the cities of their enemies." The famous Jewish Rabbi Maimonides (the Rambam) writes, "Thus, even if they were to sin grievously, they would never be completely destroyed or fall into the hands of their enemies permanently. Accordingly, this was a solemn assurance of Israel's ultimate redemption."

Not only will Abraham's descendants reap the benefits of Abraham's faithfulness, but also the nations of the world. Verse 18 states that through his children, "all the nations of the world shall be blessed because you hearkened to My voice." Abraham's obedience is a blessing for everyone. By way of Abraham's unwavering faith, trust in God, and total submission to His will, God credited this to

JESUS IS JEWISH

his account as righteousness. Israel specifically, and the nations generally, are blessed by Abraham's character.

Abraham, God's chosen covenantal partner and patriarch of the nation of Israel, doesn't fade into the pages of history like the setting sun but rather shines brightly throughout Scripture as the model and standard of faith, trust, and obedience for all.

The above summation of God's covenant with Abraham established the starting point for a consistent biblical narrative spanning from Genesis to Revelation. God's everlasting covenant partner is Abraham, including his descendants – Israel. Any reading of the Bible that supplants this relationship is in opposition to God's word.

God reaffirmed His promises to Abraham's sons later in Scripture. In the first example in Genesis 26:2-5, God bestowed the Abrahamic Covenant upon Isaac. In this passage, the Lord spoke directly to Isaac and told him not to go down to Egypt despite the famine. God used this opportunity to assure Isaac that He will keep His promises to Abraham, including passing them on to Isaac. In verse 3, God says to him, "I will be with you," "I will bless you," "I will give you and your seed all these lands," and "I will establish the oath that I swore to Abraham, your father." The Lord proceeded to reiterate the promise of multiplying his descendants to be as numerous as the stars of the heavens and that Isaac's seed will bless all the nations of the earth. Finally, God reminded Isaac why He made these everlasting promises to Abraham. He says, "Abraham hearkened to My voice and kept My charge, commandments, statutes, and instructions," a concise reminder of the type of fidelity the Lord requests from His covenant partners.

The Lord bestowed the Abrahamic Covenant upon Jacob in Genesis 28:13-14. En route to Paddan-Aram in search of a non-Canaanite wife, Jacob, the chosen one of Isaac's sons, stopped to rest and had a dream. In his dream, a ladder extended from earth to heaven and the angels of God ascended and descended on it. (Genesis 28:1-3) God conveyed the Abrahamic blessing to Jacob in this dream.

The Lord opened His monologue by again stating that He is the God of Abraham and Isaac and indeed, the land upon which Jacob rested would be given to him and his offspring. God repeated that it was Jacob's seed in whom all the families of the earth would be blessed, and it is his seed who would inherit the land. With intent and purpose, God bestowed His covenantal promises upon Jacob, son of Isaac, son of Abraham.

When Jacob woke up from his dream, emotion overcame him. He proclaimed, "How awesome is this place! This is none other

JESUS IS JEWISH

than the abode of God, and this is the gate of the heavens!" He named the place Beth-el, "the house of God," which later became the site of the earthly Temple.[37]

Abraham, Isaac, and Jacob are the Patriarchs, the carriers of God's everlasting line of blessing. These three giants of faith remain as Israel's physical and spiritual foundation. Interpretations of the Bible that fail to recognize or that contradict God's covenantal promises made to the Patriarchs are anti-Biblical.

Now that it's established that the Patriarchs and their descendants are the benefactors and partners in the Abrahamic Covenant, let's continue to follow their story.

We pick up the narrative as famine arrived in the land. Jacob, his name changed to "Israel," sent ten of his sons to Egypt to buy grain to save the lives of his household. Israel and his sons didn't know that Joseph, the eleventh of Israel's sons, who was sold into slavery years earlier by his brothers, had risen in the ranks of Egyptian politics and ruled in Egypt as the right hand of Pharaoh.

Genesis 37 through 50 records the chronicles of Israel and his sons. The narrative included acts of betrayal, attempted murder, deceit, slander, prophetic revelation, and redemption. The story reached its climax when Israel's sons bought grain from their brother

Joseph, who looked like an Egyptian, unrecognizable to them. Their powerful reunion demonstrated the beauty of repentance and forgiveness. Ultimately, Joseph invited his father, Israel, and his entire family to live in the land of Goshen with plenty of food, water, and pasture. Joseph's act of redemption saved his father Israel and his family from death by starvation. They lived as temporary residents, guests of Pharaoh in the land of Egypt. They prospered and multiplied in number.

Several generations later, a new Pharaoh rose to power that didn't know Joseph and decided to subject the people of Israel to hard labor and enslavement. The people of Israel groaned under the yoke of servitude and backbreaking oppression imposed on them by Pharaoh. God heard their cry. Exodus 2:23-25 recorded the moment when God invoked His covenant with Abraham, Isaac, and Jacob.

God decided that Israel's time for salvation had come; He demonstrated his commitment to his inviolable covenant with the Patriarchs and rescued His people. Exodus 2:25 ends with this statement: "God saw the children of Israel and God knew." He exercised the power to rescue them, to intervene and stop the atrocities committed against His covenant people. He kept his promises. God used Moses and Aaron to bring about the ten plagues in Egypt, the exodus of the Israelites from Egypt, and the covenantal ceremony at Mt. Sinai where the nation of Israel entered a perpetual

JESUS IS JEWISH

covenant of loyalty to God.

In Exodus 19 God invited Israel to be His *chosen* people. We read: "You yourselves have seen what I did to the Egyptians and how I bore you on eagles' wings and brought you to myself. Therefore, if you obey My voice and keep My covenant, you shall be my treasured possession among all peoples, for all the earth is mine; and you shall be a kingdom of priests and a holy nation." When Moses relayed these words to the people of Israel, they accepted God's invitation and answered, "All that God has spoken we will do."[38]

After they accepted the invitation, God instructed the nation, through Moses, to prepare for the covenantal ceremony. He told them to wash their clothes and garments in preparation for God's descent to the top of Mt. Sinai. On the third day a great display of thunder and lightning accompanied a thick cloud and a loud trumpet sound. Moses led the people out of the camp to meet the Lord while the entire mountain trembled violently. Then God spoke the Ten Commandments, all the people saw the voice, and became terrified. They cried out to Moses, begged him to speak for God, so overcome with fear that they might die if they continued to see the voice of God.[39]

Exodus 19:5-6 outlines the obligations of the Israelites in the covenant. They are responsible to obey the voice of God and follow His commandments. In return, God promises to make them his possession among all the nations of the earth and to make them a kingdom of priests and a holy nation.

However, the covenantal agreement contained both blessings and curses. Moses reiterated the provisions in Deut. 28:1-2. We read, "*IF* you diligently obey the LORD your God, being careful to do all His commandments which I command you today, the LORD, your God, will set you high above all the nations of the earth. All the blessings will come upon you and overtake you if you obey the LORD your God." Later in verse 15 Moses says, "*IF* you do not obey the LORD your God, to observe to do all His commandments and statutes with which I charge you today, then all these curses will come upon you and overtake you." [Italics mine]

The Bible doesn't have an agreement stipulation that says if Israel fails to follow the commands of God, God will disavow them or find another people group with whom to enter a covenant. The consequences for disobedience are clearly stated, and don't include mention that God would ever abandon Israel.

What some call the "Old Covenant" is more aptly named the Sinai Covenant or the Mosaic Covenant. It's the agreement between Israel and God, where Israel is obligated to obey the Torah. When they do, God blesses them. When they don't, He curses them. Dissolution of the covenant is *not* included in these curses.

Exodus 24 records the Sinai Covenant ratification ceremony. Moses, Aaron, Nadab, Abihu, and the seventy elders of Israel ate and drank with God. We read, "…they went up and saw the God of Israel. Under His feet was a pavement of sapphire stone, like the very heavens for clearness. And He did not lay His hand on the chief men of the people of Israel; they beheld God and ate and drank."[40]

Covenants often have signs of fealty. What is the fealty sign of this covenant?

The Sabbath.

"So, the sons of Israel shall observe the Sabbath, to celebrate the Sabbath throughout their generations *as a perpetual covenant. It is a sign between the sons of Israel and Me forever*; for in six days the LORD made heaven and earth, but on the seventh day He ceased from labor and was refreshed." [Italics mine][41]

To summarize, God entered a covenantal relationship with the nation of Israel, the descendants of Abraham, Isaac, and Jacob. In Exodus 19, God invited the entire nation into a covenantal relationship, which they accepted. Exodus Chapters 19-23 outlined the terms and conditions of the covenant. Deuteronomy Chapters

27-29 clarified the consequences of obedience and disobedience. God also gave the Israelites an enduring sign of the covenant, the Sabbath, and ratified the covenant through a meal with the elders of Israel.

At this point, you may think, "Hmmm, so where do I fit in? I'm not Jewish, and I thought that the church is now the people of God. What are you saying? I'm a little confused and unsure what to make of all of this."

Perfect.

JESUS IS JEWISH

Chapter 5

The Covenants - Part Two

The questions ringing inside your head may cause cognitive dissonance. You seem to hold two opposing truths. On the one hand, you've just read how God is in an everlasting covenant relationship with the people of Israel, and on the other, you may have been taught your entire life that those in the Church, the Jesus followers, are the people of God. Resolving this apparent problem is one of the main drivers of this book and key to revealing the concealed Jesus, so stay with me.

The next two covenants on our list are the ones God made with Moses's brother Aaron, the high priest of Israel, and then Aaron's great-grandson Pinchas. However, we will skip these covenants as they do not directly help us answer our questions: "Why does God choose to be identified as the God of Abraham, Isaac and Jacob?" and "How does God use the covenantal structure with Israel to define his relational terms with humanity?" Instead, we will examine the Davidic Covenant, which is made between God and King David, and the New Covenant, which is established between God and the house of Israel and the house of Judah.

After settling in the land of Israel, the people decided they wanted a king like the other nations surrounding them. The first king they selected was King Saul, who started out well but finished grimly when he lost in battle then committed suicide by falling on his sword. David, who served in King Saul's court for a time but was on the run from him, heard the news about King Saul's death from a soldier from the battlefield. In respect, he and all his men tore their clothes and mourned the death of their king.

Becoming king for David was not easy, even though God ordained it. A long civil war raged between Saul's house and David's house, marked by murder, intrigue, deception, and violence. This war brought a dark time in Israel's history. However, as God promised, David became the crowned King of Israel in Hebron at 30 years of age. His reign lasted 40 years.

We drop in on the story in 2 Samuel Chapter 7, where the opening verse reads, "Now when the King lived in the house, and the Lord had given him rest from all his surrounding enemies…" God gives a vision to the prophet Nathan to communicate to David. We read in verses 9 – 16:

> Now therefore, thus shall you say to my servant David, "Thus says the LORD of hosts, I took you from the pasture, from following the sheep, that you should be prince over my people Israel. I have been

JESUS IS JEWISH

with you wherever you went and have cut off all your enemies from before you. And I will make you a great name, like the name of the great ones of the earth. And I will appoint a place for my people Israel and plant them so they may dwell in their own place and be disturbed no more. And violent men shall afflict them no more, as formerly, from when I appointed judges over my people Israel. And I will give you rest from all your enemies. Moreover, the LORD declares to you that the LORD will make you a house. When your days are fulfilled, and you lie down with your fathers, I will raise up your offspring after you, who shall come from your body and establish his Kingdom. He shall build a house for my name, and I will establish his Kingdom forever. I will be his father, and he shall be my son. I will discipline him with the rod of men, with the stripes of the sons of men, but my steadfast love will not depart from him, as I took it from Saul, whom I put away from before you. Your house and your kingdom shall be made sure forever before me. Your throne shall be established forever."

Let's highlight several nuggets buried in this text. God promised David a dynasty, then peace, prosperity, greatness, and

His blessing. We notice that God's promises to David are similar to the Abrahamic promises. God promised Israel a secure and permanent home in Israel. He promised them both offspring of greatness, including the assurance that kings would come from their seed. Most importantly, God promised that His covenant with David is everlasting.

Did David and his future son, King Solomon, have any role in this covenant agreement? Yes, they were required to obey the Torah. How do we know this? If we look back at the text, we can see that it says: "When he commits iniquity, I will discipline with the rod of men, with the stripes of the sons of men, but my steadfast love will not depart from him." Iniquity refers to disobedience to the Torah, which is the only document that clearly defines sin and how to obey God. In this passage, we see God's enduring commitment to Abraham (David is his descendant), to the Torah (the eternal guide for living rightly), as well as to David and his descendants.

Even if a future king disobeys the Torah, God promises not to remove his love from them. According to God, the house of King David is an everlasting house, and He will never remove his love, blessing, or promises from it.

The final covenant we examine is the New Covenant. Note here that the New Covenant is different from the New Testament, a

JESUS IS JEWISH

crucial distinction for you to understand. In Universal Christian tradition, the Old Testament is often referred to as the Old Covenant and the New Testament to the New Covenant. This is inaccurate according to Scripture. First, no covenant is called the "Old Covenant." We already discussed the Noahic Covenant, the Abrahamic Covenant, the Mosaic or Sinai Covenant, and the Davidic Covenant. These covenants may be old from a chronological perspective, but since they are eternal covenants, they are relevant now, today, and forever. Second, the notion of an "Old Covenant" implies that it is old, passing away, and no longer necessary.

This way of thinking is logically flawed. From God's perspective, all His covenants are equally relevant.

What, then, is the New Covenant? It's not the New Testament. The New Testament is a collection of writings with eyewitness accounts of the life and teaching of Jesus from Nazareth with *letters* from the Apostles, James, and Paul, written to various assemblies throughout the Diaspora. (Diaspora refers to the dispersal or migration of the Jewish people away from their ancestral homeland.) The New Testament concludes with an apocalyptic vision written by the Apostle John. These writings may refer to the covenants as recorded for us in the "Old Testament," but they are *not* a covenant in and of themselves. This may seem like I am splitting hairs, but semantics matter, words matter. We must use correct terminology.

Knowing now that the New Covenant is not the New Testament, what is it? The New Covenant is another covenantal agreement between God and the house of Israel and Judah (all Israel). We find mention of it in Jeremiah 31:31-34:

> "Behold, days are coming," declares the Lord, "when I will make a new covenant with the house of Israel and with the house of Judah, not like the covenant which I made with their fathers in the day I took them by the hand to bring them out of the land of Egypt, My covenant which they broke, although I was a husband to them," declares the LORD. "But this is a covenant which I will make with the house of Israel after those days," declares the LORD, "I will put my law [Torah] within them, and on their heart, I will write it, and I will be their God, and they shall be My people. They will not teach again, each man his neighbor and each man his brother saying, 'Know the LORD,' for they will all know Me, from the least of them to the greatest of them," declares the LORD, "for I will forgive their iniquity, and their sin I will remember no more."

JESUS IS JEWISH

The prophet Ezekiel received a vision regarding the New Covenant as well. He writes:

> For I will take you from the nations, gather you from all the lands, and bring you into your land. Then I will sprinkle clean water on you, and you will be clean; I will cleanse you from all your filthiness and all your idols. Moreover, I will give you a new heart and put a new spirit within you; I will remove the heart of stone from your flesh and give you a heart of flesh. I will put My Spirit within you and cause you to walk in My statutes, and you will live in the land that I gave to your forefathers; so, you will be My people, and I will be your God. (Ezekiel 36:24-28)

Which group of people is God's people? The correct answer is the Israelites, in specific the house of Israel and the house of Judah, which are all the descendants of Abraham, Isaac, and Jacob. The New Covenant is *not* made with the Church or with believers in Jesus. This truth is important. Daniel Lancaster outlines the promises God made with Israel in the New Covenant in the First Fruits of Zion HaYesod workbook on page 3.20. He writes:

- Jeremiah 31:33 – God will write His Torah on their [Israel's] hearts. The LORD will be their God.

- Jeremiah 31:33 – Israel and Judah shall be God's people.
- Jeremiah 31:34 – They [Israel] shall all know the LORD.
- Jeremiah 31:34 – God will forgive their [Israel's] sin.
- Ezekiel 36:24 – God will regather the people of Israel to their land.
- Ezekiel 36:25 – God will spiritually cleanse Israel.
- Ezekiel 36:27 – God will put His spirit within them [Israel].
- Ezekiel 36:27 – They [Israel] will be faithful to the covenant of the Torah.

Lancaster goes on to write: "The astute Torah student will quickly notice that most of these promises have not yet been fulfilled. We are not there yet. The Torah is not written on our hearts yet – not completely. The process has begun, but it is not yet complete."[42]

Think of it this way. All the Old Testament covenants are for this world except the New Covenant, which is for *the world to come*. The New Covenant describes what life *will be like* in the Messianic Age. When Jesus inaugurated the New Covenant at the Passover meal with his disciples, he started it, but it's not yet here in its fullness. When we read the Passover Seder passages in the New Testament, we see that most English Bibles insert a subtitle with something to the effect of "Institution of the Lord's Supper" (this example is from the ESV). Such a rendering leads the reader away

JESUS IS JEWISH

from the text's actual meaning and insinuates that Jesus did something "new" in this passage.

A closer reading of the text reveals that Jesus participated in the Passover Seder along with the rest of Israel. He added to the significance of the Passover meal and its symbolism *rather than negating* it. He told his disciples, "When you eat the Passover meal, remember me *also*," not *instead of* the traditional elements of the meal. The bread and cups of wine consumed during the meal already have deep meaning for the Jewish people. When Jesus said, "This cup that is poured out for you is the New Covenant in my blood" (Luke 22:20), he didn't mean that the Passover celebration of Leviticus 23, came to an end. Rather, he told his apostles that this cup now has an additional meaning, *marking the beginning of the New Covenant* as outlined in Jeremiah and Ezekiel.

A common misperception in Universal Christendom is that the "older" covenants are done away with, and the "new" covenant is the only one that matters. Most Christians get this idea from misunderstood passages in Hebrews and Galatians. For instance, Hebrews 8:13 says: "In that, He says, a new covenant, He has made the first obsolete. Now what is becoming obsolete and growing old is ready to vanish."

At first glance, it does look like the author of Hebrews is

laying the groundwork for an obsolete "first covenant," but this clashes with what we know about God establishing these covenants as everlasting. Everlasting cannot be obsolete! So, either the writer of Hebrews is deviating from Torah (heaven forbid), or the Church has somehow misunderstood or mistranslated his words. *Remember, the New Covenant is the agreement for the Messianic Era, where God writes the Torah on the hearts of His people.* In the New Covenant, we see "better promises," as Daniel Lancaster outlined. These "better promises" will come to their full fruition in the Messianic Era, as Jeremiah prophesied.

Then what is being made obsolete? It's not the Torah, as is commonly understood by Christendom in reference to Hebrews 8:13. The Torah is eternal and cannot be made obsolete. Rather, it's the covenant *terms* that are being made obsolete. In the Mosaic Covenant, the Torah is not written on the hearts of the people, but in the New Covenant, it is. In the New Covenant, God will give the nation a new heart, made of flesh, rather than the hearts of stone they had under the Mosaic Covenant.

A correct reading of Hebrews 8:13 should look something like this: "In speaking of the New Covenant [the one God makes with the house of Israel and the house of Judah and inaugurated by Jesus of Nazareth], he makes the first one [the first covenant – the actual agreement between God and the people of Israel] obsolete

JESUS IS JEWISH

[because under the New Covenant, the Law/Torah will actually be written on their hearts]. What is becoming obsolete [the stipulations of the Mosaic Covenant, not the Law/Torah itself] and growing old [in comparison to the coming Messianic Age in its fullness] is ready to vanish away [the Messianic Age will be an entirely new age and the old age will vanish away; the Torah will not vanish]."

I hope that helps. There are several other passages that Universal Christendom uses to teach the idea that the Torah or the Old Covenant is done away with, and *in every case*, the teaching is due to mistranslations, misunderstandings, or misinterpretation. I know that is a bold and broad statement; however, I want you to know that verses like Hebrews 8:13 do not abrogate Torah, God forbid.

A second common misperception within Universal Christendom is that the "newest" covenant cancels or does away with a prior covenant. Again, this idea finds its roots in Replacement Theology, which teaches precisely the opposite of what the Bible says. We know now that God's *covenants are everlasting*. The irony of the obvious dichotomy between these two statements should be not only shocking but also baffling. Ask yourself: "How does God make an everlasting covenant, only to make another covenant that cancels the prior everlasting covenant?" Biblical support for the idea that one covenant cancels another doesn't exist.

TYRONE NICHOLS

The Apostle Paul explains in Galatians 3:17 that "The Law [Torah], which came 430 years later, does not cancel a covenant previously ratified by God, so as to make the promise void." Each covenant God made is not invalidated or made void by a subsequent covenant. It's no wonder we still see rainbows; the Noahic Covenant is still valid, as is the Abrahamic Covenant, the Mosaic Covenant, the covenants God made with Aaron and Pinchas, the Davidic Covenant, and the New Covenant. This is great news!

Universal Christendom taught, and still teaches, that Jesus fulfilled all past covenants; therefore, we only interact with the New Covenant. Yet, when we look with care at what is contained inside the actual New Covenant, we find that *it stands on all the prior covenants* God made with Israel.

Without the eternal nature of the Torah, the New Covenant offers no hope. Why? Without Torah, nothing exists to write on the people's hearts. Without the land of Israel, the people of Israel have nowhere to regather. Without the forgiveness of sin, Jesus's death and resurrection become groundless, useless. Let's be thankful that all prior covenants remain in effect today and pray daily that the fullness of the promises outlined in the New Covenant may soon arrive.

Many within Universal Christendom use Israel's failures

against her, claiming that she has forfeited her right to be the covenantal chosen people of God. They use her inability or willfulness to follow the agreement as a reason for God's rejection of her. To compound the problem, they claim that because the Jews killed Jesus, Israel has forever lost her status as God's partner. Therefore, they argue, God has decided to create for Himself a new group of covenant partners: the Christians, or the Church.

I would like to further explore the concept of covenant cancellation by looking at what the prophet Jeremiah had to say about the matter.

Jeremiah was an Israelite prophet whom God called upon to warn Israel of the consequences of breaking the Sinai Covenant with Him. He predicted that Babylon would come and destroy Jerusalem, taking the people into exile due to their unfaithfulness. This prediction came true, as recorded in II Kings 24 and 25 when Babylon invaded and destroyed the holy city of Jerusalem. Throughout the book of Jeremiah, he is depicted as a messenger of God's justice and grace.

Chapters 1 through 24 delineate how Israel violated the covenant and broke the terms of their agreement made with God at Sinai. Jeremiah accuses Israel of adultery. Jeremiah develops this metaphor of idolatry equaling adultery and uses the language of infidelity, prostitution, and promiscuity to describe Israel's behavior. He also accused Israel's leaders of wickedness, corruption, and abandoning the Torah and covenant, which had resulted in rampant social injustice.

We pick up the story in Jeremiah 11:3. God commanded Jeremiah to remind the people of Israel that those who do not hearken to the words of the covenant shall be cursed, which does not mean divorced, abandoned, or replaced. Jeremiah used language to remind the people of the words recorded in the Torah, which state the blessings for keeping the Torah and the curses for breaking it. Deuteronomy 27 recorded the day when Moses split the tribes into two groups, six tribes on Mount Gerizim, the other six tribes on Mount Ebal. In a loud voice, the Levites read to all 12 of the tribes the blessings and the curses. When they finished reciting each blessing or curse, all the people cried, "Amen!" This ceremony served as a powerful and meaningful ritual, instilling in the minds of the fledgling nation their duties as partners in God's covenant.

Jeremiah also reminded Israel of God's powerful intervention in rescuing them from the oppression of Pharaoh. God did this so they could worship Him. The purpose of the covenant at Sinai was for Israel to fulfill its divine destiny as a kingdom of priests, set apart and holy to God. God promised to bless them with a fertile land, often referred to in Hebrew as a "land flowing with

JESUS IS JEWISH

milk and honey."

Jeremiah also recorded Israel's lack of faithfulness to God and the curses that would come upon them if they did not repent and turn from their wicked ways. *The fact that God does punish Israel in accordance with the terms of the covenant is evidence that Israel is indeed God's chosen people.*

As stated earlier in this book, those who adhere to Replacement Theology are responsible for the Christian Church's misunderstanding of the Scriptures. One cannot find a curse in the covenant that says, "If you (Israel) do not follow my laws, I will replace you with a new group of people and cast you aside." Throughout Scripture, God promises punishment followed by promises of redemption, rescue, and hope for Israel, *despite* her unfaithfulness.

The supporters of Replacement Theology make God out to be a liar. How? If it is true that God has replaced Israel with "the Church," then the everlasting promises He made to Abraham, Isaac, and Jacob are not everlasting.

I have only briefly outlined ideas surrounding the everlasting covenantal relationship God has *with His people Israel* as detailed by Scripture. We examined Abraham, looked at Moses and the Law, peeked at the Davidic Covenant and contextualized the New Covenant. We also detailed the curses enacted upon God's covenantal partner when she fails to live up to her end of the agreement.

> Yet we are Your people,
>
> the children of Your covenant,
>
> the children of Abraham,
>
> Your beloved, to whom
>
> You made a promise on Mount Moriah;
>
> the offspring of Isaac, his only one
>
> who was bound on the altar;
>
> the congregation of Jacob,
>
> Your firstborn son whom –
>
> because of the love with which
>
> You loved him and the joy with which
>
> You rejoiced in him –
>
> You called Yisrael and Yeshurun.[43]

JESUS IS JEWISH

Chapter 6

The Parting of the Ways - Part 1 What Really Happened?

Who started Christianity?

"Why, Jesus, of course!"

But Jesus is Jewish.

The Apostles were Jewish.

His original followers were all...Jewish.

So, what happened? Did Jesus abandon Judaism? Did he leave the traditions of his forefathers to blaze a new trail and call it Christianity? To find a historically accurate answer to this question, we must examine the years 30 C.E. to 381 C.E. under a fine-focused microscope. These years, an almost 400-year period of human history, continue to influence religion, philosophy, and society. An in-depth introduction to this time is worthy of our time and effort.

In the preceding chapters, I introduced you to some of our church fathers. These men, along with several other key figures from history, played an important role in the historical narrative of

Christianity. Theologians like to call this historical period "The Parting of the Ways." The topic of "The Parting of the Ways" between Judaism and Christianity remains a challenge to study. As scholarship on this subject continues to appear, I'm sure more discoveries will soon be made which will further enlighten our understanding of the period.

Academics in the past viewed the development of Christianity as a flow of information from Judaism to Christianity. In recent years, pioneering research indicates a more reciprocal flow of information between Judaism and Christianity, but that it occurred in *direct contrast* to each other. Christianity defined itself in opposition to Judaism and Judaism described itself in converse to Christianity. Rather than it being a one-way flow of information from one group to the other, both groups defined themselves as reactions to the other.[44] Philip Alexander writes in his work *The Rabbis and Messianism*: "It is now widely recognized that emergent Christianity played a vital role in the self-definition of [R]abbinic Judaism, just as Judaism played a decisive role in the self-definition of Christianity."[45]

My focus in this book is primarily on the Gentile side of this equation, but I will refer to Rabbinic Judaism and the role it played as the two monotheistic religions split from one another.

JESUS IS JEWISH

As historians, we must, as much as humanly possible, remove any pre-conceived narratives we have been taught, learned, or absorbed by osmosis through our denominational faith paradigms and re-examine the historical evidence from a completely non-biased perspective. I know it feels like I've been beating this drum quite a bit already, but I can't emphasize it enough. Remember that building a non-biased paradigm may sound easy, but it isn't. IT'S DIFFICULT.

As I write this, I ask myself, *"What biases do I bring to the text that might affect my ability to reach the truth?"* I work hard to present only historical facts to the best of my ability and knowledge. Together, we examine the important characters of the time who played prominent roles in shaping history. I take care to help you understand not only what people said, but also what they meant according to the context and expressions of that period. In this chapter and the next three, we wear our academic hard hats and go to work. I hope by the end of this brief four-chapter introduction to the Parting of the Ways, you will be inspired to dig deeper on your own.

Let's join the story reported to us through the eyes of the Gospel writers as it relates to the life of Jesus and the political climate of the time. According to the New Testament, the group of Jewish disciples of Jesus grew to a much larger number than earlier thought. A careful word study indicates that the word "thousands" in Acts 21:20 is inaccurately translated.

When Paul arrived in Jerusalem from his missionary journeys, Peter showed him how many Jews were followers of the Messiah and zealous for the Torah. In Acts 21:20, we read: "And when they heard it [Paul's missionary report from the Diaspora], they glorified God. And they said to him, 'You see, brother, how many *thousands* there are among the Jews of those who have believed. They are all zealous for the law.'" The Greek word used in this instance for thousands is myriads (μυριάδες) and means "an indefinitely large number, but strictly means 'ten thousand' or (figuratively) a number too large to count (reckon)."[46] Why the translators chose to translate the word as thousands rather than ten thousand is difficult to answer, and I will hold my suspicions for later. The word can also be translated as an "*innumerable multitude.*" (Luke 12:1) The general sense of the word is an *indefinitely large number, but it strictly means 10,000 and figuratively means a number too large to count*. Peter did not tell Paul only a couple of thousand Jews believed in Jesus and were zealous for the Torah. He said myriads believed, somewhere between 10,000 and a number too large to count. These Jews believed in Jesus and practiced the Torah. These numbers paint quite a different picture than is taught of the early movement of Jesus. Myriads of Jews followed Jesus and loved the Law.

JESUS IS JEWISH

The Gospels present evidence for a much larger Jewish following of Jesus. According to the apostolic witnesses, the Jewish people received him with an overwhelming openness with only four recorded exceptions.[47] You can read about the four instances in the end notes.

All of them hoped to see him perform some sort of miracle. The Bible tells us that they were "amazed by his teaching" and "followed him" all the time. Jesus felt the press of crowds to the point that for him to "escape from the crowd" became rare. All four gospels present a consistent narrative of Jesus being followed by massive crowds.[48]

In Acts 2, three thousand believers joined the nascent group of Jesus followers after the Spirit of God descended upon the disciples on the Temple Mount. They told other Jews about the good news of the Kingdom of Heaven. This number increased to about five thousand in Acts 4:4 and continued to increase at a rapid pace as the miracle on the Temple Mount and the good news of the Kingdom began to spread. Many priests became believers. (Acts 6:7) By the time Peter and Paul talked in Acts 21:20, tens of thousands of Jews believed! These were *all Jewish believers in Jesus*. I point this out to reframe and correct a Universal Christian thought that the Jewish people barely accepted Jesus and therefore, all of Israel rejected him. Maybe you've heard the expression: "The

Jews rejected Christ." This teaching is contrary to evidence presented to us in Scripture.

Here are more examples: "If we let him go on like this, everyone will believe in him, and then the Romans will come and take away both our place and our nation" and "*Look how the whole world* has gone after him!"[49] Who said these things? The theopolitical contemporaries of Jesus. They worried that the movement of Jesus would overthrow them and remove them from their seats of power.

The phrase "theopolitical rulers" is a term devised by Daniel Gruber. He writes, "I have coined the phrase 'theopolitical' to convey the nature of their identity and the conflict with Yeshua. These men were politicians who manipulated the national levers of power under the pretense of serving God."[50]

"Complicated" describes the political landscape of the first century, which included back-room deals, diplomatic appointments of power by those loyal to the eagle of Rome, and political/religious alliances that wielded Rome's power. Jesus, "the quintessential Jew,"[51] became a perceived threat. He amassed such an influence among the common people, the *am ha'aretz* (the people of the land) of Israel, that the theopolitical rulers worried he would cause riots against themselves and Rome. They feared he aspired to become a

JESUS IS JEWISH

national hero who would soon throw the military and political yoke of the Roman Empire off the backs of the Jews. Concerned that the Roman ruling class would blame them, the theopolitical rulers, for not keeping the peace, they feared they'd lose their jobs and likely their very lives.

The Roman-Jewish political conflict runs the in the background of the Gospel accounts. In 57 B.C.E., Aulus Gabinius, Governor of Roman Syria, divided his dominion into five synhedria (councils), with one in Jerusalem. The Jerusalem synhedria later became the preeminent of the five, and Rome looked to it to help rule all the area's indigenous people.

Once Rome conquered a land, any land, and in this case Judea, its common practice allowed the people of the land to rule it, subject to the authority of Rome. Any person whom Rome selected to be a member of the Sanhedrin (Jewish ruling authority) received power, money, and prestige. The Sanhedrin maintained the peace, followed Roman law, remained subservient to the crown, and followed orders whenever necessary. Rome also decided it best to appoint the high priest in Jerusalem; they thought this position would hold natural sway over the local population of Jews. Rome always appointed someone loyal to Rome first and Jerusalem second. The high priest became a puppet of Rome rather than a holy guide leading God's people in Torah.

TYRONE NICHOLS

Those appointed to positions of importance remained loyal to Rome to keep their power and prestige. Rome controlled not only the purse strings but also the seats that came with Rome's benefits. To make matters worse, the High Priest at the time of Jesus turned the Temple Mount into what we might consider a modern-day swap meet. Historian Josephus records how "commerce" was the day's activity at the Temple. Even rabbinic writings decry the Bazaars[52] of the sons of Annas, infamous in New Testament history..."from the unrighteousness of the traffic carried on in these Bazaars, and the owners' greed, the 'Temple Market' was at the time most unpopular."[53] Josephus describes for us the cesspool of evil that existed around the Temple:

> As for the high priest Ananias...[he] was a great hoarder up of money...He also had servants who were very wicked, who joined themselves to the boldest sort of the people, went to the thrashing-floors, took away the tithes that belonged to the priests by violence, and did not refrain from beating such as would not give these tithes to them. So, the other high priests acted in the like manner, as did those his servants, without one being able to prohibit them; so that (some of the) priests, that of old were wont to be supported with those tithes, died for want of food...[54]

JESUS IS JEWISH

Forced to navigate political oppression, religious corruption, and cultural upheaval, Jesus remained on watch for political spies. Without fear, he engaged religious and theopolitical leaders about their dishonesty. He comforted the people of the land with the message of repentance and the nearness of the Kingdom of God, demonstrated by miracles and healings. He kept busy, diligent and on alert.

The messages of the righteous man from Nazareth captured the minds and hearts of the *am-ha'aretz* so much so that it put Rome and its appointed theopolitical rulers on notice. Something had to be done with the "instigator" from Nazareth. So, they schemed and planned to murder him.

If his following were so small, why even bother with him? This doesn't sound like an unknown fringe rabbi who found a few straggling people to be disciples, but rather someone who was a genuine threat to the current religious and political power structure, and *who at any moment, could light the match that would spark a revolution against Rome.*

The day after the crucifixion of Jesus, Roman political leaders breathed a sigh of relief that a riot had not broken out. The Jewish rulers were anxious to get back to business as usual. They had "won." They believed their plan had been executed to perfection: arrest him at night when the "crowds" were fast asleep, hold his trial in the early morning hours before anyone was aware of events, and apply such political pressure on the local Roman government to force its hand to abide by their wish or risk riots in the streets. After all, the Jewish rulers knew that if Rome felt they had a chance to squash a rebellion, and that crucifying Jesus could accomplish that goal, why not side with their politically appointed consortium?

Pilate, the Roman governor at the time, knew something was amiss after he questioned Jesus. He could see the man was innocent and even told him so. Pilate could not understand why this supposed Messiah chose not to defend himself and acted like a lamb being led to the slaughter. Jesus's Jewish theopolitical adversaries wanted Jesus dead, so Pilate washed his hands of the matter and sentenced Jesus to be placed on a Roman cross, authorizing his death.

No one expected Jesus to rise from the dead, not the Jewish religious leaders, the Roman government, or even his followers. But in case his disciples tried to come up with some off-the-wall story about his coming back to life, guards stood watch at the tomb and sealed it with a big stone too large for any one person to move.

Devastated, alone, and scared for their lives, Jesus's inner circle huddled in secrecy to avoid any fallout from being associated

JESUS IS JEWISH

with him. The Romans branded Jesus a seditionist, and the Jewish religious leaders branded him a blasphemer. To these scared disciples, it only made sense that they could soon questioned, tortured, and more than likely killed for being associated with him.

Miryam of Magdala and the other Miryam went to the tomb to anoint Jesus's body regardless of the risk. That day, the third day of the weeklong Feast of the Unleavened Bread celebration, the High Priest waved the first sheaf of barley before the Lord as an offering from the harvest to come. The women likely knew they would be reported for visiting the tomb, maybe even followed to see if they would lead the authorities to where the disciples were hiding. In their minds, the risk was worth paying tribute to their Master. A little earlier in the day in Jerusalem on the Temple mount, while the High Priest lifted his first fruits offering, a great earthquake struck the area and an angel of the Lord rolled away the boulder. The angel's appearance was like lightning, and his clothes white as snow. The guards were so terrified at the sight of him that they dropped like dead men.

When the women saw this scene, they were startled. The angel spoke to them and said, "Don't be afraid. I know you are looking for Jesus, who was executed at the stake. He is not here because he has been raised – just as he said! Come and look at the place where he lay. Then go quickly and tell the other disciples that

He has been raised from the dead. You will see him soon. Now quickly...go!"[55] [56]

"And lo, upon Christ's resurrection, the Christian Church was birthed."

Nope. that's *not* what it says.

These days were the "Counting of the Omer," the 49-day period on the Jewish calendar between the First Fruits, the day after Pesach (Passover), and Shavuot (Pentecost). Each day contains spiritual significance as each is part of a countdown to the anniversary of God giving the Torah on Mt. Sinai. For the first 40 days of the Omer counting, Jesus visited with more than 500 of his followers: first, his closest disciples; then his outer circle of seventy; and finally, those who had been with him for most of his public ministry. (This isn't the exact order in which Jesus visited people after his death. I wanted to give you a sense of whom he visited and how many.)

On the fortieth day of the counting of the Omer, Jesus gathered his disciples together on the Mount of Olives and gave them his farewell address. The disciples, still longing for Jesus to take up residency in the Temple and usher in the Messianic Age, asked him, "Lord, when are you going to *restore self-rule to Israel*?"

JESUS IS JEWISH

He answered, "You don't need to know the dates or the times; the Father has kept these under His own authority. But you will receive power when the Holy Spirit comes upon you; you will be my witnesses both in Jerusalem and in all Judea and Samaria, indeed to the utter ends of the earth." (Acts 1:6-8)

"And lo, upon Christ's return to the heavens, the church was birthed."

No, again. That's not what it says.

You might protest: "Don't Jesus's words mean something like 'And by the way, we will not be restoring self-rule to Israel, but self-rule will be given to the Church because I am discarding the Jewish people due to their rejection of me, and I am going to establish a new covenant people of God called the Christians'?"

No, that isn't what he said.

Most Christians find it hard to understand that Jesus knew self-rule would be restored to Israel as the Law and the Prophets said. But, if there was ever an opportunity for Jesus to set the record straight that the Church was being birthed, this was it… right before he ascended into the clouds.

But he didn't.

TYRONE NICHOLS

Whether one believes the account of Jesus's resurrection or not, it remains a historical fact that the disciples believed it. They believed utterly, to the point they were all willing to die for their Master.

Peter and Paul were both martyred during the "persecution of the Christians" under Emperor Nero. Peter demanded he be crucified upside down since he felt he was not worthy of dying in the same manner as his Lord. Andrew took the good news of the Messiah to Asia Minor (modern-day Turkey and Greece) where he was eventually crucified. The sword pierced through Thomas in Syria for sharing the good news. Phillip was cruelly put to death by the proconsul in North Africa. Matthew was stabbed in Ethiopia, and Bartholomew met his death in Southern Arabia after witnessing in Armenia and Ethiopia. James was stoned and then clubbed to death in Syria. Simon was killed after refusing to worship the sun god in Persia. Matthias was burned to death in Syria. John was exiled to the isle of Patmos, where he penned the final book of the New Testament, The Revelation, and lived out his days in solitude.[57]

Would you live and die like this for a lie you *knew* to be a lie?

So, the question remains: "When did Christianity begin?"

JESUS IS JEWISH

Chapter 7

The Parting of the Ways - Part 2 What Really Happened?

Jesus told his disciples to wait in Jerusalem after his ascension for the gift that the Father would send, the *Ruach Ha Kodesh* (Holy Spirit). Acts recorded that about 120 disciples gathered in an upper room and devoted themselves to prayer. (Acts 1:15 and Acts 2:1)

Seven weeks prior, the Jews celebrated Passover, a festival that marks the Israelites' liberation from Egyptian bondage. During this festival families gathered for the Seder meal, a ritual feast that involved retelling the story of the Exodus.

The second day of Passover, called First Fruits, marked the beginning of another religious observance: the Counting of the Omer, mentioned in Chapter 6. This was a time of spiritual reflection and anticipation, lasting 49 days. The counting concluded on the 50th day with the feast named *Shavuot*, or Pentecost, from the Greek word for fifty.

This festival commemorated the revelation of the Torah on Mount Sinai. Throngs of Jews from all nations came from their faraway homes, bearing sacrifices for the celebration. Not a simple journey to Jerusalem, the pilgrimage stood as an act of faith and obedience in their allegiance to God.

The disciples gathered in an upper room with others, about 120 people. A sudden sound came from the sky like the roar of a violent wind. Flames like tongues of fire rested on the disciples' heads and the Spirit of God filled them all. They began to talk in different languages so that Jews traveling from the Diaspora heard the message of Jesus in their own tongue. They were amazed and accused the disciples of being drunk! They asked, "How is it possible that these men from the Galil can speak our language?" (Acts 2:7-8) The Parthians, Medes, Elamites, residents of Mesopotamia, Judah, Cappadocia, Pontus, Asia, Phrygia, Pamphylia, Egypt, the parts of Libya near Cyrene, Rome, Jews by birth and proselytes, Cretans, and Arabians, each heard speaking in their native tongues. How could this be?

Then Peter stood up to speak.

Was this the seminal moment when the Church was birthed, and Peter established himself as the first pope for all time?

No.

Peter, a devoted follower of Jesus of Nazareth and observant

JESUS IS JEWISH

Jewish believer in the God of Abraham, Isaac, and Jacob, directed the audience's attention to the prophecy of Joel, which states that in the eschatological era, the Holy Spirit will be poured out upon all humanity. Joel continues, "Your sons and daughters [Jews] will prophesy, your young men will see visions, your old men will dream dreams..."[58] He calls the *men of Israel* in Acts 2:22-31 "to listen to the fact that Jesus of Nazareth was a man demonstrated to you to have been from GOD by the powerful works, miracles, and signs that GOD performed through him in your presence. You yourselves know this...But GOD has raised him up and freed him from suffering and death! Look what it says in the Torah about him, 'I saw the LORD always before me; because he is at my right hand, I shall not be shaken. Therefore, my heart is glad, and my whole being rejoices; my flesh also dwells secure. For you will not abandon my soul to Sheol or let your holy one see corruption. You make known to me the path of life; in your presence is the fullness of joy; at your right hand are pleasures forevermore.'[59] Therefore, since he [King David] was a prophet and knew that GOD [the Jewish God of Abraham, Isaac, and Jacob] had sworn an oath to him that one of his descendants would sit on his throne...he was speaking about the resurrection of the [Jewish] Messiah!"[60]

Peter continued, "LET THE WHOLE HOUSE OF ISRAEL know for certain that God has made him both Lord and Christ, this Jesus whom you crucified!"[61] [ALL CAPS mine] The Jewish listeners on the Temple Mount that day were stung with conviction and cried out to Peter, "Brothers, what should we do?" Peter answered them, "Teshuvah (repent), turn to GOD, and be immersed in the authority of Jesus the Messiah into forgiveness of your sins, and you will receive the gift of the Spirit of God. For the promise is yours [the Jewish people], for your children, and for those far away – as many as God may call!" Three thousand Jews were added to the disciples' number that day.

A couple of days later around the afternoon prayer time, Peter declared, "Men of ISRAEL...the God of Abraham, Isaac, and Jacob has glorified his servant Jesus..." [ALL CAPS mine][62] By Acts 21:20, Peter told Paul, "You see, brother, how many tens of thousands of believers there are among the Jews, and they are all zealous for the Torah!" Nowhere in the book of Acts can we find any hint or clue that the Church began on Pentecost. This day is all about God fulfilling His promises to His covenant partners, the Jews, by sending the Messiah.

I know some of you are thinking, "Hmmm...Well, something happened because I go to church. I don't go to synagogue. If the Church neither began with the death and resurrection of Jesus, nor his ascension into heaven nor at Pentecost, then when and how did it happen?"

JESUS IS JEWISH

In Acts Chapters 6 and 7, we are introduced to Stephen, a young Hellenized Jew from the Diaspora. He returned to Jerusalem to be close to the Temple and joined the Nazarene sect, as he believed that Jesus was the Jewish Messiah. In Jerusalem, Stephen regularly attended a Greek-speaking synagogue called the Synagogue of the Freedman. An active and effective member of the Nazarene sect, he was arrested for supposedly speaking blasphemous words about Moses and God. Jews in his synagogue who did not follow Jesus did not appreciate the message of the Messiah and had him brought before the High Council to defend himself.

In a trial setting very similar to that of the Apostle Paul, which happens later in the book of Acts, Stephen was asked, "Are the accusations true?"

What accusations?

Rumors were being spread that Stephen was teaching against the Temple, against Moses, and against the Scriptures of Israel. If we are going to find any hints of the early establishment of the Church, maybe we can find them in Stephen's testimony.

If you have a moment, please read Stephen's trial in the seventh chapter of Acts. If you do, you will find Stephen giving a very Israel-centric defense. What follows is my paraphrase of his testimony, with major points highlighted for our discussion.

The God of glory appeared to Abraham, our father, and promised to give him the land and descendants, even though he had none at the time of the promise…The sons of Israel (Jacob) grew jealous of Joseph and sold him into slavery…Joseph found favor in the Pharaoh's eyes and was placed as second in command of all of Egypt, thereby saving his father's family by moving them to Egypt…Moses encountered God at the burning bush and revealed His name by saying, "I am the God of your fathers, the God of Abraham, the God of Isaac, and the God of Jacob, I have heard my people's cry, and I have come to rescue them by sending you to Egypt…" This same Moses, who led our people out of the land of Egypt, said, "God will raise up a prophet like me from among your brothers…" Our fathers wandered in the desert for 40 years, worshiping the LORD in the Tent of Witness, which had been made according to the pattern Moses had seen from God…The tent of the meeting remained with our people as we entered the Promised Land and remained as such until the days of King David…David's son Solomon was given the privilege of constructing a dwelling place of God – the same dwelling place where we worship today.

Until this point in Stephen's defense, could the High Council find fault with anything? No. He presented an impeccable history

JESUS IS JEWISH

lesson. This Jewish man knew his people's history and Scriptures (Torah) well. Stephen lived as a pro-Temple, pro-Torah, and pro-Israel Jew. *At this place in his testimony, he connected the Jewish Messiah, Jesus, to the people of Israel, which led to his martyrdom.*

He first quoted the prophet Isaiah, "Heaven is my throne, says Adonai, and the earth is my footstool. What kind of house could you build for me? What kind of place could you devise for my rest? Didn't I make all these things?" (Isaiah 66:1) He then struck at the heart of the matter:

> You stiff-necked people (Exodus 32:9) with uncircumcised in heart and ears, (Leviticus 26:41) you always resist the Holy Spirit. As your fathers did, so do you. Which of the prophets did your fathers not persecute? And they killed those who announced beforehand the coming of the Righteous One, whom you have now betrayed and murdered, you who received the law as delivered by angels and did not keep it![63]

When Stephen accused them of killing the Messiah, they ended their silence and yelled at the top of their lungs. In one accord, they rushed at him, threw him outside the city, and stoned him. Paul, who would later become the champion of Jesus's message to the

Gentiles, witnessed with approval the entire episode.[64] They did not stone Stephen due to his attempt to start a new religion or to defend a new religion. They killed Stephen because he accused them of being just like their fathers, who killed the prophets. In their case, they killed The Prophet. Dr. Bjoraker, a professor at The King's University, sums up nicely what we can take away from Stephen's testimony:

> Stephen speaks as a Jew eager for his people to return to the first things of Israel. He shows a high regard for Moses and the Temple. (Acts 7:30 – 42; 44-50)
>
> Stephen spoke as a Jew to fellow Jews, in the tradition of the great prophets of Israel who preached against their people's idolatry. (Acts 7:51-53)
>
> Stephen reminded them that the Temple itself does not save, but God alone saves. The Temple built by human hands cannot contain God. (Acts 7:49-50) This was not a refutation of the Temple; it was a rebuke upon the religious leaders who put their faith in the Temple (as a god-idol worship) rather than in the One whose reason the Temple exists. This is why some accused Stephen of speaking against the Temple, as logic would dictate. He had given this

JESUS IS JEWISH

same message before.

Stephen's speech catalyzed the expansion of the early Messianic Movement (within Judaism) from Jerusalem to Judea and Samaria and the ends of the earth.[65]

What about the Gentiles who came to believe in Jesus after the rapid expansion that resulted from Stephen's speech?

Cornelius (Acts 10) became the first Gentile who expressed faith in the Messiah after the resurrection of Jesus through the ministry of Peter. After Peter visited with him, the issue arose about what to do with him and how to include him in the commonwealth of Israel due to his Gentile status. Should he keep the entire Law of Moses? Many devout, believing Jews held to the opinion that he should. Full conversion of Gentiles to Judaism was the norm and is commanded in the Torah. So, any Gentile who came to Judaism by faith in Jesus of Nazareth should become a full-fledged proselyte.

The Apostle Paul (or Rabbi Shaul), a previous persecutor of Jews who placed their faith in the Messiah, met Jesus on the road to Damascus in the form of a miraculous vision and became a believer in Jesus. After his experience, Paul traveled throughout the Diaspora, preaching the good news of the Jewish Messiah to the

Jews first, then to the Gentiles. Upon hearing the good news, many Gentiles believed and joined themselves by faith in Jesus of Nazareth to the commonwealth of Israel. They identified themselves as fellow heirs to the covenant promises of God.

While Paul was in Antioch, men from Judea came to correct Paul and teach the newly believing Gentiles that, according to Torah and according to tradition, if one truly wanted access to the Kingdom of God, he or she must convert to Judaism. They charged Paul with error in his theology. He taught that non-Jews could be connected to Israel by faith in Jesus, but the leaders protested that he was leading the Gentiles in Antioch astray. The Judeans' arguments swayed the Gentile believers against Paul. When presented with the Jewish law about circumcision, most were perplexed and perhaps convinced that Paul was wrong in that they did need to become proselytes.

Paul and his traveling companion Barnabas disagreed with the men from Judea, and confusion amongst the Gentiles and Jews ensued. In order to resolve the matter, the synagogue leaders in Antioch (remember there were no "churches" yet – I will discuss the importance of this in a later chapter) decided to send Paul, Barnabas, and some of the Gentile believers back to Jerusalem, where they were to seek the guidance of the Apostles and the elders.

JESUS IS JEWISH

Upon arrival, Paul reported all the amazing things God did among the Gentiles in the Diaspora and how God opened a door of faith to the Gentiles.[66] There were believing Pharisees in Antioch and on the Jerusalem Council who held to the opinion that "(y)ou can't be saved unless you undergo *b'rit-milah* (circumcision) in the manner prescribed by Moses!" Thus, the *sheilah* (a question that requires a Jewish legal ruling – a halachic ruling) was put before the Apostles in Jerusalem.

What do we do with the Gentiles?

Acts recorded for us that some of the members of the party of the Pharisees who believed in Jesus as the Messiah stood up and said, "It is necessary to circumcise them and direct them to observe the Torah of Moses."[67] An inter-Jewish debate followed over Gentiles who had received the gift of the Holy Spirit upon belief in the Messiah, and thus claimed citizenship in the commonwealth of Israel and a share in the life to come.

Of course, a major debate erupted. Paul taught *halachah* that went against established Jewish legal rulings. His teaching seemed preposterous, but the controversy had to be settled. The Apostles and elders met to investigate this matter. They decided to search the Scriptures to see how to handle a new, troublesome, and controversial *sheilah* (question), oy-vey! The new *sheilah* came about because Paul taught Gentile inclusion into Israel by faith alone, faith in the Jewish Messiah. Paul's position contradicted 1500 years (give or take a few decades depending on your chronology) of Jewish tradition and practice regarding Gentile conversion. What a controversy!

"After a lengthy debate, Peter agreed with Paul."[68] Wow. Peter's opinion as one of the original twelve disciples held great sway with the other Apostles and elders. It was the perfect lead-in for Paul and Barnabas to give their testimony to the assembly about the miracles God had done through them. Gentiles could come to faith and receive the gift of the Spirit without becoming proselytes.

Finally, after the testimonies of Peter, Paul, and Barnabas, James the brother of Jesus and leader of the assembly rose to give his final ruling. I imagine you could've heard a pin drop as the divided, believing group of Jewish men leaned in to hear the final verdict.

James began: "Brothers, hear what I have to say. Peter had told in detail what God did when he first began to show his concern for taking from the Gentiles a people to bear his name. And the words of the Prophets are in complete harmony with this, for it is written:

JESUS IS JEWISH

After this, I will return;

and I will rebuild the fallen tabernacle of David.

I will rebuild its ruins,

I will restore it,

so that the rest of mankind may seek the Lord,

that is, all the Gentiles who my name has called,

says Adonai, who is doing these things. [Italics mine][69]

James continued, "All this has been known for ages. Therefore, my opinion is that we should not put obstacles in the way of the Gentiles who are turning to God. Instead, we should write them a letter telling them to abstain from things polluted by idols, from fornication, from what is strangled, and from blood. From the earliest times, Moses has had those who proclaim him in every city, with his words being read in the synagogues every Shabbat."[70]

No one discussed the start of a new religion called Christianity. No one even thought of such a possibility. Gentiles turned to God through faith and connected themselves to the commonwealth of Israel. The only topic on the table? How best to include Gentiles in Israel.

TYRONE NICHOLS

The proverbial gavel dropped, and James gave the ruling: legal conversion isn't necessary.

As an aside, Universal Christendom uses Acts 15 to prove that following the Torah's commands no longer applies to the Jew or the Gentile. This was never a consideration with James. Jewish obligation to the Torah remained a given. The crucial question pivoted around whether the Gentiles should be under the same obligation as the Jews for Torah observance. Next, if they didn't have to legally convert to Judaism, how could they be included into the commonwealth and not cause ritual impurity for the observant Jewish brothers and sisters?

James used the Torah to justify Gentile inclusion into the commonwealth of Israel. From now on, they would be people called by the name of God. A majority of the elders supported the decision, as can be seen in the letter written to the assemblies in Antioch, Syria and Cilicia, where they stated, "…it seemed good to the Holy Spirit *and to us.*" (Acts 15:25) [Italics mine]

At the end of his ruling, James emphasized that rabbis in the synagogue taught Moses (the Law) every Sabbath and encouraged these Gentile believers in the Jewish Messiah to attend, hear his laws, and learn to obey them. From the outset, James, the Apostles, and the elders did not place the burden of the entire law upon the

JESUS IS JEWISH

new Gentile believers. The Gentile believers didn't need to follow legal conversion but *did need to learn about the laws of Moses*. James and the elders decided to write a letter highlighting four rulings they expected the Gentiles to keep. Jeremiah 12:16 says, "If [the Gentiles] will diligently learn the ways of My people...they will be built up among My people." On this amazing ruling, Rabbi Lichtenstein comments:

> They [the apostles and elders] also knew the words of the Master: "I did not come to annul the Torah," etc., and that whoever annuls one of the least commandments will be called "least." He also said, "Unless you have a greater righteousness than the Torah scholars and the Pharisees, you will not enter the kingdom of heaven;" likewise in Matthew 7: "Those who do the will of my Father;" and "Anyone who hears these words of mine and does them." And if he did not annul the Torah, neither did his apostles have authority to annul the Torah. (E.g., "If Rabbi did not teach this; where did [his disciple] Rabbi Chiya get it?" [b. Yevamot 43a]).[71]

The discussion in Acts 15 centered only on legal conversion of Gentiles. The documentation in the Torah decided the matter. The idea of abolishing Torah never entered the mind of James or the others. Would the Apostles use the Torah to decide their ruling, then discard Torah, the very writings that showed them what to rule? Absurd. Whether a disciple of Jesus or not, Jews know the requirement to observe Torah is incumbent upon all Jews. The abolition of Jewish observance of the Law of Moses? Ludicrous, heretical, and grounds for expulsion from the Jewish community.

Paul's gospel (the gospel to the Gentiles) stated that "This mystery is that the Gentiles are fellow heirs, members of the same body, and partakers of the promise in Christ Jesus through the gospel"[72] As Paul traveled on his missionary trips and proclaimed the good news of Jesus "to the Jew first and then to the Gentile," did he place upon the Gentiles only the four decrees as outlined in Acts? *Of course not.* He didn't teach belief in Jesus *along with* nullification of the Ten Commandments.

The four decrees given by the Apostles to the Gentiles established a baseline for ethical and moral conduct, which allowed the Jews and Gentiles to fellowship with one another. These decrees protected the Jewish community from ritual uncleanness and eliminated obstacles that could have separated the Jewish and Gentile members of Messiah's new community. To join this Jewish community of faith, Gentiles agreed with these four decrees then further agreed to study Moses (The Torah) in their walk with Messiah.

JESUS IS JEWISH

Chapter 8

The Parting of the Ways - Part 3 What Really Happened?

Up to this point in history, the first Jewish followers of the Jewish Messiah observed Torah and its instructions. The Gentiles who planned to enter the Jewish community followed a set of four specific decrees or "laws" to simplify fellowship and demonstrate respect and appreciation for the entire community. Paul, Peter, James, the Apostles, and the elders made a new ruling; they removed the requirement for legal conversion to Judaism.

Gentile followers of Jesus became welcome in the Jewish community when they placed their faith in God, acknowledged the Jewish Messiah, Jesus, as their own, agreed to the four decrees, and continued study of Torah in the synagogue. Jewish believers understood that God made a way for Gentile acceptance into the commonwealth of Israel by faith in the Messiah. In Acts 15, we see nascent stages of an assembly of Jews and Gentiles worshiping the God of Abraham, Isaac, and Jacob under the Tent of David, with Jesus as the common denominator. The assembly consisted of observant Jews faithful to the Torah and the beloved traditions of the fathers, and with grafted-in Gentiles accepted in the commonwealth through faith in Jesus. This community formation happened within the borders and confines of first-century Judaism and covenant promises of God.

Leading up to Acts 15 we learned, "no one, as far as we know, called himself a Jewish Christian or spoke of belonging to an entity called 'Jewish Christianity.' The terms are invented ones, introduced to describe a supposed phenomenon of early Christianity." The Apostle Paul self-identified as a man who "worships the God of our ancestors as a follower of The Way, which they [the religious Jews] call a sect."[73] Gentiles included in the commonwealth of Israel through "The Way" believed in and studied the Jewish Law and the Prophets. The Apostle Paul, aligned in support of this new sect, reiterated that he, too, remained a staunch believer of all that was in accordance with the Law and written in the Prophets.

The new sect did not last long.

By 325 CE, we find ourselves at the Council of Nicaea in modern-day Turkey, where "Christianity" became the official religion of Rome. The Christianity formalized at the council stood a far cry from the Apostles' idea of a bi-*ekklesia* within Judaism.[74] The council made sure it distanced itself from Jewish trappings, an action that later contributed to anti-Semitic beliefs in Christianity. With intent, those who formed the Nicaean Creeds ensured they

JESUS IS JEWISH

conflicted with and opposed Judaism. These creeds exacerbated tensions between Judaism and Christianity then, and to this day.

The council rejected Judaism in its totality and established its own distinct identity. This fact is irrefutable. For example:

> I renounce all customs, rites, legalisms, unleavened pieces of bread, and sacrifices of lambs of the Hebrews, and all the other feasts of the Hebrews, sacrifices, prayers, aspirations, purifications, sanctifications, and propitiations, and fasts and new moons, and Sabbaths, and superstitions, and hymns and chants, and observances and synagogues. Absolutely everything Jewish, every Law, rite, and custom, and if afterwards I shall wish to deny and return to Jewish superstition, or shall be found eating with Jews, or feasting with them, or secretly conversing and condemning the Christian religion instead of openly confusing them and condemning their vain faith, then let the trembling of Cain and the leprosy of Gehazi cleave to me, as well as the legal punishments to which I acknowledge myself liable. And may I be an anathema in the world to come, and may my soul be set down with Satan and the devils.[75]
> - The Constantine Creed

We learned the Council not only wrote anti-Semitic creeds, but they also adopted pagan, anti-biblical holidays and feast days.

> I accept all customs, rites, legalism, and feasts of the Romans, sacrifices, prayers, purifications with water, sanctifications by Pontificus Maximus (high priest of Rome), propitiations, and feasts, and the New Sabbath "Sol dei" (day of the Sun), all new chants and observances, and all the foods and drinks of the Romans.[76]

If the above quotes don't startle you, please re-read them.

In less than 300 years, "Christianity" swore off all things Jewish. The Constantine Creed demanded that all customs, rites, and laws be of Roman origin. It changed the Sabbath day to Sunday, the day of a pagan god, Sol (the sun).

Let's return to our story at the end of Acts Chapter 15.

The Apostle Paul left the Jerusalem Council encouraged by the support of the Apostles and elders and the official stamp of approval to proclaim his gospel to the Gentiles. He traveled around the Roman world and used the Mediterranean Sea to reach various places and peoples along the coast.

JESUS IS JEWISH

You might be wondering, "If the early believers started as a sect within Judaism, how did the term 'Christian' come about?"

This term first appeared in Acts 11:26, where it reads: "The disciples were called Christians (Χριστιανούς) first at Antioch." Notice that *people outside the sect* of "The Way" used the term "Christian" and applied it to believers in Jesus. We don't read that disciples called themselves Christians. We see the term "Christian" again in Acts 26:28, where King Agrippa said to Paul, "In a short time would you persuade me to be a Christian (Χριστιανούς)?"[77] Paul didn't use this term to describe himself during his trials; *Agrippa used it to describe Paul*. The third and final time this term appears in Scripture is when those who persecuted followers of Jesus used this name *as a convenient group description.* Followers of "The Way" didn't give themselves this name. "Let none of you suffer as a murderer, or thief, or evil doer, or as a meddler. Yet if anyone suffers as a Christian (Χριστιανούς), let him not be ashamed, but let him glorify God in that name."[78] The word Christian means "a follower of Christos," the Greek word for the Hebrew Bible's concept of Messiah, the Anointed One.

The heathen population in Antioch likely coined this phrase to describe the Jewish and Gentile believers of Jesus in the synagogue. The Bible doesn't record for us what the believers called themselves other than "disciples." Others labeled them as a sect

105

called "The Way," or a sect of the Nazarene, or even Christian. In its original context, the term Christian described believers in Jesus, *both Jew and Gentile, within the context of Judaism.*

Gentile believers began to act arrogantly toward and separate from their Jewish brothers, which caused a schism in the believing community. After that, Gentiles carried the label "Christian." These seeds of separation may be seen as early as Paul's letter to the Romans, in which he admonishes the Gentiles about their behavior as adopted sons and daughters in their new family, the family of Israel.

God tasked the Apostle Paul with a daunting mission; impart the gospel of the Messiah to Jewish and Gentile congregations dispersed throughout the Diaspora and provide instruction on how to coexist. Paul sent a significant portion of his epistles to communities composed of both Jews and Gentiles, written in response to inquiries such as: "How are we to navigate these challenges? How can we maintain fellowship when my Gentile brother may partake of meat offered to idols?" or "He does not observe the sacred festivals, as he is new to the faith and believes they are not mandatory. What should be our course of action?" Given the plethora of issues that Paul encountered during his ministry, you can imagine the magnitude of his undertaking.

JESUS IS JEWISH

In the Diaspora, Gentiles came to faith in Messiah as new believers in such numbers that they overwhelmed the number of Jewish believers. Gentiles hadn't lived with an appropriate context for Torah, Israel, the Temple and the one true God. Unschooled in Jewish topics, they needed integration into Israel and Israel's God. Author and expert on Paul, Mark Nanos, highlights this thought regarding Gentile decorum within a synagogue community. He writes:

> ...of their obligation to "subordinate" themselves to the "governing authorities" of the synagogues to which they were attached, including such matters as obedience to the operative halakhot for defining proper behavior for "righteous gentiles" (i.e., the apostolic decree, Noahide Commandments), and the payment of taxes and other community obligations. That is, Paul and the Christian Jews and gentiles of Rome both understood their community(s) as part of the Jewish community(s) when Paul wrote Romans, with Christian gentiles identified as "righteous gentiles" who were now worshiping in the midst of Israel in fulfillment of the eschatological ingathering of the nations. (15:5-12)[79]

Since they did not need to go through legal conversion, these

Roman believers tended to flout their status in the Kingdom of God over their Jewish brothers. They perhaps believed their "faith alone" status within the community was a "greater gift" than those obligated by covenant to follow Torah. In his letter to the Romans, Paul gave them a "vision of them worshiping the One God in one voice in the midst of the circumcised, thus fulfilling Israel's eschatological aspirations of all the nations one day recognizing Israel's God as the God of all humankind: 'Rejoice, O Gentiles, with his people.'" (15:10; cf. vv. 4-12)[80]

The book of Romans, Paul's masterpiece, defined the Gentiles' role within the commonwealth of Israel in his "olive tree" theology. He taught that Gentiles are grafted into the root of Israel and the root of Israel supports Gentiles. Dr. Dan Juster writes the following:

> He (Paul) likens the community of salvation to an olive tree. Some natural branches were broken off, but not all (see Rom. 11:17), and wild branches were grafted in, that is, non-Jews who had no "cultivation" as a covenant people. Paul warns them not to boast, but to stand in awe, for the root of salvation history in Israel supports them, not they, the root.
>
> They are to stand in awe, for if God did not spare

JESUS IS JEWISH

> natural branches, He would not spare them unless they stand in humble faith. Now Paul begins an argument again concerning Israel. In verses 23 and 24, we read, "God has the power to graft them in again…how much more will these natural branches be grafted back into their olive tree" (RSV). And this is exactly what will happen: Lest you be wise in your conceits, I want you to understand this mystery, brethren: a hardening has come upon part of Israel until the full number of the Gentiles come in, and so all Israel will be saved…(Romans 11: 25-26 RSV)[81]

Paul pointed the Romans toward the proper attitude, demeanor, and behavior they should have for their Jewish brothers: one of humility, as the Jews supported the Gentiles, not vice-versa. Paul emphasized that ethnic Israel remained elect. Promises given to them by the prophets would be fulfilled when he wrote: "As regards the gospel they are enemies of God, for your sake; but as regards election they are beloved for the sake of their forefathers. For the gifts and call of God are irrevocable."[82]

Historical Christianity took this verse to mean that Jews became enemies of God and disqualified themselves from God's promises. *That's the opposite of what Paul said.* Paul's final thought stated that the Jews remain beloved by God and the gifts and call of

God to them remain irrevocable. Historical Christianity changed the Jewish calling to "revocable," and in essence, called Paul and God liars.

The question of "identity" or "election" stood at the heart of the controversy over Gentile inclusion into the commonwealth of Israel. Paul's letters taught that the Jews are and will remain the people of God. They remained the "elect," they weren't "unelected." Again, he wrote, "The Jews are still His chosen people, because of His promises to their ancestors Abraham, Isaac, and Jacob. For God's gifts and His call are irrevocable, they can never be withdrawn." (Romans 11:29)

The believing Gentile, through faith in the Messiah, was grafted into the Olive Root of Israel and became a fellow participant and heir in the promises God made to Abraham, Isaac, and Jacob. God keeps His promises, and this is great news for the believing Gentile. The Gentile's assurance of inclusion into Israel, as well as their everlasting destiny, rested on the truth that God's promises to Israel remain in force.

The epistle of Paul to the Romans, along with his other letters, appealed for unity within the assembly of the Messiah; unfortunately, the Gentile believers in Rome failed to embrace his written instruction. Paul knew these Gentiles had a false sense of

JESUS IS JEWISH

superiority, characterized by detachment from Moses and the Torah. He opposed these tendencies, as they led to an attitude of condescension toward their Jewish brothers in the Messiah. This attitude of arrogance found its ultimate expression in the Council of Nicaea, where ill-willed efforts further consolidated Christianity as a religion distinct from, and opposed to, Judaism.

Recognize that other broader historical contexts shaped the background of the New Testament texts and played a significant role in the separation between Christianity and Judaism in the 2nd, 3rd, and 4th centuries. Jewish people who didn't believe that Jesus is the Messiah remained at odds with their brothers and sisters who did.

At the heart of this debate stood the identity of Jesus of Nazareth. Proto-Rabbinic Judaism (an academic term to describe Judaism before what we know today as Rabbinic Judaism) worked hard to distance itself from the sect of the Nazarenes for two main reasons. First, from a Proto-Rabbinic Judaism point of view, the sect of the Nazarenes chose the "wrong" Messiah. Second, the Nazarenes included Gentiles as welcome members of their community without having them undergo ritual conversion. Proto-Rabbinic Judaism believed these "unconverted" Gentiles caused a continual state of ritual impurity in Jews associated with these Gentiles.

While the internal struggle for ideological victories ensued between the sect of the Nazarenes and the family of Judaism, Rome made plans to crush the Jews, and to put an end to their antagonistic behavior toward Caesar.

In the mid-first century, tensions between the Jews and Rome escalated to a tipping point when Caligula announced that he intended to set up a statue of his own in the Jerusalem Temple. Unrest and riots ensued. Ad hoc Jewish forces came together to defend the Temple and Jerusalem from the approaching Roman army. To everyone's amazement, rag-tag groups of Jewish militants repelled the attack of the legions of King Agrippa II, supported by Gallus' XIIth "Fulminata." Within Judea, people viewed this early victory as a blessing, a providential sign that God stood with them and they could throw off Rome's oppression. For the moment, Jews controlled Judea, readied themselves for Rome's response, and believed they would see prophecy fulfilled in their day.[83]

Roman forces instead reconstituted and galvanized under new leadership. Vespasian added the Legion XV Apollinaris, called up by his son Titus, re-launched their assault and overcame the Jewish revolutionaries. "Vibrations from the Roman armies approaching drumbeats created no small stir among the Jewish people, prompting mass evacuations, even before the great eschatological war was officially contested and decided in

JESUS IS JEWISH

Jerusalem."[84]

The emerging movement of the sect of the Nazarenes remembered the prophetic words of their Master Jesus and fled to the North, along with many of the general population, to avoid the coming devastation. Some saw this action as a betrayal of the Jewish people. Dan Jaffee, in his book *Studies in Rabbinic Judaism and Early Christianity*, gave a picture of internal dissension caused by the zealots, political groups within greater Judaism who followed the path of violence, assassination, and intrigue in order to accomplish their primary goal – a free Israel. These zealots had gained control of some Jewish people. We read in Dr. Seif's book quoting Dan Jaffee:

> Was the abandonment a result of betrayal? Not at all! "Internal upheavals led to the departure of many" disconcerted Jews, as frenzied and murderous Zealots usurped power in Jerusalem and took control of the struggle. Josephus is very clear on this matter: "Many there were of the Jews that deserted every day and fled away from the Zealots." (Wars, 4.377)[85]

Did this herald the moment when Messianic Jewish believers separated from their Jewish brothers? No. P. Sanders writes "nothing Jesus said or did which bore on the Law led his disciples after his death to disregard it," i.e., Temple participation. Fidelity to the ancestral religion is evident everywhere, as we shall see.[86]

The Romans destroyed the Temple on the 9th of Av (Jewish calendar month) in 70 C.E. and dealt a deathblow to Judaism and Israel. The effects of this single event cannot be overstated. Without the Temple, Judaism fell into shambles. Both the early movement of the Messiah and first-century Judaism lost the center of their religious universe. After the war, many Jews, including the disciples of Yeshua, returned to Jerusalem to try to reconstitute their religion without its central pillar of identity, the Temple. An early church father named Eusebius referred to the fact of a Messianic Jewish presence and leadership in Jerusalem through 132–135 C.E.[87] This presence formed an unbroken line of Jewish believers in Jesus who oversaw the Messianic assembly in Jerusalem until 135 C.E., one hundred five years after his resurrection.

In faithful steadfastness, the early movement of Jesus-believing Jews remained loyal to the land, the people, and the Scriptures of Israel. After the Bar-Kochba revolt in the early second century, the remaining Messianic believers, along with the rest of the Jews, fled Israel. Dr. Seif writes, "The Jerusalem branch of the Messianic movement ended in Jerusalem when Jerusalem ended for the Messianic Jews."[88]

JESUS IS JEWISH

After the Bar-Kochba revolt, Romans forbid Jews access to Jerusalem. Eusebius writes, "…when the city came to be bereft of the nation of the Jews, and its ancient inhabitants had completely perished, foreigners of the Church colonized it, too, it was composed of Gentiles, and after the Jewish bishops, the first who was appointed to minister there was Marcus."[89]

Without the Temple and a homeland, Judaism scrambled to reconstruct itself in the Diaspora. The hub for the Messianic movement centralized in Antioch, about 250 miles north of Jerusalem, where already approximately 22,000 Jews attended its several synagogues.[90] At the same time, according to Jewish historiography, a council of rabbis convened at Yavneh, a city on the southern coastal plain of Israel, to reconstitute, rebuild and reframe Judaism without the land and Temple of their faith.

Dr. Boyarin of UC Berkeley brought into question the historical veracity and true actions of the council at Yavneh. But according to the Jewish Virtual Library, the Sanhedrin that functioned in Jerusalem moved to Yavneh by permission of Vespasian in 69 C.E. We read: "After the Temple was destroyed, so was the Great Sanhedrin. A Sanhedrin in Yavneh took over many of its functions, under the authority of Rabban Gamliel. The rabbis in the Sanhedrin served as judges and attracted students who came to learn their oral traditions and scriptural interpretations."[91]

TYRONE NICHOLS

The rabbis of Yavneh functioned in a "crisis" atmosphere and an exclusivist ethic motivated them; they aimed to define orthodoxy [without the Temple] and rid Judaism of all those who would not conform to their vision of it.[92] According to Boyarin, the council may be a myth, created by rabbis of later generations to ascribe orthodoxy in antithesis to Christianity. Boyarin writes:

> ...although traditional scholarly historiography refers to Yavneh—however characterized in detail—as a founding council that "restored" Judaism and established the rabbinic form as hegemonic following the disaster of the destruction of the Temple...it is more useful to approach Yavneh as an effect of a narrative whose purpose is to shore up—even this may be presuming too much—the attempt at predominance on the part of the Rabbis in the wake of the greater debacle following the Fall of Betar in 135 CE. That which the Rabbis wished to enshrine as authoritative, they ascribed to events and utterances that took place at Yavneh, and sometimes even to divine voices that proclaimed themselves at that hallowed site. This, together with the challenges to "Jewish" identity provided by the growing development and importance of Gentile Christianity (that is, the Christianity of those who were neither

JESUS IS JEWISH

genealogically Israel nor observers of the commandments but claimed, nevertheless, the name Israel), formed the background for the invention of Jewish orthodoxy by the Rabbis.[93]

With Boyarin's assumptions and caution noted, we learn that by 90 CE, according to Jewish history, a functioning Sanhedrin in Yavneh appeared whose work defined the future of Judaism without the Temple. Only 45 years later, they would find themselves defining Judaism without the land as well. To the outsider, Judaism seemed finished with their Temple destroyed and the people dispersed. Emperor Hadrian in 136 C.E. renamed Jerusalem "Aelia Capatolina," issued a decree forbidding Jews to live there, and built a pagan temple over the site of the second Temple.

By 136 C.E., Rabbinic Judaism in Yavneh and Gentile Christianity in Rome bracketed the nascent forms of "Messianic Judaism" in Antioch. (I use an anachronistic term for the early Jesus movement since "Messianic Judaism" as a title did not exist at the time.) With inclinations toward both Judaism and Gentile Christianity, Messianic Judaism found itself in a precarious position, pulled in two directions. Scholars continue to search for "source" documents to get a clearer picture of how Gentile Christianity and Judaism defined themselves in antithesis to one another. An example of this dichotomy exists in a document written in the mid-second century titled, "A Dialogue with Trypho."⁹⁴ In it, the vibrant debate surrounding the nature of God and the nature of Jesus comes to life. The work highlights the ultimate question of the age, which is: "What is monotheism and which group is best able to define it?"

As for Judaism, the decisions of the council at Yavneh slowly made their way throughout the Jewish world, with one ruling being that of *Birkat ha-minim* [curses against the heretics]. "Worded more like an imprecation (see Tanḥuma [Buber ed.], Vayikra 3), in its invocation of divine wrath against internal enemies to Jewish integrity and against external enemies of the Jewish people, it differs from the other petitions."⁹⁵ The *Birkat ha-minim* is the benediction concerning heretics recited in the weekly *Amidah* (the *Shemoneh Esreh* prayer). Within Judaism, debate arose and still exists as to when the 12th benediction appeared in the Amidah. It's an important component of self-definition for Judaism and reads:

> For the apostate let there be no hope. Let the arrogant government be speedily uprooted in our days. Let the nozerim [sect of the Nazarenes] and the minim [heretics] be destroyed in a moment. Let them be blotted out of the Book of Life and not be inscribed together with the righteous [Torah observant Jews who are descendants of Abraham]. Blessed art Thou Lord our God who humbles the arrogant.⁹⁶

JESUS IS JEWISH

Meanwhile, Messianic Jewish believers found a home base in Antioch consisting of Torah-observant Jews who believed that Jesus was the prophesied Messiah. They worshiped alongside Gentile believers in Jesus, trying to figure out how to co-exist in a bi-ecclesiastical synagogue community.

Let's look at a snapshot of the rather muddled conditions around 136 CE. In the Yavneh synagogue, the early stages of Rabbinic Judaism formed as it defined itself against Gentile Christianity. Meanwhile, Gentile "Christianity," already in Rome, claimed divine apostolic succession and fostered an attitude of arrogance and anti-Semitism toward the Jews, the exact opposite attitude Paul asked them to display. Messianic Judaism in Antioch faced challenges with Gentile and Jewish worship co-existing in the same space, indicating further issues to come.

TYRONE NICHOLS

Chapter 9
The Parting of the Ways - Part 4 What Really Happened?

Many factors complicated the theological landscape around 136 CE. A three-fold division emerged between Gentile Christianity, the Nazarenes and Judaism. Although the early movement of Jesus and Rabbinic Judaism had differences, to some it appeared to be a disagreement over nuances of Torah and the identity of the Messiah.

Gentile Christianity presented a different issue. According to the rabbis of Yavneh, Gentile Christianity "appropriated" the Jewish concept of the Messiah, transformed him into a deified human figure and established the institution of the Universal Church. By 325 C.E. at the Council of Nicaea, Gentile Christianity became a religion that removed the Messiah from his original context and placed him inside a Roman Christian framework. A central debate among the bishops at Nicaea involved the nature and identity of Jesus of Nazareth. This identity crisis didn't involve the nature of his office, "Christ" (Messiah), but the actual makeup of his personhood. Was he deity? Was he divine? Was he human? Was he all of these? The Nicaeans believed that Christ is God in essence while the Arians held to the belief that Jesus was the Son of God but

JESUS IS JEWISH

was not God Himself. This dispute dominated the Christian universe and Roman politics for several hundred years; it eventually split the Western (Catholic/Latin) and Eastern (Orthodox/Greek) churches along these theological dividing borders.

The nascent pluralistic Christian movement developed in different directions, each strain carrying with it a central creed that set apart one sect from another. These sects included "The Way" movement led by the Apostles and Paul. Others emerged: Gnostic Christians, anti-Jewish Marcionites, Ebionites – possibly known as Jewish Christians[97] – and, as explained above, Roman Gentile Christianity, which evenly split between the Nicaeans and the Arians.[98] During the embryonic stages of what became Christianity, these groups competed with one another for adherents and religious dominance. All were, in some form or another, persecuted under Roman law until Constantine attempted to unite the Empire by a forced, one-sided creed, that Jesus was, in fact, God. Western bishops agreed, of course.

These ideological and theological clashes, which seemed settled at Nicaea, weren't. The Gentile church split into Roman Catholicism and Eastern Orthodox Christianity over the definition of Jesus's intrinsic essence. Athanasius, the champion of the Nicaean or homoousian (meaning "of one substance") position, held that Jesus had to be both fully God and fully man. He argued that the death of a mere human being could not redeem us, grant us immortality, and resurrect our bodies. Arius, the champion of Arianism, argued that the idea of the Eternal God becoming man remained as offensive to them as it was to the Jews. If God lowered Himself to become man and live in a human body, this lowered the high status of God. The Arian position postulated that Jesus was divine but not deity. God granted Jesus his divine status due to his moral accomplishments, miracles, acts of kindness, and sacrifice (martyrdom) to redeem mankind from sin; God elevated Jesus to His own right hand as the Son of Man, Son of God. Due to his excellence, Jesus became the model for righteous behavior and the hope for mankind's prize of immortality. For the Arians, Jesus could not be God, since God, being perfect by nature, is inimitable.

Richard Rubenstein summarized the Arian position:

> How could an all-powerful, all-knowing, all-good Creator experience temptation, learn wisdom, and grow in virtue? How could he suffer on the Cross and die the death of a human being? Surely, when Jesus cried out, "My God, my God, why hast Thou forsaken me?" he was not talking to himself! When he admitted that nobody knows the day and hour of Judgment, "not even the angels of heaven, nor the Son, but the Father only," he was not just being

JESUS IS JEWISH

modest. And when he told his disciples that "the Father is greater than I," he meant exactly what he said.[99]

Rubenstein continued by saying the Nicenes, on the other hand, insisted that Jesus is the Lord Christ and has always existed, he is "immutable and unalterable," and he is "the image not of the will nor of anything else except the actual existence (hypostasis) of the Father."[100]

Blind to the irony, both "Christian" sides agreed that God rejected the Jews. See Appendix D for what Dr. Rosner calls the Shadow Side of Nicea.

Emperor Constantine desired to find a peaceable middle ground between the two positions. He convened the bishops from the East and West at Nicaea, and hoped the meeting would enable them to agree upon language amenable to both sides. Constantine wasn't neutral in the debate; he agreed with the Nicene position and wanted to assure the final document reflected the Western viewpoint that Jesus is God.

During the council, neither side budged from their strong beliefs. The Arians (mostly Eastern bishops) maintained that Jesus was the Son of God but begotten by God and thus subservient to

Him. The Nicaeans disagreed with vehemence. They argued that the ontological nature of Christ was "one" with God, or God Himself.

To unite the Roman Empire both politically and spiritually, Constantine demanded that each bishop at the council sign the finalized document under pain of excommunication. The western bishops decided with ease and signed. The eastern bishops refused because they couldn't agree with an unthinkable sin. They accepted their excommunicated status. The lack of consensus and the ultimate failure of the council haunted Constantine for his entire reign.

The debate focused on a single word: *homoousios*. This non-biblical term became a crucial word in Western Gentile Christian theology. Ousia meant "essence" or "substance." *Homo* meant "the same." This Greek philosophical concept came from elite intellectual circles where people often discussed it. Many bishops took offense that a Greek word became included in a biblical creed. In an odd twist, the idea of including the Greek philosophical term in the manifesto wording became *the very test of faith* to identify those who didn't accept Jesus's identity as God.

The Nicene Creed described Jesus Christ as:

> (T)he Son of God, begotten from the Father, only-begotten, that is, from the *ousia* of the Father, God

JESUS IS JEWISH

> from God, light from light, true God from true God, begotten not made, *homoousios* with the Father, through whom all things came into being. (Kelly, Early Christian Creeds, 215–216. Kelly translates ousia as "substance" here, and the creed as recited today translates *homoousios* as "consubstantial" – of the same substance.)[101]

This word caused immense distress in members of the Council. The essence of Christ became the point of departure and ultimate schism in the Universal Church. Between 325 CE and the Council of Constantinople in 381 CE, the Nicene faction and the Arian faction found themselves at war, excommunicating one another from their respective churches and positions of leadership. Athanasius, the Alexandrian Bishop, and leader of the Nicene movement, known for his sharp mind and inclination for violence, found himself excommunicated five different times by whichever Augustus sat on the throne. Arius, the leader of the Arian sect, became excommunicated multiple times due to his beliefs and actions. While not as prone to violence as some other leaders, Arius did have a group of street thugs who rioted on his command.

In the second half of the 4th century, three boyhood friends from Cappadocia, Basil of Caesarea (Basil the Great), his younger brother Gregory of Nyssa, and their best friend Gregory of

Nazianzus, developed theological ideas that made it possible for the conservative Arians and the Nicene Christians to find common ground. They put forth a theory which included the Holy Spirit (most Christians understood Him as a part of God, as introduced by Tertullian in the mid-200s) and championed the Spirit's inclusion in the Godhead. They created a new theological term, which expressed the oneness of God inside of a tri-essence. They said, "The Father, the Son, and the Holy Spirit are three separate beings, each with his own individual characteristics—they are three hypostases. But they are one and the same in essence—they are *homoousios*."[102] Gregory of Nyssa writes:

> [T]he difference of the hypostases does not dissolve the continuity of their nature nor does the community of their nature dissipate the particularity of their characteristics. Do not be amazed if we declare that the same thing is united and distinct, and conceive, as in a riddle, of a new and paradoxical unity in distinction and distinction in unity.[103]

The real effect of this new terminology distinguished the Christian "Godhead," which now included Jesus and the Holy Spirit, from the *echad* (singular in essence) God of the Jews and radical Arians.

JESUS IS JEWISH

As a result, Christians who accepted this triune God, distributed over three Persons, no longer shared Jehovah with their Jewish forebears or the Supreme Being with their pagan neighbors, nor could Jews or pagans claim to believe in the same God as that worshiped by the Christians.

Doctrinally, this is the point at which Christianity breaks decisively with its parent faith [Judaism] and with other forms of monotheism that, insofar as they use family metaphors, consider God a Father and the persons created in His image Sons and Daughters. For Nicene Christians, incorporating Jesus into the Godhead was a way to preserve and extend the worship of Christ without sacrificing monotheism. For others, defining Jesus as God incarnate sacrificed monotheism by definition.[104]

Arianism contained the idea that a person could improve his or her behavior and not wait for the end of the world for righteousness. It represented a fundamental compulsion in Christianity: the drive to imbue worldly reality with the spirit of Christ and so renew human civilization. St. Augustine differed with this hopeful exuberance for mankind's ability to repair themselves and the world. He contended that without the presence of the "city of God" in the form of the organized Church, humanity would be devoid of hope.

As Theodosius I ascended the throne of Rome in 379 C.E., he inherited an empire in decline. War plagued the realm, Goths rebelled, tax revenues dwindled, social unrest and religious division ran rampant. In an effort to bring unity, he resolved to put an end to the Arian controversy and adopted a modified version of the Nicene Creed at the Council of Constantinople in 381 C.E. Theodosius believed that Nicene Christianity, with its emphasis on the deity of Christ, its pessimistic view of human nature, and its prominent role for bishops and saints better suited the aspirations and concerns of Christians in a time of rapid change and diminished communal expectations. He deemed unified control under the Nicene banner as the only viable path forward.

In 382 C.E., Theodosius decreed Christianity the official religion of the Roman Empire, which brought the movement begun by Constantine full circle. The emperor concluded that his official announcement would heal a fractured Church and, with the addition of the Holy Spirit to God's definition, strategized that many Arian detractors would support his declaration due to the circumspect language in the creed, which included both Jesus and the Holy Spirit in the Godhead. Theodosius did not concern himself with his detractors because he was ultimately in charge of the official Roman

JESUS IS JEWISH

religion and had the power to enforce his edict. At minimum, all heretics would be excommunicated, and executed at maximum. Still, some Western bishops disagreed with the modified Nicene Creed and petitioned for some word changes. They argued that a clause known as the *filoque*, "and the son," needed to be added to the words "the Holy Spirit proceeds from the Father." These bishops wanted to make sure that the Holy Spirit proceeded from both the Father and the Son, and not from the Father only. This insistence exposed the ongoing quarrel between the Catholic/Latins and Orthodox/Greeks about Jesus's stature as God. The Nicene-Constantinopolitan faith looks to Jesus as equal to God in all things. The Eastern bishops held to the belief that the divine Father and the divine son were not equal, with the Father greater than the son. Theodosius failed to unite the East/West schism and the Universal Church remains split to this day.

From the perspective of Roman Catholicism, the Council of Nicaea represents a pivotal moment in the resolution of the Arian controversy. The Nicaean theology, which posits that Jesus is God and co-equal with God, emerged victorious with only slight modification at the Council of Constantinople. A majority of Western Europe converted to Catholicism, which understands Jesus as the second Person of the Trinity and the Holy Spirit as the third Person. This exacerbated the division between East and West and theological differences between the two worlds of Christianity grew.

TYRONE NICHOLS

In Rome, the Pope excommunicated emperors in Constantinople whom he considered heretics. The bishops in Constantinople ignored him, which created long periods of silence between them. As time passed, Eastern and Western Christianity became separate religious confessions of faith. The rift that divided Christianity into Catholic/Latin and Orthodox/Greek traditions remained ingrained in the fundamental differences between Western and Eastern Christianity.

For the purposes of this book, the brief discussion about formative stages of Gentile Christianity emphasized the point that Christianity *formed itself outside the theological walls of Israel* and created a new religion. Every Christian creed excluded the God of Abraham, Isaac, and Jacob. Work to create those creeds excluded advice from His chosen elect. Jews received vilification and demonization as Christ killers and Gentile Christianity said Jews forfeited their right to be the chosen people of God.

The historical Jesus, a devout Jew, observed the Torah, kept the Sabbath, celebrated the festivals, honored the traditions of his ancestors, and affirmed that Heaven and Earth would pass away before anything in the Torah did, right down to one "jot" or "stroke." Jesus remained, and remains, a Jew in every sense of the word. Christianity may venerate him today, but he bears little resemblance to the faith and way of life he himself practiced.

JESUS IS JEWISH

Chapter 10
When Matthew Used the Word "Church," What Did He Mean?

Matthew 16:18 reads, "And I tell you that you are Peter, and on this rock, I will build my church."

"Finally! We found it! The place where the church is born in the New Testament."

Sorry, but again, no.

At the start of this book, I stated that Jesus never went to church. This may have surprised you if you hadn't considered it before. Maybe you even wanted to put the book down.

"What do you mean he never attended church? My New Testament has 'church' written everywhere! And even if you convinced me that Jesus never went to church, his disciples sure did and so did the Apostle Paul! So, what are you talking about?"

Be patient with me, allow me to explain. The answer could change the way you read the New Testament for the better, and could be a major mile marker on your journey to find the truth.

TYRONE NICHOLS

To fully grasp Matthew's use of the term "church," let's explore a first-century understanding of the word "synagogue." Jesus taught in the synagogue. When we encounter the word "synagogue," we tend to apply a 21st-century understanding and impose it on first-century reality. But wait! That's an anachronistic interpretation, and may lead us astray. Our 21st-century mind understands "synagogue" as Dictionary.com defines it: 1) A Jewish house of worship, often having facilities for religious instruction; 2) An assembly or congregation of Jews for the purpose of religious worship; and 3) the Jewish religion; Judaism.

Anders Runesson gives a different insight. He states that the nature of the first-century synagogue can't be understood with only one word. "There are twenty-five Greek, Hebrew, and Latin terms used in antiquity to designate what we translate into English as 'synagogue,' none of which are identical to the rise of the later rabbinic synagogue in the 5th century, which gave birth to all modern mainstream forms of Judaism."[105] [106]

To truly understand Matthew's word "church," we scrub our modern-day understanding of "synagogue" and then rebuild it from its foundation.

Ekklesia is the Greek word used by the Septuagint (the Greek translation of the Hebrew Tanakh, or Old Testament) to convey the meaning of two Hebrew words. These words are *edah* (עדה) and *kahal* (קהל). According to the Fully Updated Strong's Concordance, the Hebrew word edah is almost always translated in the Septuagint as *sunagoge*. *Sunagoge* in the first century did not mean "synagogue," i.e., a specifically Jewish religious meeting place, but rather a common word that meant gathering the "congregation" (Exodus 4:15, 12:3, 17:1, 34:31). Its primary usage described the gathering of all of Israel. For example, the Lord told Moses to "gather the entire edah at the entrance to the Tent of Meeting." (Lev. 8:3)

The Hebrew word *kahal* means "community, assembly or association of communities." The Hebrew phrase *ha'kahal et ha'edah* meant "gather the congregation or gather the assembly." (Gen. 49:5-6, Lev. 16:17, Num. 19:20, Dt. 10:4, 1 Sam. 17:47.) In Daniel Gruber's book *The Separation of Church and Faith, Volume 1, Copernicus and the Jews*, he writes:

> In the Septuagint, *kahal* is translated alternately by the synonymous Greek words – *sunagoge and ekklesia*. The words simply meant "meeting," "gathering," "community," or "assembly." Neither word in itself contained any religious meaning or connotation. Neither word was connected with any particular people group.[107]

TYRONE NICHOLS

In Matthias Konradt's monograph *Israel, Church and the Gentiles in the Gospel of Matthew*, he confirms that Septuagint translators chose *ekklesia* to convey the meaning of *kahal* and *ekklesia* can refer to more than one group or gathering.[108]

Other ancient Greek texts used the word *sunagoge* in a variety of ways. Plato used it to mean "a bringing together or uniting" or "forming an army in a column." Thucydides used the word in the sense of "mustering an army for war." Polybius used *sunagoge* for "a gathering in of harvest," and Aristotle used it for "a collection of writings."[109] Standard Greek texts used *ekklesia* as an assembly, as did Herodotus and Thucydides. Thucydides and others also used *ekklesia* as "an assembly of the citizens regularly summoned, i.e., the legislative assembly." Athenians, for instance, brought together two types of *ekklesia*, the ordinary *(kuriai)* and the extraordinary *(sugkletoi)*."[110]

Gruber added clarification of the usage of *ekklesia*:

> The word *ekklesia* as used by the Septuagint translators was not a Christian word, nor even a religious word. It did not connote or imply anything Christian. Indeed, at the time of the Septuagint, nothing "Christian" existed. Everywhere in the Greek world, every people had the *ekklesiai*, i.e.,

JESUS IS JEWISH

their meetings and meeting places." He continues, "The word *sunagoge* did not denote or imply anything Jewish. It did not even denote or imply anything religious. It just meant, 'meeting,' 'gathering,' 'assembly,' or 'meeting place.'"[111]

For the most part, authors of the Messianic Writings (New Testament) wrote in Greek to communicate Hebraic concepts and words; they often drew from Septuagint texts to remain consistent in translation and communication of ideas.

In the New Testament, *sunagoge* appears approximately 50 times with a slight favor toward meaning a "meeting place" rather than a gathering. (See Acts 13:43 as an example.) Luke knew the term *sunagoge* didn't conjure up religious imagery; instead, he added a descriptor to the *sunagoge* to which he referred. That's why he wrote "...there was a *sunagoge* of the Jews." (Acts 13:5, 17:1,10) To the modern reader, this may seem redundant. However, the first-century reader needed the specific designation since *sunagoge* only meant a meeting or meeting place for any group of people.

According to Lee I. Levine in his work *The Ancient Synagogue - The First 1000 Years*, the buildings where Jews chose to meet also "were used as a courtroom, school, or hostel, or for political meetings, social gatherings, keeping charity funds, slave manumissions, meals (sacred or otherwise) and, of course, religious liturgical functions."[112] These buildings functioned as centers for the community, so authors of the apostolic writings described the sunagoge to which they referred.

In Matthew 10:17-20, Jesus instructed his disciples about missionary journeys and what to expect. He said to be on their guard "against men; they will hand you over to the local councils and whip you in their *sunagogai*." We don't read about disciples of Jesus being whipped until Paul and Silas (let's call them second generation Jewish disciples of Jesus not a part of the Twelve). Jewish authorities flogged Paul and Silas when they included Gentiles in the commonwealth of Israel through faith in the Jewish Messiah.

Matthew wrote sunagoge nine times in his gospel.[113] Most scholars believe he spoke either Hebrew or Aramaic and used the word *kahal*, which translated as *sunagoge*.

As Konradt points out, the translators of the Septuagint used the Greek word *ekklesia* to communicate the Hebrew word *kahal* for "congregation." Multiple examples of this use exist in the apostolic writings. Let's look at a few examples.

Hebrews 2:12 reads, "I will tell of your name to my brothers;

JESUS IS JEWISH

in the midst of the congregation will I sing your praises." The Greek word used for congregation is *ekklesia*. Hebrews 2:12 quotes Psalm 22:23 which reads, "I will tell of your name to my brothers; in the midst of the congregation, I will praise you." The Psalmist used *kahal*, the Hebrew word for congregation.

Author Daniel Gruber gives another example:

> He [Moses] was in the *ekklesia* in the desert, with the angel who spoke to him on Mount Sinai and with our fathers; and he received living words to pass on to us. (Acts 7:38) What is the meaning of *ekklesia* here? To what does it refer? Keep in mind that Stephen was not speaking Greek, he did not use the word *ekklesia*. That is simply Luke's Greek translation of what Stephen actually said. Speaking to a Jewish audience in Jerusalem, Stephen was speaking in first-century Hebrew or Jewish Aramaic. Beyond all question, he used the word *kahal* to indicate the assembly/congregation/community of Israel.
>
> Luke used *ekklesia* for *kahal*, just as it had been used throughout at least the three centuries from the beginning of the Septuagint to his day. Stephen was specifically speaking of the assembly of the

congregation of Israel. To then translate Luke's use of *ekklesia* into English 'church', as the KJV does, is almost inexcusable. It presents a gross distortion and misrepresentation of what Stephen was saying, rather than a translation. Stephen knew nothing at all of church and Moses knew less.[114]

When Matthew wrote the word "church," what did he mean?

You probably connected the dots by now, but just in case, let's read two more comments on Matthew. First, "Matthew [was written] in the context of Second Temple formative Judaism(s). It is written from the perspective…that Matthew [wrote] to a group of Christian Jews who were still in contact with non-Christian Jews in the synagogue."[115] Second, Anthony J. Saldarini argues that Matthew's gospel addressed a Christian-Jewish community rather than a Jewish-Christian community.[116] Saldarini believes that the Matthean comments on Law, Messiah, and Jewish authorities stemmed from someone inside the Jewish community and represented first-century Judaism.[117]

Turner's point, and Saldarini's, show that Matthew wrote inside a Judaic "ecosystem." We understand Matthew's use of the term *ekklesia* the same way Septuagint translators used the word, to translate the Hebrew word *kahal*.

JESUS IS JEWISH

Matthew didn't use the word "church" to signify a Christian institution, because to this point in history, such an institution didn't exist. Matthew couldn't have known what "church" even meant. The Greek word *ekklesia* had meaning, but not the word "church" as we understand it in the 21st century. Matthew used it for *kahal*, the congregation or assembly.

Another question you may have is, "Did Matthew use the word *ekklesia* to refer to a synagogue, the 21st-century type?"

The 21st-century understanding of the institution called the Jewish synagogue formed when Rabbinic Judaism led the Jewish religious way of life in the 5th century. The first-century type of synagogue developed earlier than the time of Jesus. According to Lee Levine in his chapter called "Origins," the synagogue found its roots at "the city gates" (reaching as far back as Genesis 23:10, 18), the focal point of communal activity, a finding supported in both biblical and non-biblical literature.[118]

Other activities at city gates included meals, prophetic activity, judiciary rulings and settlement of personal affairs, public announcements, and religious functions [such as the reading of the Torah].[119] A conqueror might set his throne there as a sign of victory, a king perhaps sat there to hear his people's grievances. How the *sunagoge* (gatherings) at the city gates migrated to buildings in the 2nd temple period is unknown according to Levine. The *Mishnah* is valuable to us as it adds to our discussion on three counts: 1) It attests to the early practice of Torah reading in a local setting; 2) it tells us that the community at large performed the reading, in this case by those unable to participate in the Temple worship in Jerusalem; and 3) a synagogue per se is not mentioned, but a general reference is made to gathering in towns. Although later renditions of this tradition of reading the Torah, followed by most commentators, introduced the notion that these scriptural readings took place in the local synagogue, such interpretations are wholly unwarranted. The *Mishnah* mentions only "towns," and the specific place may have been the gate area or some other public space.[120]

In Matthew 4:23 the narrator states: "Jesus went throughout Galilee, teaching in their *synagogues* and proclaiming the good news of the kingdom and curing every disease and every sickness among the people." Now we know that Jesus visited the sunagoge, the central meeting place of the town, not a building called a synagogue in the 21st-century understanding of the word. By the first century, the local *sunagoge* (gathering/assembly) took up residence in homes or buildings used for various and assorted *ekklesiai* (groups, congregations, assemblies – see Levine).

Anders Runesson writes, "any interaction in public synagogues in the first century indicates involvement in Jewish

JESUS IS JEWISH

Society...." He goes on to say:

> The Matthean Jesus and his disciples...campaign across the land in public institutions [sunagoge – my insertion] and elsewhere, clearly aiming at setting in motion a mass movement to save Israel, or more precisely, to rescue the "lost sheep of the House of Israel." When we read Matthew in such public institutional settings, we are reminded that what we separate and call "religion" and "politics" were, in antiquity, interwoven aspects of communal life.[121]

At the beginning of this chapter, I quoted Matthew 16:18: "I tell you that you are Peter, and on this rock, I will build my church, and the gates of Sheol will not overcome it." How should we now understand Matthew's use of the word *ekklesia*? He didn't use the word "church," it's not likely that Jesus used *ekklesia* when speaking to Peter. Most scholars believe Jesus didn't speak Greek to his disciples. More than likely, Jesus used the Hebrew word *kahal* (or an Aramaic word for it), which Matthew translated into the Greek word *ekklesia*, as the Septuagint translators did before him.

Jesus referred to an assembly with its meaning in the Hebrew Scriptures, the *kahal* of Israel. Gruber made an excellent point in this regard. He wrote:

If Yeshua [Jesus] had been proclaiming that he was going to build a community that could not be found in the Biblical Hebrew context, then he would have been putting himself outside the God-given, Biblical definition of the Messiah. God had promised long before to make Israel a community of nations.

Messiah comes to fulfill what God promised, not to annul or abandon it. God had promised to make Israel His community/*kahal*/*ekklesia* of nations.[122]

We established that Matthew used the Greek word *ekklesia* in the same vein as the Septuagint translators. We now explore how a first-century audience understood the word *kahal*.

Deuteronomy 23:3 says, "No Ammonite or Moabite or any of his descendants may enter the assembly of the LORD." The Septuagint translated *kahal* of the LORD as *ekklesian kuriou*. In English, it means the "community/congregation/assembly of the LORD." Psalm 40:9 reads: "I proclaimed Your righteousness in the great *kahal*. Behold, you know, O LORD, my lips did not conceal it." Deuteronomy 10:4 says, "The LORD wrote on these tablets what he had written before, the Ten Commandments He proclaimed to you on the mountain, out of the midst of the fire, on the day of the *kahal*. And the LORD gave them to me." In each of these verses,

JESUS IS JEWISH

any literate first-century reader of scripture understood that an adjective or identity marker went with the word *kahal* to identify which *kahal*. In Deut. 23:3, it's the LORD's *kahal*. In Psalm 40:9, it is the great *kahal*. In Deut. 10:4, it's the gathering of the entire nation of Israel, the *kahal* of Israel.

In Matthew 16:18, Jesus identified that He initiated his own *kahal*. When Peter spoke his God-given revelation to Jesus, "You are the Messiah, the Son of the living God," he electrified the moment in time when Jesus proclaimed the beginning of his *kahal*! Jesus claimed – as His own – an assembly of followers and disciples who understood that he, the Jewish Messiah defined by the Torah, fulfilled scriptural prophecies.

That the English translators translated the Greek word *ekklesia* into an anachronistic word "church" supported their supersessionist paradigm. Why? Because the word "church" purposefully directed the reader away from the biblical *ekklesia*, the *kahal* of Israel and into a new entity no longer associated with Israel or the Jewish people. Jesus and Matthew didn't use a word that signified an establishment called Christianity, for such an institution didn't exist for another 300 years!

We need to think in terms of Jesus building his *kahal*, his *ekklesia*, his assembly/congregation from the perspective of the

Jewish Messiah who came to keep the promises of His Father, and that he came to rescue both the lost sheep of Israel and Gentiles who are called by His name.[123]

If I've not adequately put forth convincing arguments that use of the term *ekklesia* should point us toward a *kahal* within Israel, more specifically Jesus's *kahal* within Israel, and if you might still believe that *ekklesia* should semantically point to the word "church" with all of its 21st-century linguistic entrapments, look how this misguided translation of "church" makes Jesus's statement look strange and disjointed.

The second verse in Matthew that uses the word *ekklesia* is Matthew 18:17. "If he refuses to listen to them, tell it to the church. And if he refuses to listen to the church, treat him like a Gentile or a tax collector."

What does it mean that Jesus instructed the "church" to treat an unrepentant brother like they would a Gentile or tax collector? If we use a 21st-century understanding of "church," aren't the Gentiles included in the "church?" Isn't the "church" a Gentile institution? Why would Jesus speak to them in a derogative manner? Why did he place them in the same category as hated tax collectors?

When Jesus made this statement, the community of Israel

JESUS IS JEWISH

considered Gentiles as outsiders. Pious Jews didn't partake in a meal with Gentiles, enter their homes, or associate with them *in any way*. Jesus's statement is incomprehensible unless we understand that he used the term *kahal*, translated by Matthew as *ekklesia* and that inclusion of Gentiles *hadn't yet occurred*. Jesus referred to a "brother" who doesn't listen, and that unheeding brother should be treated as an outcast *from the community of Israel*, not outcast from a Gentile community.

In Jesus's time, Gentiles joined the commonwealth of Israel through a proselytization process of lessons and study during a year or more of time, which guaranteed the participant would be "born again" into Israel ("born again" applied to the person when the proselyte completed the process) and received by his new family of Jews as a fellow recipient of the promises made to Abraham and his descendants. Paul later wrote to the Romans that Gentiles became grafted into the olive root of Israel by joining the *ekklesia* of Jesus (through faith), making them fellow citizens as Gentiles in the *kahal/ekklesia* of Israel.

Chapter 11
The Apostle Paul or Rabbi Shaul?
Part 1

With our simple but straightforward understanding of the development of Universal Christendom, I invite you to study the Apostle Paul. Did he play a role in this development as we understand through our historical lens? Let's examine whether common Christian perceptions of Paul hold up against the New Testament text.

We've conducted an intensive examination of a historical, accurate-as-possible timeline of Universal Christianity's development. We outlined how Jews, Torah, and the traditions of the Fathers bore no influence in its formation.

We've learned that a biblical, canonical narrative doesn't include the establishment of an institution called Universal Christianity. I imagine some readers disagree, but allow me to develop the idea further.

Consider Paul. Within the ivory towers of academia, people recognize that the Jesus of history and the Jesus of the Bible are, in fact, Jewish. If Jesus didn't start Christianity, then by default, Paul

JESUS IS JEWISH

did, for two reasons: one, he authored most of the New Testament, and two, he bore the moniker, "Apostle to the Gentiles."

Who was the Apostle Paul? For the past two millennia, the Church answered this question with a resounding anti-Jewish and anti-Torah opinion. Post-holocaust scholarship took a fresh look at Paul and examined his loyalties, personal ethos, and commitment to practicing first-century Judaism. Scholars such as Mark D. Nanos, David H. Stern, James Dunn, E.P. Sanders, D.T. Lancaster, Paula Fredrikson, and Professor Franz Delitzsch shed light on understanding Paul from a first-century, pro-Torah, pro-Jewish perspective. This significant new area of academic study received the moniker "The New Perspective on Paul" or "The Radical New Perspective on Paul."

Most of today's Universal Church doctrine and praxis misunderstands Paul and his epistles. If the Church misunderstands Paul and his message to his first-century audience, perhaps we mistake the essence and function of Christianity in the Kingdom of God?

If asked to answer the question "Who was the Apostle Paul?" most people in the Universal Church might give an answer like this one at Ask.com:

"Paul, according to the Bible, became a Christian after meeting with Jesus Christ on his way to Damascus to persecute the disciples of Jesus in Jerusalem. He was previously called Saul but changed after becoming blind for some time and a servant of God called Ananias restored his sight.[124]

Many Christians might add something like: "After Jesus changed Saul's name from the Jewish 'Saul' to the Christian 'Paul,' Paul renounced Judaism and became a Christian. He spent the rest of his life spreading the gospel and writing his letters." This description falls apart after careful analysis and critical exegesis.

Let's examine Paul's testimony first. We'll review and analyze his statements about himself during his trials recorded in the book of Acts, and his self-descriptions in the third chapter of Philippians. We'll delve into two challenging passages that clarify Paul's testimony and his theology.

The book of Acts records a series of trials in which Paul defends himself against accusations by religious Jewish leaders. These trials provide the best place to conduct our examination of Paul.

Let's set the stage.

JESUS IS JEWISH

At the time of events recorded in Acts, assassinations and violence escalated in Jerusalem. Political turmoil and sectarian infighting plagued the city as men and partisan parties vied for control. While still in Philippi, the prophet Agabus warned Paul and his traveling companions not to go to Jerusalem due to the chaos in the city.[125] As a fervent Torah observer, Paul disregarded the danger and travelled to Jerusalem along with his delegates and other celebrants to the feast of Shavuot (Pentecost).

As Paul and his Diaspora delegates approached Jerusalem, we imagine the palpable excitement they experienced upon seeing the Temple, some for the first time. They brought this unanswered question with them: "Would the *ekklesia* (assembly) of the Messiah, led by the Apostles, receive me and my new Gentile converts and welcome them as brothers of Israel?" Paul knew the believing community divided over Gentile inclusion into the commonwealth of Israel without full conversion. His arduous task weighed on him; convincing his opponents that God chose the Gentiles.[126]

The brothers received them gladly, and Paul recounted to them "all the things God had done for the Gentiles through his service." He introduced the council to the representatives from Syrian Antioch, Galatia, Macedonia, Thessalonica, and Corinth, cities with Gentile populations. He detailed how God worked in their lives. As each delegate presented himself before James and the elders and offered gifts on behalf of the community, the elders glorified God and gave thanks for what the LORD was doing in the Diaspora.

The elders in Jerusalem, too, brimmed with good news. They shared with Paul and the Gentile delegation that "many tens of thousands of believers among the Judeans were all zealous for the Torah!"[127] The Messiah inspired the Jews to greater obedience to Torah and caused a new hunger for God among the believing Jews. The message of the good news of the Messiah spread among the Jewish people and their numbers grew into the tens of thousands. All of them believed in Jesus and passionately followed Torah.

Not all the news was pleasant. Rumors circulated within the Jewish disciples of Jesus that Paul taught his assemblies to abandon the law of Moses (claiming Paul was anti-Torah), not to circumcise themselves (anti-*halachah*), and not to follow the traditions (oral traditions).[128] These speculations remained a grave concern to the Jewish disciples. If true, Paul would be discredited within the *ekklesia* of the Messiah. The elders and Paul needed a strategy for Paul to prove to his brothers and sisters in the Messiah that these allegations were lies. This plan needed to accurately portray Paul's teachings to his Gentile converts as pro-Torah, pro-*halachah*, and pro-oral traditions.

JESUS IS JEWISH

To help establish his innocence, they decided Paul would pay for four Jewish community members ready to fulfill their Nazirite vows. When the community saw Paul fulfill his Nazirite vow and pay for others to do the same, they would realize his adherence to Jewish customs and beliefs. "Then everyone will know that they have heard an empty report about you and that you, too, are walking in the statues of the Torah."[129]

Fulfilling a Nazirite vow required obligatory participation in the sacrificial system, still in operation after the death and resurrection of Jesus. Numbers 6:13-21 outlines the requirements necessary: burnt offerings, sin offerings, peace offerings, grain offerings, and wine libations. Paul's visible participation in the sacrificial rites signaled that he did not believe the death of Jesus abolished the sacrificial system.

You just heard the needle bring the record to a screeching halt. Right?

Paul participated in the Temple sacrifices after the death of Jesus.

Whoa.

For further research, I suggest you read the book by Daniel Lancaster, *What About the Sacrifices*, published by First Fruits of

Zion. Lancaster explains the significance and everlasting purposes of the sacrificial system.

Paul's involvement in the sacrificial system poses a significant challenge for Christian commentators. Some argue that Paul's actions show deceit and duplicity, and suggest that he did this to persuade as many Jews as possible to accept the Messiah. This interpretation paints a negative image of Paul and accuses him of being a liar.

Instead, the actions of Paul in Acts 21 sent a strong and clear message to the elders and the Jewish followers of Jesus in Jerusalem that the rumors about him were false. Paul remained a devout Jew who observed the Torah.

Given this evidence, how do we interpret some of his more controversial passages that appear to be anti-Torah? Before delving into this topic, we examine Paul's words and actions in more detail.

I) The Temple

His Nazirite vow fulfilled, Paul returned to the Temple. Some Jews from Asya (Asia Minor) "saw him in the Temple; stirred up the whole crowd and laid hands hands on him."[130] The Jews from Asya either didn't hear the message that Paul paid for his and four other men's Nazarite's vows or they were skeptical about his true

JESUS IS JEWISH

motives. They cried out, saying, "Men of Israel, help! This [pointing at Paul] is the man that speaks rebellion [sedition against Rome] in the ears of all men and in all the earth against this people [the Jews] and the Torah [Moses] and this place [the Temple], and [to top it off] he has brought to the Temple, Gentiles, and profaned the holy place!"[131] These pious Jewish men who didn't believe in Jesus leveled these charges against Paul.

When these men stirred the Jewish crowd into a frenzy, the mob seized Paul and hauled him outside the Temple.[132] A riot ensued. The Levitical guards instantly placed the Temple on lockdown as disorder and bedlam escalated. Roman guards, posted in prominent positions around the city, stood ready to keep the peace in conditions like this. The tribune at the Roman garrison near the Temple Mount received a report of the riot, and he rushed soldiers and centurions into the fracas.

The crowd wanted to kill Paul.

Then they saw the tribune and his soldiers bearing down on them.[133] The tribune shoved his way through the crowd, corralled Paul, and bound him in chains. He asked the instigators: "Who is this, and what has he done?" Shouts of accusation echoed from various locations in the crowd. "One said this, and another said that."[134] The cacophony of noise prevented the tribune hearing the truth. The tribune chose to retreat to the safety of the garrison and protect Paul.

The angry mob saw an opportunity to incite a full-blown riot and trailed behind the soldiers shouting, "Get rid of him!" Paul requested permission from the tribune to address the crowd. The tribune recognized the potential repercussions if he mishandled the prisoner and that perhaps Paul could appease the agitated crowd. He agreed to Paul's request and hoped that the Jew from Tarsus might resolve the misunderstanding and bring peace.

As Paul stood on the steps and gave his defense, the crowd quieted to listen. Paul said: "I am a Jewish man! I was born in Tarsus, which is in Kilikya [a city on the south coast of Turkey], but I grew up at the feet of Gamaliel. I was taught Torah in all its details and am zealous for God like all of you are today."[135]

Paul admitted that his zeal for the Torah drove him to persecute Jews who followed "The Way":

> However, on my way to Damascus around noon, suddenly a brilliant light from heaven flashed all around me! I fell to the ground and heard a voice saying to me, "Shaul! Shaul! Why do you keep persecuting me?" I answered, "Sir, who are you?" "I

JESUS IS JEWISH

am Yeshua from Nazareth," he said to me, "and you are persecuting me!" Those who were with me did see the light, but they didn't hear the voice of the one who was speaking to me. I said, "What should I do, Lord?" And the Lord said to me, "Get up and go into Damascus and there you will be told about everything that has been laid out for you to do." I had been blinded by the brightness of the light, so my companions led me by the hand into Damascus.

A man named Hananyah, an observant follower of the Torah who was highly regarded by the entire Jewish community there, came to me, stood by me and said, "Brother Shaul, see again!" And at that very moment, I recovered my sight and saw him. He said, *"The God of our Fathers* determined in advance that you should know his will, see the Tzaddik [the righteous one] and hear his voice; because you will be a witness for him to everyone of what you have seen and heard. So now, what are you waiting for? Get up, immerse yourself and have your sins washed away as you call on his name."

After I had returned to Jerusalem, it happened that as I was praying in the Temple, I went into a trance, and

TYRONE NICHOLS

I saw Yeshua. "Hurry!" he said to me. "Get out of Jerusalem immediately, because they will not accept what you have to say about me." I said, "Lord, they know themselves that in every synagogue I used to imprison and flog those who trusted you; and that when the blood of your witness Stephen was being shed, I was standing there too, in full agreement! I was even looking after the clothes of the ones who were killing him!" But he said, "Get going! For I am going to send you far away – *to the Gentiles*!"[136] [Italics mine]

Up to this point in Paul's story, the hushed crowd listened to his words. Perhaps they remembered his reputation as a fanatical rabbi and persecutor of "The Way." But when he said that Jesus sent him to the Gentiles, the crowd erupted. "Rid the earth of such a man! He's not fit to live!"[137]

"As they were crying out and flinging off their cloaks and throwing dust into the air, the commander ordered Paul to be brought into headquarters. He said Paul should be examined by lashing, so that he might find out why they were shouting against him so."[138]

This scene began the final chapters of Paul's life. We soon

JESUS IS JEWISH

find him in prison, in chains, and on trial on charges of heresy and treason for his obedience to take the message of the Kingdom to the Gentiles in the name of Jesus.

Why did the crowd grow angry when Paul began to talk about Gentiles? According to Judaism at this time, unless Gentiles went through ritual conversion and became proselytes, *halachic law forbid* their inclusion as fellow heirs in the commonwealth of Israel and in the promises of God. Paul's non-Jesus-believing Jewish countrymen opposed him, and his message brought controversy to the camp of Jesus's disciples. Again, the question of Gentile inclusion into Israel and how that could be legally accomplished caused unceasing arguments and tension.

Paul defended himself from court to court and appeared before ruler after ruler. In every account he gave, he *portrayed himself as a faithful Torah-observant Jew who was loyal to the Fathers and devoted to the Temple.*

Before examining the specific statements Paul used to defend himself, bear in mind that all of Paul's declarations during these trials took place toward the end of his life.

Paul goes on trial in six different venues:

i. The Temple – explained above (Acts 22) and not repeated below
ii. Before the Sanhedrin – The tribune took Paul to the Sanhedrin to allow them to determine if Paul had done anything wrong. (Acts 23)
iii. Before Felix – (Acts 24)
iv. Before Festus – (Acts 25)
v. Before Agrippa and Bernice – (Acts 26)
vi. Before the Jewish community in Rome – (Acts 28)

First Fruits of Zion's lead educational teacher completed several commentaries on the Torah. D.T. Lancaster has completed remarkable work regarding Paul in the First Fruits of Zion publication called Torah Club. Many of the following ideas can be found in Torah Club, Volume Six. Using Lancaster's framework, let's inspect Paul's testimony in each of the six trials to ascertain a proper portrait of the rabbi from Tarsus.

II) Before the Sanhedrin

The day after the Roman tribune arrested Paul in the Temple, he escorted Paul, bound in chains, to the Sanhedrin. This assembly consisted of 70 rabbis, most of whom were either Sadducees or Pharisees (Paul's sect). Shim'on Gamaliel sat in the office of leader of the Sanhedrin, a seat that his father Rabbi Gamaliel, Paul's teacher, once occupied.

JESUS IS JEWISH

In Acts 23:1, Paul initiated his defense against the indictments of heresy. "Brothers, in the blamelessness of my heart I have walked before HaShem (God) until this day." Lancaster writes the following about Paul's opening statement:

> A Jewish man's duty to God consists of Torah and the commandments. Paul's opening declaration means "I have remained Torah observant to this very day." The Greek word *politeuomai* means "to live as a citizen." The verb is adopted in Jewish literature to express the specifically Jewish ethic of "conducting oneself according to the Torah."[139]

Paul knew that some on the council were Pharisees and some were Sadducees. These two groups disagreed with one another on the issue of the afterlife and Paul calculated that he could use this contentious dispute to his advantage. He called out, "I am a Pharisee, the son of a Pharisee, and it is for the hope of the dead and their rising that I am being tried."[140] Paul knew that he would not receive a fair trial from the Sadducees, and with a chance that the Pharisees might help him because he was one of their own, he raised this divisive topic in his testimony.

He claimed that he saw the risen righteous one, Yeshua of Nazareth, on the road to Damascus and used this as evidence that life continues after death. "When he had said this word, a dispute began between the Pharisees and the Sadducees, and the assembly was divided. For the Sadducees say there is no resurrection and no angel and spirit, and the Pharisees confess them both."[141]

Pandemonium ensued. The Pharisees cried out, "We find nothing wrong with this man! What if a spirit or angel has spoken to him?"[142] The Pharisees agreed that the issue revolved around whether spirits and the afterlife were real, not who or what spoke to Paul! The heated debate rose to such a passionate level that the tribune removed Paul from the fray before the group tore him to pieces. The soldiers grabbed Paul and escorted him back to the fortress.

Note these two points in Paul's defense before the Sanhedrin. First, Paul did not say that he *was* a Pharisee, he said "I am a Pharisee." He declared his membership in the Pharisaical sect that educated him and to which he still belonged. He used this connection to his advantage. Second, Paul maintained his testimony about his encounter with the risen Lord on the road to Damascus. He stated his belief in an afterlife and resurrection of the dead and argued from that to the possibility that he saw Jesus. In Paul's mind, he remained a loyal, Jewish Pharisee and followed Jesus.

JESUS IS JEWISH

III) Before Felix

The Roman tribune in the garrison learned about a conspiracy to kill Paul. Someone hired members of the Sicarii (a Jewish group of assassins) to attack and kill him. The tribune placed the prisoner under the protection of Felix, governor of Judea and Samaria who resided in Caesarea.

Governor Felix held the trial. Chananyah the high priest in Jerusalem, some elders, and one attorney named Tartullos arrived to present their case against Paul. The prosecution declared that Paul brought pestilence, provoked contentions among the Jews, and headed the *notzrim* (The Way).

They said Paul defiled the Temple. They claimed he ought to be prosecuted according to the laws of Torah.[143] The combined indictments, if proven correct, incurred the death penalty.

Paul stepped forward with a confident heart. He knew these allegations were false. He told Felix, "You will be able to confirm that not more than twelve days have passed from the time I went to Jerusalem to worship. They did not find me in the Temple arguing with anyone or stirring up commotion among the people, and not in synagogues, nor the city. They have no proof for what they are charging me."[144]

Paul continued, "But this I confess to you [Felix], that according to the Way (which they call a sect), I worship the *God of our fathers*, believing *everything written* in the Torah and the Prophets. [I serve the God of my Fathers and I follow all that is written in the Torah, *while* a member of the sect they call The Way.] In God I have a hope – which these men also wait for – that there will surely be a resurrection of both the righteous and the unrighteous. Therefore, I do my best always to have a clear conscience before both God and men."[145] [Italics mine]

Paul acknowledged he belonged to "The Way," but he continued to believe in and live out a Torah-obedient lifestyle. Like his Pharisaical brothers, he believed in the hope of the resurrection of the dead, both the righteous and the wicked, and asserted this belief should not be grounds for finding him guilty of these charges. Paul reaffirmed he did everything with integrity before both God and man, because he believed everyone would one day stand before the righteous Judge and give an account of their lives.

Paul reminded Felix why he went to the Temple in the first place. "Now at the end of many years I came to bring donations to my people and to offer *korbanot* [sacrifices]. And with these *korbanot*, Jews from Asya (Asia Minor) found me after I had been purified in the Temple, not in a crowd of people or in a commotion."[146]

JESUS IS JEWISH

Paul denied starting a riot, emphasized that he visited the Temple to honor God, bring alms, offer sacrifices, fulfill vows, and worship God. When he offered sacrifices at the Temple, he did so without hesitation or questions.

Some people in the Universal Church struggle with Paul's participation in the Jewish sacrificial system, since according to Christian theology, the death of Christ abolished this system. Paul's testimony shows this wasn't true in the time between Christ's ascension and before the destruction of the Temple.

Paul finished his defense before Felix. "And these men from Asya, who stand before you and testify against me...let them please tell what wrong they found in me when I stood before the Sanhedrin, except for this one issue that I called out when I stood in their midst, 'I am being tried before you today for the resurrection of the dead.'"[147]

Paul concluded with the facts: he had committed no crimes, made no trouble, loved the Temple, worshiped God the same as his forefathers, and loved the Torah. The single reason for his trial? An inter-Jewish debate about the resurrection of the dead.

After the trial, Paul remained in prison, not because Felix found Paul's actions illegal, but under the guise of not understanding

The Way, he wanted a bribe from Paul. "And he was waiting for Paul to give him a bribe so that he might release him, and for this reason, he called him many times and spoke with him. At the end of two years, Festus arose [as governor] in Felix's place. Since Festus wanted to show kindness to the Jews [for political reasons], he did not release Paul from prison."[148]

In his third recorded defense, this time before Governor Festus, we see Paul held steadfast and denied he offended his fellow Jewish brothers. He loved the Torah, he loved the Temple, he loved God, and he loved Jesus, which didn't preclude him from his Torah obedient lifestyle.

IV) Before Festus

Eight days into Festus's rule, he ordered the guards to bring Paul to him for a hearing. Paul's Jewish accusers came and accused him of many unsubstantiated things. Paul again defended himself by saying, "I have not sinned in anything – not against the religion of the Jews [Torah observance], the Temple, or Caesar [as a seditionist]."[149]

To appease the Jewish leadership and preserve peace, Festus proposed another trial of Paul before the Sanhedrin in Jerusalem. Paul realized that his accusers still wanted to kill him. A return to

JESUS IS JEWISH

Jerusalem meant a death sentence for Paul. He responded:

> I am standing right now in the court of the Emperor, and this is where I should be tried. I have done no wrong to the Judeans, as you very well know. If I am a wrongdoer, if I have done something for which I deserve to die, then I am ready to die. But if there is nothing to these charges, which they are bringing against me, no one can give me to them just to grant a favor! I appeal to the Emperor![150]

Festus consented to Paul's request. "You have appealed to the Emperor; you will go to the Emperor."[151] Paul's appeal to Caesar seemed the optimal solution for Festus. He avoided condemning an innocent man, he preserved peace and crucial political ties with the Jewish leadership, and he stayed neutral in the internal Jewish dispute. The Jews believed they benefitted now that Festus had to send Paul to faraway Rome.

V) Before King Agrippa and Bernice

King Agrippa and Bernice (his sister, the Queen) arrived in Caesarea, on the coast of Israel, to pay their respects to Festus. They wanted to ensure their relationship with the new Roman procurator began well. As rulers of Caesarea Philippi, a city in north Israel, they relished good standing with both Jews and Romans alike. Festus brought Paul's case to their attention. Festus explained to Agrippa and Bernice the unique aspects of Paul's situation and that "the accusers disputed with Paul about certain points of their religion, and particularly about somebody called Jesus, who had died, and whom Paul claimed, was alive."[152] None of the allegations demanded the death penalty, according to Festus, but the Judeans thought so. He hoped Agrippa could shed some light on the situation. To further complicate matters, Paul (a Roman citizen) had appealed to Caesar and would soon go to Rome.

On the day after King Agrippa and Bernice arrived, the court of Festus held a grand audience. Festus informed Paul this gathering stood as an opportunity for King Agrippa and Bernice to hear his testimony. Many prominent Romans in the city, as well as the King and Queen with their entourage and Governor Festus, sat in an auditorium-like setting, and waited to hear from the controversial man known as Rabbi Shaul (Paul).

The audience quieted as Paul shuffled in chains toward the center of the auditorium.

"You may speak on behalf of your soul," Festus said to Paul. Paul looked around the room and may have marveled at this opportunity and at the irony of it. Lancaster writes, "As a free man,

JESUS IS JEWISH

he would have never been given the occasion to declare the good news of Jesus to such an audience. As a prisoner, he stood before kings and queens, governors and magistrates, the upper echelon of society. As he looked around the room and took in the moment, Paul breathed a prayer for strength and wisdom, and commenced with one of the most polished of all the speeches Luke records for us in the book of Acts."[153]

Paul appealed to the wisdom of Agrippa and honored him in front of the assembly. "King Agrippa, I consider myself fortunate that it is before you today that I am defending myself against all the charges made against me by Jews because you are so well informed about all the Jewish customs and controversies. Therefore, I beg you to listen to me patiently."[154]

Paul framed his testimony in light of his Torah-observant, Pharisaic life:

> All Jews know how I lived my life from my youth on, both in my own country and in Jerusalem. [Remember, Paul was from Tarsus.] They have known me for a long time; and if they are willing, they can testify that I have followed the strictest party in our religion – that is I have lived as a Pharisee. How ironic it is that I stand on trial here because of

my hope in the promise made to our Fathers...why do you people [looking at his accusers] consider it incredible that God raises the dead?[155]

Paul stated that as member of the Pharisaical sect of Judaism, he lived in accordance with their strict interpretation of Torah. He reminded the audience he awaited trial in Rome due to his Pharisaic belief in the resurrection of the dead, which the Sadducees fiercely opposed. Agrippa knew of this bitter theological divide between the Pharisees and Sadducees. As a Herodian, Agrippa inclined toward the Sadducean worldview. Paul mentioned it, as he believed he provided context for Agrippa.

Regarding Jesus, Paul reminded them that years ago, he did all he could do to combat Jesus and his followers. "I received authority from the high priest, I myself threw many of God's people in prison; when they were put to death, I cast my vote against them. I would go from one synagogue to another, punishing them and trying to make them blaspheme; and in my wild fury against them, I even went so far as to persecute them in cities outside the country."[156]

The audience may have wondered, "Why would he tell the truth about himself in such an unashamed, authentic manner?" To admit that he caused severe persecution against those he later joined

JESUS IS JEWISH

increased the irony and complexity of Paul's testimony. Paul recounted his experience on the road to Damascus while he traveled under the full authority and power of the high priest. "I saw a light from heaven, brighter than the sun...We all fell to the ground, I heard a voice, 'Shaul! Why do you persecute me?'"

"Who are you, sir?"

"I am Yeshua..." (Acts 9:3-9)

Paul continued, "So King Agrippa, I did not disobey the vision from heaven. On the contrary, I announced first in Damascus, then in Jerusalem and throughout Judea, and to the Gentiles, that they should turn from their sins to GOD and then do deeds [*mitzvot*] consistent with repentance [*teshuvah*]. It was because of these things [the fact that I took this message to the Gentiles] that I was seized in the Temple and they tried to kill me. However, I have said nothing but what both the prophets and Moses said would happen – that the Messiah would die, and that he, as the first to rise from the dead, would proclaim light to both the people [the Jews] and the Gentiles."[157]

All the Jews received and understood Paul's message of repentance (*teshuvah*), "Repent and turn toward God." All Jewish prophets preached this same message since the beginning.

TYRONE NICHOLS

John the Immerser preached teshuvah, as did Jesus. "Repent [teshuvah] for the Kingdom of Heaven is at hand." Paul's message proclaimed two new truths that traditional Jewish leadership found almost impossible to accept: one, that Jesus is the Messiah, because, in their view, he didn't fulfill all prophecies related to the Messiah; and two, that Paul, a Jew, delivered this message to Gentiles at the command of Jesus.

Everything in Paul's testimony as recorded for us in Acts 26 is Jewish. His message of "repentance that leads to salvation" is the same message preached in the books of Moses, in the books of the Prophets, by John the Immerser, and by Jesus. "Repent, turn to God, and perform deeds appropriate to repentance." Paul performed the duties and acts of Torah, as stated in his monologue. He associated with Pharisees and considered himself a Torah-observant Pharisee. He claimed that the message he brought to both Jew and Gentile remained consistent with the Law and the Prophets. Paul understood the Law and the Prophets not only demanded the message of repentance be shared with the Gentiles, but that the Jewish Messiah would suffer and die as an atoning sacrifice for Gentile sins as well as those of the Jews.

Festus responded to Paul, "You are out of your mind! All this learning has driven you crazy!" But Agrippa and Bernice knew Paul's rational arguments agreed with Mosaic Law. Perhaps they didn't agree with him, but they understood him. Agrippa asked, "In this short time are you trying to convince me to become Christian?" When Agrippa said these words, Paul surmised that his message had pierced Agrippa's mental armor and thus responded, "Whether it takes a short time or a long time, I wish to God that not only you, but also everyone hearing me today, might become just like me except for these chains."[158]

What did it mean to be just like Paul? From his testimonies, we must conclude it means to be a Torah-observant Jew, faithful to the message of repentance, committed to the traditions and customs of the Jewish people, and devoted to the Jewish Messiah, Jesus. This portrait stands at odds with Universal Christianity's view of Paul.

We'll take a closer look at some of his letters later, but next, let's evaluate Paul's final testimony. Agrippa mentioned to Festus, "This man has done nothing that deserves either death or prison. If he hadn't appealed to the emperor, he could have been released."[159] Innocent Paul traveled to Italy.

VI) Before the Jewish community in Rome

The book of Acts Chapter 27 details the harrowing voyage that Paul and his traveling companions endured on their way to Rome. They survived a disastrous shipwreck when the ship ran aground, they swam to safety, they faced malnutrition, Paul miraculously survived a poisonous snakebite, and they had to hunt for a second ship to continue their journey.

While in Rome the guards allowed Paul to entertain visitors and meet with the local Jewish leaders. Paul recounted his astounding testimony to these leaders. He reassured them that, "I have done nothing against either our people or the traditions of our fathers." Again, Paul confirmed his life and message were consistent with Torah and traditions of the fathers. In fact, Paul said, "I am in chains *because of the hope of Israel.*" [Italics mine] Although these Roman Jewish leaders hadn't heard of Paul, they had heard about those who followed the sect of the Nazarene.

From morning till evening, Paul explained matters before them, gave witness about the Kingdom of God, and made use of the Torah of Moses and the Prophets to persuade his new audience about the merits of Jesus. Convinced by what he said, some people believed, while others refused.[160]

Religious leaders of Paul's time accused him of being anti-Torah, anti-Jewish, anti-Moses, and a non-observant Jew who taught that the law had been abolished due to the actions of Christ, *Christianity developed its theology around these misguided beliefs.*

JESUS IS JEWISH

Christianity believes Paul helped start a new religion. He didn't. He lived the Jewish Torah-observant life as a Pharisee, he honored Moses by being Torah-observant, and he preached repentance and the good news of the Messiah within the context of a thorough Jewish framework. Paul's own words showed that none of his accusers spoke the truth.

Today, in the 21st century, we must ask ourselves: Do we continue to consider Paul a liar? Do we stand with his accusers? Or do we re-examine Paul and his message in a way that is thoroughly pro-Torah, pro-Jewish, pro-Moses, pro-traditions, and pro-Jewish Messiah — as Paul himself said?

TYRONE NICHOLS

Chapter 12

The Apostle Paul or Rabbi Shaul?

Part 2

Moving forward, we'll consider Paul's statements with utmost care and note that his personal testimony is the crucial foundation of his epistles. Paul remained devout Jew, followed the Torah, and believed in the Messiah prophesied by the Jewish prophets. Traditional Christianity doesn't understand Paul's writings this way.

When we understand Paul's foundation, we also understand Mark Nanos, an esteemed Pauline scholar, who has played a vital role in the re-examination of Paul in post-Holocaust scholarship. Nanos wrote in his book *The Mystery of Romans*:

> I locate in the author of Romans a very different Paul; a thoroughly Jewish Paul, functioning entirely within the context of Judaism, giving priority to Israel, even willing to give his life in the place of the Jewish people in the tradition of Moses to ensure their irrevocable stature as God's beloved for whom restoration is certain.[161]

JESUS IS JEWISH

Why does Nanos hold this strong opinion of Paul in contrast to that of the Church? The quote below came from a Christian website, www.belief.net, which attempted to answer the ironic question, "Was Paul Jewish?"

"Most scholars believe so, though they have argued about his commitment to Judaism both before and after his conversion to Christianity."[162]

Did Paul convert to Christianity? Without one shred of evidence, the above statement describes Christianity's concept of Paul: a Jew who persecuted Christians, met Jesus on the road to Damascus, and "converted." Paul's teachings are now considered the main source of Christian doctrine.

Let's look closer.

The study of Paul in post-Holocaust scholarship gives us a deeper understanding of him as a first-century Judean Pharisee who became a follower of the Jewish Messiah. Academic research indicates that Paul's transformation on the road to Damascus was not a switch to a different religion named "Christianity."

President and founder of First Fruits of Zion, Boaz Michael, produced a series entitled *HaYesod*, in which he relays the following:

Paul's experience on the road to Damascus was a much deeper experience than a simple religious conversion from one group to another. He met the living Messiah, the same Messiah he and the Pharisees had been anticipating for centuries, the same Messiah who lived his life within the framework of the Hebrew Scriptures. Like Yeshua [Jesus] himself, Paul remained a Jew, faithful to the ways of his people and loyal to the Torah.[163]

After meeting the Messiah, the Apostle Paul spent three years in Damascus, where he studied and taught the Torah. When Paul returned to Jerusalem to share and explain his encounter with the Savior, the Jewish disciples of Jesus doubted his testimony and looked with skepticism on his claims, and rightly so. Paul once persecuted and sentenced to death those who confessed belief in the resurrected Jesus before his experience on the road to Damascus.

After Peter and the Apostles in Jerusalem, Jesus's closest companions, accepted Paul, they all studied the Scriptures and the words of the Messiah together. The group in Jerusalem first understood Jesus as Messiah only in the confines of Judaism and as a logical extension of Jewish faith within the framework of the Hebrew Scriptures. After Paul's message added in Gentiles, he and others spent their entire lives with Jewish and Gentile people and introduced members of both groups to the Jewish Messiah.

JESUS IS JEWISH

I reiterate why Paul's gospel, which he often called "my gospel," created controversy in the Jewish community. It granted Gentile people access to the Kingdom of God when they took on a life of discipleship under Jesus of Nazareth but did not require conversion to Judaism. Paul's message, enclosed inside the truth of the Bible/Torah, departed from tradition and orthodoxy. Paul and the disciples used the Tanakh (the Hebrew name for the Hebrew Scriptures) to strengthen their claim of Gentile inclusion, but the idea caused many in the Jewish population to question Paul's allegiance to the Jewish people and his status in the community.

In the third chapter of Philippians, Paul reminds the reader of his pristine Jewish qualifications. He didn't disavow Jews and Jewish credentials as many Christian commentators assert, but compared his impeccable Jewish resume to the greatness of knowing the Messiah! He listed the following criteria as proof of his flawless Jewish status:

1. B'rit-milah (circumcised) on the eighth day
2. By birth belonged to the people of Israel (as compared to proselytes who become Jewish by ceremony and Torah law)
3. From the tribe of Benjamin (Paul knows his ancestral background)

4. A Hebrew-speaker, with Hebrew-speaking parents (he speaks the tongue of his fathers)
5. In regard to the Torah, a Parush (he uses the present tense to describe his relation to the Pharisees; in essence he said, "I am a Pharisee")
6. In regard to zeal, a persecutor of the Messianic community
7. In regard to the righteousness of Torah, blameless (Paul does not say he was blameless, but says he is blameless as it relates to following Torah).

Paul's gospel ostracized him from this Jewish, Pharisaic fraternity. He suffered loss of prestige and status in the eyes of men. He "gave it all up" (the prestige his Jewish standing provided him – *not the Torah*) and "regarded it [the status] as garbage" to gain the Messiah. Paul did not stray from the ways of the Hebrew Scriptures. With zeal, he followed the ways of Torah his entire life.[164]

Paul's teachings are intricate, leading to frequent misinterpretations that have, in turn, shaped Christian theology in distorted ways. Many of my Christian friends would likely be taken aback to discover that, even after his encounter with Jesus on the road to Damascus, Paul continued to live as a Torah-observant Jew, a fact to which he himself attests. What makes Paul's writings so challenging to grasp? And why has there been centuries-long confusion surrounding them?

JESUS IS JEWISH

The apostle Peter says, "He [Paul] writes the same way in all his letters, speaking in them of these matters. His letters contain some things that are hard to understand, which ignorant and unstable people distort, as they do the other Scriptures, to their own destruction."[165] For us to comprehend Paul and his teachings in the context of his time, we must be willing to discard, or at least suspend, our 21st-century, Christian-influenced portrait of him and *shift our intellectual perception to first-century Judaism*. This is no easy task. If portions of Paul's letters were "hard to understand" for some in the 1st century, imagine how much more work we need to do as 21st-century truth seekers!

Christendom has warped Paul's letters into anti-Torah and anti-Jewish form. Paul wrote all his letters as he lived his life: pro-Torah and pro-Israel. Isn't it right to honor his life and writings from his worldview?

Let's look at a couple of misunderstood passages from Paul in the New Testament to further develop the portrait of Paul as an authentic, first-century Torah-observant Jew. I don't present an exhaustive exploration into the controversial passages that Christendom claims as proof that Paul is anti-Jewish and anti-Torah. Instead, I give the reader two important tools: a firm *hermeneutical* (principles of interpretation) and *exegetical* (critically looking at the text) foundation to use in your study of Paul's teaching. Though "the majority of New Testament scholars have maintained a fundamental antithesis between Paul and Judaism,"[166] we can be encouraged on our journey to revise the traditional narrative of "Paul, the Jew-who-became-Christian" to find "Paul, the Jew-who-embraced-his-[and our]-Jewish-Messiah."

In Romans 2:13 Paul wrote, "For it is not merely the hearers of Torah whom God considers righteous; rather it is the *doers of what Torah says* who will be made righteous in God's sight." In Romans 3:31 we read, "Does it follow that we abolish Torah by trusting? Heaven forbid! On the contrary, we confirm Torah!" And in Romans 7:12, "So, *the Torah is holy; that is, the commandment is holy, just, and good.*" In his first letter to the Corinthians, he wrote in Chapter 7 verse 19, "Being circumcised means nothing [being Jewish], and being uncircumcised means nothing [being Gentile]; what does mean something *is keeping God's commandments [the Torah].*" In his first letter to Timothy, Paul explained the purpose of Torah. In Chapter 1 verse 8 he wrote, "We know that *the Torah is good*, provided one uses it in the way the Torah itself intends." I realize that the version of the Bible you read may not have translated the word "Law" as "Torah"; however, in Paul's vernacular he is referring to Torah and it should be understood as such. [All italics mine]

These verses provide samples of Paul's pro-Torah theology.

JESUS IS JEWISH

At its core, his theology contains a Jewish *hashkafa* (worldview) rooted in the Judaism of his era. My paraphrase is, "The doers of what the Torah says are made righteous in the eyes of God, and faith in Jesus does not abolish this understanding. This is no different than what Jesus taught when He said, 'If you love me, you will obey me.'"

Believers in Jesus as God's Messiah "do" Torah; faith in the Messiah confirms Torah. The Torah is holy, just, and good. As members of the body of Messiah, being Jewish is of no consequence, as being Gentile is of no consequence. Paul elaborates on this idea when he says: "There is neither Jew nor Gentile, neither slave nor free, nor is there male nor female, for you are all one in the Messiah." Paul doesn't discount the distinctives of each group, only that our collective *status* in God's Kingdom makes us all equal; *we are all co-heirs to the promises of God*. What matters in the Kingdom is that we live out God's commands, His Torah. Paul's theology centers on reverence for and observance of the Torah. He strives to rightly divide the Torah and to make it applicable to all citizens in the Kingdom of God.

So how does this work? How do Gentiles and Jews fellowship together as believers within the context of Judaism? How do Jews include Gentile believers who've received the gift of the Holy Spirit, but haven't become Jewish according to *halachah*?

TYRONE NICHOLS

The proselytization ritual, according to the Jewish norms of that time, included months if not years of study with a rabbi, circumcision, the mikvah (ritual immersion), and sacrifice on the Temple Mount. When a Gentile undertook the ritual conversion to Judaism, he or she followed Jewish *halachah* (legal rulings) during the process, which led to the moment when the Gentile became legally and fully Jewish, obligated to keep the entire Torah for the rest of his or her life.

Paul traveled around the Diaspora and taught that this custom (legal conversion) no longer applied to Gentiles who came to faith in the Messiah. What?!?

Paul argues in Romans 2:25-29 that for a Gentile to gain access to the commonwealth of Israel and be a fellow heir to the promises of God, "legal conversion" is not necessary. Paul maintains that inclusion into the commonwealth, for the Gentile, was a matter of a circumcised heart. Let's read the passage together.[167] [168]

Daniel Lancaster inspired the following paraphrase in his audio series on the book of Romans:

> For circumcision [Paul's shorthand for "legally Jewish"] is indeed of value if you do what the Torah

JESUS IS JEWISH

says. But if you are a transgressor of Torah, your circumcision [legal Jewish status] has become uncircumcision [the same as being legally Gentile]. Therefore, if an uncircumcised man [a legally Gentile man] keeps the righteous requirements of the Torah, won't his uncircumcision [legal Gentile status] be counted as circumcision [legal Jewish status]? Indeed, the man who is physically uncircumcised [legally Gentile] but obeys the Torah, will stand as a judgment on you who have had a b'ritmilah [circumcision, therefore legally Jewish] and have Torah written out but violate it! For the real Jew is not merely Jewish outwardly; true circumcision [Jewish status] is not only external and physical. On the contrary, the real Jew is one inwardly: and true circumcision [Jewish status] is of the heart, spiritual not literal; so that his praise comes not from other people, but from God. [Paraphrase of Romans 2:25-29]

Through Paul's new "law," Gentile believers now become sons and daughters of Abraham by way of a circumcised heart (a heart of faith) and a heart that practices Torah.

Paul's message caused a major controversy in first century

Judaism. Jewish traditions required that qualified recipients of the promises of God had to be *legally* Jewish – either a person born of a Jewish mother or person born as a Gentile then born a second time as a Jewish proselyte. Only sons of Abraham had access to the covenant promises, and only the sons of Abraham were obligated to follow Torah. If a foreigner wanted to be viewed in the eyes of God as a son or daughter of Abraham, established traditions said he or she had to go through the legal rituals of proselytization.

Caution: both Jews and proselytes had to meet one absolute prerequisite to be considered eligible for inheritance in the Kingdom; faith/belief in the One True God. That faith drove and still drives the Jew and the Gentile-turned-Jew to observe the commandments.

Faith and repentance accompanied by actions of obedience to the Torah bring the believer into the commonwealth of Israel and a share in the afterlife. *Obedience to the Torah is the outworking of the inner heart of faith of the Jewish believer.* This theology is reiterated by James, the brother of Yeshua, when he writes, "Thus, faith by itself, unaccompanied by works [acts of righteousness as defined by Torah] is dead."[169]

Christianity assumes that the Jews believe a Jew is "saved" by obedience to the Torah. *No.* For the Jew, obedience is a matter of

JESUS IS JEWISH

the heart, of faith. Obedience to the Torah is the action that proves their faith in the One True God.

Both James and Paul look to Abraham as the model for faith. James writes, "You see his [Abraham's] faith worked with his actions, by the actions his faith was made complete; and the passage of the *Tanakh* was fulfilled which says, 'Abraham had faith in God, and it was credited to his account as righteousness. He was even called God's friend. You see that a person is declared righteous because of actions and not because of faith alone.'"[170] This is exactly what Paul says in Romans 2:13 "...it is the doers of what Torah says who will be made righteous in God's sight."

Am I saying that Paul is teaching a works-based salvation model? Doesn't Paul say, "For by grace you are saved through faith, and that not of yourselves; it is the gift of God – not by works so no man can boast?" (Eph. 2:8-9)

Yes. God's grace saves us, and it is *activated* by our faith in Him. Faith is the first step, like for Abraham, but not the only step. *I can't work my way to being saved, but my works show that I am saved.* God will see my good works and credit them to me as righteousness. Isn't this what Jesus taught? "Let your light so shine before men that they may see your good works and glorify your Father in heaven. Do not think that I have come to abolish the Law [the Torah] or the Prophets; I have not come to abolish them, but to fulfill them!" [Fulfill - to fill full, to live rightly and interpret rightly God's Torah.] (Matt. 5:16-17)

In Chapter 3 of Romans, Paul answers the question his Jewish readers might have after they read his opening salvo regarding "legal Jewish status." My paraphrase of their question reads, "Is there any distinction between Jew and Gentile? If a Gentile can also become a Jew on the inside, by faith, then what advantage does the Jew have?" Paul worded their question this way, "What is the value of being circumcised [being legally Jewish]?" His answer was "MUCH IN EVERY WAY!" [Emphasis mine]

"In the first place, the Jews were entrusted with the very words of God. If some of them were unfaithful, so what? Does their unfaithfulness cancel God's faithfulness? Heaven forbid!"[171] Paul stressed that God's faithfulness to the Jews doesn't depend on the faithfulness of the Jews themselves. God's promises stand, and God keeps His Word. The Jewish nation receives *blessings* for keeping their end of the covenant obligations conferred upon them at Sinai and *curses* if they fail to keep the commandments.

Scriptures don't say that God will "divorce" his covenant partner and find a new one. The Torah *does* say the LORD's covenant partner *may be punished* due to her own actions and lack

JESUS IS JEWISH

of obedience, but God's faithfulness to her will never go away. Never.

From the words at the end of Chapter 2 and the beginning of Chapter 3 in Romans, we conclude that mankind is saved by faith in the Divine Creator. *Obedience to the Law saves neither the Jew nor the Gentile.* Torah observance is the Jewish nation's covenant responsibility before God to be the light to the world. Observance done with the right heart is meritorious and brings blessings upon the Jewish nation as she fulfills her side of the covenant.

Now, let's go back to Paul's controversial message.

In the assembly of the Messiah, and in the context of the Commonwealth of Israel, Paul taught that legal conversion of the Gentile to become Jewish was no longer *necessary*. This ruling doesn't release the Gentile from Torah because Torah defines righteous actions and defines them now. Torah wasn't discarded and isn't discarded now. Remember, Jesus said that he didn't come to abolish the law, only to fulfill it in the sense of keeping it.

Paul reiterated this message to the Galatians:

> What the Messiah has freed us for is freedom! Therefore, stand firm, and don't let yourselves be tied up again to a yoke of slavery. Mark my words-I

Sha'ul [Paul] tell you that if you undergo b'rit milah [the rites of legally becoming Jewish, including circumcision] the Messiah will be of no advantage to you at all! Again, I warn you: any [Gentile] man who undergoes b'rit milah [becomes legally Jewish] is obligated to observe the entire Torah! [Why? Because it is the Jews' obligation, as a covenant partner with God, to observe all of the Torah.] You [Gentiles] who are trying to be declared righteous by God through legalism [through ritually becoming Jewish] have severed yourselves from the Messiah! You have fallen away from God's grace! For it is by the power of the Spirit, who works in us because we trust and are faithful, that we confidently expect our hope of attaining righteousness to be fulfilled. When we are united with Messiah Yeshua, neither being circumcised [status of being legally Jewish] nor being uncircumcised [status of being legally Gentile] matters; what matters is trusting and faithfulness expressing itself through love. [My paraphrase of Galatians 5:1-6]

This passage is about how a Gentile enters the Kingdom, not about annulment of Torah. Gentile believers enter the Kingdom by faith in Messiah. Anyone who thinks conversion to become legally

JESUS IS JEWISH

Jewish or any type of Torah observance *as a means of salvation/gaining entrance to the Kingdom* is taking on a yoke of slavery. Adherence to Torah is *not* slavery.

Lancaster summarizes historical Christianity's incorrect understanding of Galatians 5:1-6 in the following:

> Christianity is freedom; Judaism and the Torah is slavery. The Christian who observes the Jewish law renders Messiah of no advantage because the Messiah came to cancel the Jewish Torah and set men free from those rituals. In Messiah, Judaism has now come to an end. In fact, if a Christian keeps the Old Testament law, he severs himself from Messiah, falls from grace, and is in danger of damnation.[172]

How do we reconcile this historical Christian interpretation with Paul's statement in Romans 7:12: "So then, the law [Torah] is holy, and the commandment is holy, righteous, and good"? *We can't reconcile these statements.* Christendom teaches Christians are "free" from the Law, and Paul says the exact opposite. He states that the Law is holy, and the commandments are holy, righteous, and good.

Perhaps another way to think about this idea is helpful.

According to Paul, the Gentile believer in Jesus becomes a son of Abraham (*b'nei Avraham*) by faith, just as Abraham believed in the LORD and the LORD credited Abraham's faith to him as righteousness. *For Paul, it made no sense why a Gentile would want to undergo conversion to become Jewish when he or she was already included in the commonwealth of Israel by faith.* "Paul saw it as a type of slavery: working to achieve a status that is yours already. Not that the Gentile believers already had Jewish status – not at all. They were not Jewish, but they were sons of Abraham by faith and part of the greater people of God."[173]

Paul wrote this to the Galatian Gentiles to counter the claims of some Jews in their community that full conversion stood as the only way to become fellow heirs with the community of Israel. The Messiah connected the believing Gentile to Israel as a son of Abraham by faith, making legal conversion unnecessary. Again, why try to gain entrance into the kingdom when you've already gained entrance?

Paul clarified this to some believing Gentiles in Galatia who were confused. To ensure they'd be considered part of the Kingdom of God, they listened to opposite reasonings; Paul's reasoning on one hand and the reasoning of Jewish men on the other, who believed entrance to the Kingdom required conversion. These men insisted Paul tried to change 1500 years of Jewish tradition and

JESUS IS JEWISH

halachah about how a non-Jewish person entered the family of Israel. Confusion persists even today.

We see why Paul became such a controversial figure in the Jewish community. He argued that Gentiles could be equal inheritors of the commonwealth of Israel through discipleship under the wings of the Jewish Messiah and faith in the God of Abraham, Isaac, and Jacob.

What is the relationship between the Gentile believer in the Jewish Messiah to the Torah? Does Paul show that the Gentile believer is not obligated to the Torah? Does Paul teach that the Torah was nailed to the cross and "done away with?"

We look at Colossians next, but before we do, let's ask ourselves some commonsense questions.

First, why does the Christian Church abide by nine of the Ten Commandments but change one of them? The Church agrees not to have other gods besides God, not to worship idols, not to take the LORD's name in vain, to honor your father and mother, not to murder, not to commit adultery, not to steal, not to bear false witness, and not to covet.

The Church affirms the Law in nine, then discards Sabbath observance, the fourth commandment. Why?

TYRONE NICHOLS

For argument's sake, let us suppose the Church believes it follows the fourth commandment, though not literally as with the rest of the commandments. Who gave the Church permission to change the day of the week considered as the Sabbath? Most in the Church believe that it's what Paul said to do. Paul told the Church that we have "died to the Law through the body of the Messiah" (Romans 7:4) and that we have been "released from the law, having died to that by which we were bound, so that we serve in newness of Spirit and not in oldness of the letter!" (Romans 7:6)

If this is so, why does Christianity follow *any* of the Ten Commandments? Are we not "dead" to all of them in the body of the Messiah? Are the Ten Commandments only sort of a guide?

Second question: If Jesus said that he did not come to abolish or nullify the Law, why do Paul and the Church abolish it? Are Paul and people in the Church elevated to authority above Jesus?

Jesus said not one jot or tittle would pass away until the New Heaven and New Earth arrive. Yet does Paul, about 15 years later, discard the very words of the Messiah and nullify the Torah by teaching its obsolescence, its nullification? We must be missing something. Did Jesus teach that the Torah is done away with? Did Paul receive permission somehow to create a new religion—an anti-Torah, anti-Jewish religion only about freedom from the Law, only

JESUS IS JEWISH

about grace in God, and only about guidance by the Spirit of God?

In Colossians 2:13-17, Paul wrote:

> When you were dead in your transgressions and the uncircumcision of your flesh, He made you alive together with Him, having forgiven us all our transgressions, having canceled out the certificate of debt consisting of decrees against us, which was hostile to us; and He has taken it out of the way, having nailed it to the cross.[174]

"Exactly! See? Paul taught that Torah was nailed to the cross! Jesus did away with it when he was executed."

Yes, that's the "correct" Christian interpretation, but it relies on an incorrect understanding of one phrase.

The "certificate of debt" is not the Torah; this certificate contains the *decrees against us*, it's the *record* of our sins nailed to the cross. The Greek word used here to describe "a certificate of debt" is *cheirographon*. It means, "a note of indebtedness, written in one's own hand as a proof of obligations…A common thought in Judaism is that of God keeping accounts of man's debt, calling in the debt through angels and imposing a just judgment based on the records kept in the ledger."[175]

Paul said this "certificate of debt" nailed to the cross is the ledger of our indebtedness to God, the record of all debts (our sins), which one day we will have to repay. The Torah itself is *not* the certificate of death and is *not* hostile to us; rather it's a light that guides our path and points out our sins and their repercussions. *Our sins themselves and the consequences of them* are hostile to us.

Thank God for the Torah in that it points this out for us! Jesus nailed our certificate of debt, the list of our sins, to the cross! He decided to pay the debt for us with his life! He paid the price of our sins! What somber but welcome news!

Paul continued in Ephesians 2:13-16:

> But now, you who were once far off have been brought near through the shedding of the Messiah's blood. For he himself is our peace – he has made us both one and has broken down the wall which divided us by destroying in his own body the enmity occasioned by the Torah, with its commands set forth in the form of ordinances. He did this in order to create in union with himself from the two groups a single new humanity and thus make shalom, and in order to reconcile to God both in a single body by being executed on a stake as a criminal and thus in

JESUS IS JEWISH

himself killing that enmity.

To what enmity does he refer? It's the enmity that existed between Jew and Gentile, not an enmity that existed between the Gentile and Torah! What is the dividing wall, then? It's called the *m'chitzah*. In Greek the word is *mesotoichon*, which means the middle wall or the dividing wall.

This wall stood in the Temple to keep Gentiles from the inner courts. It marked the line where the Gentiles could go no further. It meant "Only Jews allowed past this wall." According to Paul, Jesus's death broke down this physical wall of hostility between the two people groups as a symbol that the *invisible* wall of separation also had disappeared. Jesus rendered Gentiles and Jews the same in status before God and access to God.

"Surely," you may say, "Paul did away with the Kosher food laws and the Jewish calendar, which does away with the Torah, right? In Colossians 2:16-17, didn't he, like Jesus, declare all foods clean as well as normalize all days so that one is not any more special than another?"

No. This passage is also misunderstood.

Paul advises "to not let anyone pass judgment on you in connection with eating and drinking, or in regard to a Jewish festival or the new moon, or Shabbat, which *are* [emphasis mine] a shadow of the coming things, and the body is of the Messiah." In this case, translators mistranslated this verse based on their theological predispositions.

Most translators changed the word "are" to the word "were," implying that the new moon and Shabbat are a thing of the past and no longer relevant for today. The Greek verb used here is *"eimi,"* which is like our verb "to be." It's used here in the present tense indicative mood ("right now" mood), as in "I am the way." When translators changed the verb to the past tense, they did injustice to what the author wrote, which is the sense of "being" or "continual being." Jesus "fills the feast full," quite the opposite of annulled or canceled.

What's the thinking about the dietary laws? Most Christians point to Romans 14 to confirm that Paul declared all foods clean. Romans 14:1-3 says:

> Now as for a person, whose trust is weak, welcome him-but not to get into arguments over opinions. One person has the trust that will allow him to eat anything, while another whose trust is weak eats only vegetables. The one who eats anything must not look down on the one who abstains; and the abstainer

JESUS IS JEWISH

must not pass judgment on the one who eats anything, because God has accepted him.

This verse looks as if Paul abolished the Levitical food laws. Did he?

Let's inspect what Jesus taught about Levitical food laws first. Many people in Christendom point to Mark 7:1-23 to show that Jesus annulled the food laws. If he'd violated any Torah law, including food laws, he'd be disqualified as the Messiah and as our Savior, and his sacrifice would mean nothing to us.

In Mark 7:1-4, Jesus framed the debate around eating ritually *clean* bread with ritually unclean hands. Jesus said, "Listen to me, all of you who understand! There is nothing outside of a person that can contaminate him by going into him. Rather, the things coming out from him contaminate the person. Whoever has ears, let him hear!" (Mark 7:14-16)

To understand this passage clearly, know that the "traditions of the fathers" (oral traditions within Judaism) gave context to the discussion. Jesus leveled a charge at the Pharisees, saying, "You invalidate the Word of God [Torah] by your tradition [tradition of the elders/sages] which you have handed down; and you do many things such as that." By saying this, Jesus told the religious leaders some of the traditions surrounding the laws of God invalidated the commands!

The issue revolved around the tradition of "washing of hands" (*n'tilat-yadayim*) before eating. This group of Pharisees believed if Jesus did not wash his hands before eating "clean" food, in this case bread, the bread would be tainted due to the status of his unclean, unwashed hands.

Let me clarify.

The question is, "Can 'clean' food become 'defiled' by 'ritually unclean hands?'" One side of the issue said food handled by ritually unclean hands defiled the person who ate it. "According to Maimonides, the Pharisees attempted to avoid eating any foods defiled by contact, and they believed that doing so [not eating defiled food] led to the sanctification of the soul."[176]

The Master disagreed and offered a counter argument, with which rabbinic law agrees today. Rabbi Buchler wrote a succinct consensus. "The supposition that unwashed hands could defile to such a degree that the food could in its turn defile the body of him who ate it...is contrary to rabbinic law."[177] Jesus taught that nothing clean – the bread – when eaten by "unwashed" or ritually unclean hands, could render the food "unclean" and thus make the eater of

JESUS IS JEWISH

the food unclean.

Biblical scholar and member of the Jerusalem School of Synoptic Research, David Bivin, writes:

> In this context, Jesus and his contemporaries are not discussing categories of permanent prohibitions (which by Biblical definition are impure or unclean), for instance forbidden food such as camel meat, rabbit meat or pig meat (Deuteronomy 14:7-8), but rather items such as cups and hands that are not essentially unclean but have, according to rabbinic *halachah*, the capability of contracting uncleanness, that is, of going in and out of a state of purity. If this was the discussion, then Jesus was not declaring "clean" what the Bible declares, "unclean." His answer to the question "Does touching food with unwashed hands ritually contaminate it?" was an acceptable Jewish response in the first century. The Jewish sage Jesus ruled, "No, it does not." Bread that is touched by an unwashed hand does not lose its state of ritual purity and become a carrier of impurity. It does not introduce impurity into one's body.[178]

Jesus's answer didn't do away with the Levitical food laws.

TYRONE NICHOLS

He clarified his position on an internal Jewish legal debate around the nature of clean and unclean hands. Remember, anyone who claimed to be the Messiah would not and could not violate the Torah. *Torah is the only document that outlines and delineates the Messiah's qualifications.* If Jesus abolished or negated the Torah *in any way*, he would disqualify himself from the position of Messiah.

According to the Torah laws, ritual uncleanness because of contact with specific animals, certain animal carcasses, bodily fluids, leprosy, or a corpse, isn't sinful, but is a ritual status that rendered a person unclean. Ritual uncleanness prevented a person from participation in Temple services until he or she completed a ritual purification process.

The two sides debated within the Jewish religion whether unclean hands turned ritually clean food to unclean food. The Torah Club quotes Rabbi Lichtenstein:

> Yeshua meant by this to say, "Since contamination is an external condition, one need not be so stringent in it, for it is not among the weighty commandments, and thus one must not add decrees upon it that one may not eat without [ceremonially washed hands]." In his statement in verse 20, the meaning is, "These are things that contaminate the (true and inner) man

JESUS IS JEWISH

but eating without [ceremonially washed hands] does not contaminate the man."[179]

Mark portrays Jesus's authentic Jewishness in the halachic debates with other teachers. By his declaration that clean foods cannot make an Israelite unclean if he or she eats with unwashed hands, Jesus defends the Torah and upholds the Levitical *Kashrut* laws. (Lev.11)[180]

Did Paul's statement that "all foods are clean" contradict Jesus's teachings? To better understand Paul's perspective, let's go back to Romans 14 to view his remarks in context and comprehend his message in full. Mark Nanos writes about Paul's theological *hashkafa* (worldview) in his book *The Mystery of Romans*:

> Conceptually, Paul did not see faith in Jesus Christ as a break with Israel and his fellow Jews of the Diaspora. He certainly had not left the Jewish faith. Jews were the historical community of the One God, whether they believed in Jesus as the Christ or not. Thus, to be a Christian, whether Jew [which would be natural to Paul] or Gentile [which was a wonderful new reality that had always been part of Israel's eschatological expectation], would have immediately made one a "brother" to all Jews,

whether they were Christians or not.[181]

I disagree with scholars when they use "Christian" or "Jewish-Christian" to describe a first-century Jew who believed in Jesus as his Messiah. The assembly of the Messiah included Jews who believed in Jesus as the long-awaited Jewish Messiah and Gentiles who joined themselves to the Jewish community through faith in Jesus. At that time in history, *no one* would have considered himself or herself a member of a *new religion or a new faith.*

I prefer to substitute the term "Christians" with "Jews or Gentiles who placed their faith in Jesus" and "non-Christians" with "Jews or Gentiles who have not placed their faith in Jesus" for the sake of clarity. You'll see these replacements enclosed in brackets in the quotes below. Nanos writes:

> These tensions are easily resolved by recognizing that the "weak" are the same [Jews who have not placed their faith in Jesus] whom Paul has been defending throughout the entire letter to the "strong" [Jews or Gentiles who placed their faith in Jesus] as those to whom the gospel is given first, although not exclusively. The "strong" [Jews or Gentiles who placed their faith in Jesus] are ready to dismiss these [Jews who have not placed their faith in Jesus]

JESUS IS JEWISH

contemptuously as "enemies" of the gospel; however, Paul seeks to explain that they are not enemies as it may appear-they are God's "beloved" (11:28), and even their current suffering is on behalf of the "strong" [Jews or Gentiles who placed their faith in Jesus] (11:11, 30). Paul expects the "strong" [Jews or Gentiles who placed their faith in Jesus] to begin to understand their responsibility to serve those who may appear to be antagonistic "neighbors" as their beloved "brethren." They are to welcome the "weak" [Jews who have not placed their faith in Jesus] (14:1) and unite with them in glorifying God (15:5-6), "for Christ has become a servant to the circumcision [legally Jewish] on behalf of the truth of God to confirm the promises given to the fathers." (15: 7 – 8)[182]

Nanos again writes:

The "weak" [Jews who had not placed their faith in Jesus] had faith in the same God but were not [Jews or Gentiles who placed their faith in Jesus] – they were Jews who practiced the historical faith of Israel: faith in God, the One Lord of all humankind, even if they displayed no faith in Jesus as the Christ, or in the Gentile claims of co-participation in Israel's blessings ("good things"). No, the "weak" were not [Jews or Gentiles who placed their faith in Jesus] – the "weak" were [Jews who had not placed their faith in Jesus].[183]

This categorization of the "strong" and the "weak" denotes respect for the Jew who has not placed their faith in Jesus and their practice of the Law from a perspective of genuine faith. Nanos concludes:

> In other words, the issue is not [Jew or Gentile with faith in Jesus] freedom from the Law. Rather, the implicit critique is of faith that fails to recognize that Jesus is the Christ, the Lord of Israel, and also the Savior of the world. For Paul, their faith is not deficient because it includes the practice of the Law and Jewish customs; it is deficient in that it is just not yet able to recognize that the promises have been fulfilled in Christ.[184]

The "strong," Jews or Gentiles with faith in God and the Jewish Messiah Jesus, set the example through humility, care, and kindness toward the "weak," those Jews with faith in God but not Jesus. They enlighten the "weak," not condemn the "weak," and

JESUS IS JEWISH

respect those who adhere to *Kashrut* laws as outlined in Leviticus 11. The priority for the strong is not that they abstain from food or drink to which they believe they are entitled, but *choose to abstain* from food or drink so they do no harm to the weak person(s) who hold to a stricter Levitical diet.

Remember: Paul, throughout his writings, asserted if others believe he abandoned the Law and the Prophets, they misunderstood him. He emphasized he kept the Law. He taught the Gentiles, if they joined the commonwealth of Israel by faith in the Messiah, to practice the righteousness of the Law. The Gentile believers should not behave in such a way that made allegations against Paul true. Even if their opinions differed on food laws, they needed to demonstrate a lifestyle that the "weak" will see as acceptable to God. The "strong" are not to provoke the "weak" in case the "weak" malign "The Way," but respect the "strong" in their service to God.

To reiterate, when we re-read Romans 14, we interpret "weak" to mean Jewish men and women of faith who are not disciples of Jesus but remain faithful to the One True God. "Strong" denotes believing Jews and believing Gentiles in the Messiah. This will help clarify Paul's position on food laws, and you will hear his heart when it comes to unity within the body of Messiah.

TYRONE NICHOLS

Now let's turn our focus to Romans 14:14: "I know, that is, I have been persuaded by the Lord Jesus the Messiah – that nothing is unclean in itself. But if a person considers something unclean, then for him it is unclean." Two different Greek words clarify what Paul is saying. Paul's ruling has nothing to do with abolishing the Kashrut laws of Leviticus 11 and everything to do with helping his community resolve an eating issue between *akathartos* (unclean) and *koinos* (common) food.

"When used in reference to Jewish dietary law, *koinos refers to otherwise kosher food rendered unfit for consumption by contact with* idolatry, non-Jews, or some other source of defilement."[185] *Akathartos*, on the other hand, "is used in reference to Jewish dietary law and refers to the meats which the Bible has declared unclean and forbidden."[186] Paul *never* uses the word *akathartos*, which is unclean and forbidden food, but only *koinos*, kosher food unfit for consumption due to contact with ritually impure items.

"I know and am convinced in the Lord Jesus that nothing is *koinos* in itself; but to him who thinks anything to be *koinos*, to him is *koinos*."[187] In this verse, *Paul didn't change Torah and call unclean foods clean.* He said if someone considers an otherwise kosher food as *koinos*, that is, defiled in some manner that makes it unclean, then to that person it's unclean. Don't judge the person! Give grace. If you are the strong and one of your weaker brothers or

JESUS IS JEWISH

sisters believes a food to be *koinos*, and you disagree, be the stronger person. Defer to your brother or sister who is convinced that it's unfit to eat and don't eat it. This is the way *to win your weaker brother or sister over to the truth of the Messiah.*

In verses 18 and 19, Paul writes, "Anyone who serves the Messiah in this fashion both pleases God and wins the approval of other people. So then, let us pursue the things that make for peace and mutual up building." Paul remained pro-Torah on food laws and observed Torah himself.

I haven't defended every controversial statement of Paul's which Christianity supposes is anti-Torah and anti-Jewish. You received some primary tools for your exploratory journey into your paradigm and your view of Paul as a pro-Torah, pro-Israel, first-century apostle of the Messiah. Now you can use them.

When you understand Paul as a pro-Torah observant Jew, the entire Bible falls in place. The consistent narrative from Genesis to Revelation emerges: the story of the Creator God who enters a covenant relationship with Abraham and his descendants and blesses the entire world through them. To Paul, God is the One who keeps His covenants and fulfills His promises by sending Messiah to reconcile His people and the world to Himself.

TYRONE NICHOLS

Chapter 13
Jesus Is Jewish

Most colleges and seminaries only emphasize Greek and Roman historical and cultural backgrounds of the New Testament when students study the life of Jesus.[188] Though these two cultures played a significant role in human events, they didn't form or shape daily life for Jesus of Nazareth. In this section, we delve into the daily life and cultural backdrop of Jesus. What societal norms and customs shaped his world? How did he engage with these practices, and what routines marked his day-to-day activities? To what divine principals did he adhere?

The Greco-Roman culture was not Jesus's culture though it existed in the background of his life. Born and raised Jewish, he had Jewish parents, participated in the Jewish feasts, studied at the Jewish Temple, and lived an authentic first-century Jewish life.

Is this common knowledge? Perhaps. Most mainline Christian denominations overlook the obvious fact that Jesus is Jewish in every sense of the word, and have done so for more than 1800 years. This Jesus-isn't-Jewish viewpoint resulted in religious confusion, church wars, denominational splits, anti-Semitic inclinations and actions, and misguided theology. Without question,

JESUS IS JEWISH

the Church removed Jesus from his Jewish context, culture, people, and Scriptures.

Our task? Remove Jesus from his Gentile attire and dress him in the authentic clothing of first-century, Middle Eastern, Hebraic culture. Similar to the story of Joseph who became unrecognizable to his family, the Gentile Church chose to hide Jesus in "Egyptian" clothing.

Replacement Theology began early in the 2nd century and crystallized through the 3rd and 4th centuries. The Universal Church severed itself from the authentic Jewish faith of the Apostles, Paul, and the early Jewish believers. Not one of these early disciples called themselves "Christian."

Scholars around the world seek to restore Jesus to his Jewish context and bring his teachings and his historical background to their original Jewish form. Scholar Brad H. Young says it this way: "Jesus was Jewish. He spoke Hebrew. He lived and worked in the land of Israel when his people, the Jews, suffered under the cruel yoke of the mighty Roman Empire. He lived his entire life *as a religious Jew.*"[189]

To reject Jesus's Jewishness seems disingenuous at best and poor scholarship in the extreme. Most Christian pastors, educators, and scholars rob him of his Jewish lineage, social settings, culture, and maintain a misleading narrative about him.

Some scholars like James H. Charlesworth get it right. "Knowledge of the first-century religious, social, and political situation is essential to developing a more honest and true portrayal of Yeshua [Jesus]."[190] Some academics like Frederick J. Murphy express their findings in passionate terms. "Every page of the New Testament attests to Christianity's deep roots in Second Temple Judaism. Our increased knowledge of Judaism in the time of Jesus makes the New Testament come alive."[191]

Universal Christianity forgot, or never learned, what the rabbi from Tarsus, the Apostle Paul, implored us to remember; that Gentiles *become branches grafted into the root of Israel*. The root supports us, not the other way around. Promises God gave to Abraham include the grafted-in branches, giving Gentiles hope and confidence that God keeps His word and includes us in the commonwealth of Israel and the world to come. This happens through faith and obedience to the Jewish Messiah and his faithfulness to God. Let's understand Jesus in light of the *Tanakh* (the Jewish name of the "Old Testament") and his halachic teaching on the Torah.

When we step out of our Gentile Christian paradigm and into

JESUS IS JEWISH

the structure that works and fits with first-century Israel, we discover our Jewish Jesus. Everything he teaches can be seen with clarity only through the multiple lenses of Torah, Jewish tradition, and the daily, weekly, and annual customs of Judaism he kept. His life events show his family and cultural life saturated in Judaism; at the age of eight days, circumcised (*brit-milah*), redeemed as the first-born (*pidyon ha-ben*), attended and taught in synagogue, celebrated the feasts as outlined in Leviticus 23, and celebrated *Chanukah* (John 10:22). Everything about his life shouts a committed Jewish religious upbringing and lifestyle.

As a child, Jesus learned his culture and history in a *Galilean Beit Midrash*.[192] His knowledge and discernment about the Hebrew Scriptures astonished learned rabbis in the Temple when he was only twelve years old. He loved the House of God so much that his parents accidentally departed for Galilee after a festival without him. He stayed behind to learn from rabbis in the Temple courts. He participated in regular Shabbat services and often read from the Hebrew scrolls. When he taught and healed, Jewish people followed him and listened with astonishment to his innovative and insightful teachings on the Torah. Religious leaders of his day questioned him about his interpretation of the Torah. He stunned them and the crowd with insights, authority, and wisdom. He corrected some of the Pharisees as to the error of their interpretation of Moses and over-reliance upon the traditions of the Jewish Fathers.

TYRONE NICHOLS

The Pharisees in first-century Judaism, too often portrayed as Jesus's enemies, stood as his "brothers" whom he debated on legal rulings and theological misunderstandings. The book of Acts records many of his Pharisaical brothers cast their lot with him, willing to lose their lives for their Master. His authentic prophetic call to repentance reverberated in the ears of his fellow kinsman and conjured up images of the prophets of old, who called for *teshuvah* (repentance) and a return to God. He loved Jerusalem and its people and wept for their inability to recognize him for who he was. He willingly gave his life for the people in God's beloved city despite being rejected by some of them.

Jesus's parents kept the routine of an observant Jewish household in the first century. They shared constant religious rhythms: daily prayers, weekly Sabbath observances, new moon observances, and annual festivals. Deuteronomy 6:7 makes it clear the highest calling of any Jewish parent is to educate children in the ways of Torah and help them acquire a respectable vocation. Jewish parents followed Rabban Gamaliel's guidance when he wrote, "The study of Torah combined together with an occupation is good, because the demands of the two of them keep sin out of one's mind; but the study of Torah that is not combined with an occupation will end in naught." (m. *Avot* 2:2) Joseph likely purposed in his heart to set Jesus on a traditional Jewish course.[193] The Talmud says, "A father is obligated to his son, to circumcise him, redeem him, to

JESUS IS JEWISH

teach him Torah, to find a wife for him, and to teach him a trade...Rabbi Yehuda said, 'One who does not teach his son a trade, teaches him to be a bandit.'" (b. *Kiddushin 29a*)[194]

From the beginning of Jesus's life, Joseph followed the commands of Moses. Joseph and Mary ensured Jesus's circumcision occurred on the eighth day (Luke 2:21), Joseph paid the redemption price for a firstborn son (Luke 2:23), and according to Justin Martyr, Joseph taught Jesus the trade of working with his hands, "for he was in the habit of working as a carpenter when among men, making ploughs and yokes." (Justin Martyr, *Dialogue with Trypho*, 88)[195]

As did all devout Jewish families, Joseph and Mary traveled up to Jerusalem to participate in the yearly Passover celebration with their young son. "His parents went to Jerusalem *each year* to celebrate the Festival of Pesach. When he was twelve years old, they went up to Jerusalem according to the law of the festival." (Luke 2:41-42) [Italics mine.] This verse gives us insight into the family customs of Jesus. His parents participated in the feasts as prescribed in Leviticus 23 to lovingly show fidelity to their God and obedience to His commands. At age 12, Jesus neared the time of his bar mitzvah and adulthood; this Passover may have been his first opportunity to participate in the Jewish sacrificial rituals associated with the festival.

TYRONE NICHOLS

While in Jerusalem at least one Passover season, Jesus spent time with the sages in the Temple, astonished them with his insights, and learned from the dialogue. "At the end of three days, they found him in the Temple. He was sitting in the midst of the teachers, listening to them and asking them questions. All those who heard him were amazed at his intelligence and his answers." (Luke 2:46-47) Mary and Joseph, on their way home, panicked after they realized Jesus wasn't with them in their traveling group. They returned to Jerusalem and found him sitting among the respected Torah teachers of the day. Despite his parents' surprise, Jesus pointed out that they should have looked for him in the Temple, as it was "the place that is my Father's house." (Luke 2:49)

In Luke 4:16 we read, "He went to Nazareth, where he had been brought up, and on the Sabbath day he went into the synagogue, as was his custom. He stood up to read…" Where did Jesus go on the Sabbath? To the synagogue. How often did he do this? It was Jesus's custom. Our Master did not come to belittle the synagogue or the Jews who worshiped according to the Torah. Instead, he attended on a regular basis and participated in liturgical prayers and public Scripture reading.

One Sabbath, Jesus read from the scroll of Isaiah. Scholars know that Jews read the entire Torah throughout the year. (Acts 13:27) On this Sabbath no one knows whether Jesus chose the

JESUS IS JEWISH

passage to read, or if it was the required reading of the day. He read Isaiah 61:1-2: "The Spirit of the Lord God is upon me, because He anointed me to preach the gospel to the poor. He has sent me to bind up the brokenhearted, to proclaim release to the captives and freedom to prisoners; to proclaim the favorable year of the LORD…" Just as other rabbis of his era, Scripture notes that he, too, sat down to teach, and proclaim, "Today this passage is fulfilled in your hearing." (Luke 4:21) Without a doubt, Jesus's words meant "It is I of whom this passage speaks. I am the *Anointed One*." Using the Scriptures of Israel, Jesus announced his God-given mission.

Word about the Anointed One spread throughout Galilee. The gospel of Mark recorded that "multitudes of people [Jews] followed him" (Mark 3:7-8), fascinated by what he did and taught. The Galilean healer became popular. Sick and lame people no longer waited patiently to meet him and at times forced, shoved, and pushed their way through the crowd to get next to him.[196] When wicked spirits saw him, they shouted, "You are the Son of God!" (Mark 3:11) Yet Jesus loved those afflicted, and he "healed them all." (Matthew 12:15-16)

In one instance, after a day of teaching and healing, a dense crowd grew restless, so he escaped into the bow of a boat to avoid the crush of people. Jesus sat in the boat near shore to teach the crowd gathered at the edge of the water. Jesus spoke in parables, a conventional rhetorical device used in rabbinic teaching. (The Hebrew word for parable is mashal.)[197]

Christian tradition often misunderstood meanings of the Master's parables, and assumed deep mysteries, secrets, and even esoteric meanings behind each one rather than the plain meaning.[198] This practice of *eisegesis* (imposing personal interpretation onto the text) began with the first Christian councils in the 3rd through 5th centuries. For instance, St. Augustine's work, *The City of God*, contains this type of biblical interpretation, although Augustine knew very little Greek and no Hebrew.[199] Despite his limitation in understanding the underlying languages, his thoughts have had profound impact on Christian theology for millennia.

Jesus employed educational techniques like the parable and focused on everyday Jewish themes in his teaching, such as "the Kingdom of Heaven" and "repentance," which is also found in the teaching of the sages.[200] Another common misperception is that Jesus used the mashal (parable) to hide the true meaning of his teachings. Only the select "righteous ones" worthy enough to understand them received the wisdom. *The reverse is true*. The multitudes didn't grasp the basics of the Kingdom and Jesus used parables to convey the message in simple and understandable language. His disciples understood the message and responded to it. Most of the crowd had not.[201]

JESUS IS JEWISH

A most famous and misunderstood teaching of Jesus is often referred to as "The Sermon on the Mount." Dr. Joel Willits, a leading authority on the Gospel of Matthew, argues that Matthew 5 through 7:12 is not one long "sermon," but an anthology of Jesus's most poignant teachings during his ministry.[202] It is his *halachah* on Torah.

Jesus said in Matthew 5:17, "Do not think that I have come to abolish the Law or the Prophets; I have not come to abolish them but to fulfill them." Traditional Christianity understands "fulfill" to mean he himself fulfilled Torah, and in his fulfillment of Torah he abolished Torah for us.

Job done, right?

I remind you that Universal Christianity suggests the Torah is old and getting older, soon to pass away, if it hasn't already. When we read the passage through our developing Jewish paradigm, a different meaning appears. By using the terms "abolish" and "fulfill," Jesus told His disciples that he *interprets and obeys the Torah correctly*. Matthew 5:17 is Jesus's endorsement of the unchanging, ongoing authority and validity of the Torah of Moses. Consider the following example from a rabbinical book called the *Mishnah*: "Whoever *fulfills* the Torah in poverty, will *fulfill* it later on in wealth; and whoever *abolishes* the Torah in wealth, will *abolish* it later in poverty." (m. Avot 4:9) This is one example of many which demonstrate the proper understanding of the words "fulfill" and "abolish." A rabbi who *misinterpreted* the Torah abolished it. A rabbi who *properly interpreted* the Torah fulfilled it. Viewed from outside their Jewish context, these words took Universal Christianity down a road the Master never intended.[203]

In Matthew 5:18, Jesus further emphasized the eternal nature of the Torah when he said, "not a single jot or tittle shall pass away from it until all has been fulfilled." He cautioned against nullifying even the smallest of commandments in verse 19, warning that those who did so would be considered the least in the Kingdom of Heaven, while those who uphold and teach them will be considered great. The commonly held Universal Christian belief that the Torah has been annulled is misguided. Jesus came to accurately interpret and practice the Torah and viewed it as a durable document until the arrival of the New Heaven and the New Earth after the Millennium Kingdom. He extoled those who live by and teach the Torah, in contrast to those who misunderstand and do not properly observe it.

D.T. Lancaster, author of the Torah Club's *Chronicles of the Messiah*, reinforces this point of view:

> The Second Century Rabbi Gamliel ben Shimon (who was no friend to the Jewish believers)

nevertheless understood Yeshua's [Jesus's] words and intention to mean that one must neither add to the Torah nor subtract from it. He quotes the Master as saying, "I did not come to destroy the Torah of Moses nor to add to the Torah of Moses." (Falk, Harvey, Jesus the Pharisee, pp. 19)[204]

In Matthew 5:17, Yeshua [Jesus] endorsed the ongoing, unchanging authority and validity of the Torah of Moses in the strongest possible language. He endorsed the whole Torah, not only the Ten Commandments. All gospels and epistles should be interpreted in light of his emphatic statement, including the entire Sermon on the Mount, which should be understood as His affirmation of the unchanging and enduring Torah.[205]

Following Matthew 5:17–19, Jesus continued to elaborate on several important *halachic* subjects regarding Torah to clarify the true intent of the Law. In first-century rabbinic fashion, he touches on the following topics:

- The Beatitudes – the internal disposition of a true follower of Torah – (Matt. 5:3-12)

TYRONE NICHOLS

- The Light of the World – the external purpose of the practitioners of Torah – including transmitting and teaching the Torah – (Matt. 5:14-16, Luke 8:16-17)
- The eternal nature of the Torah – (Matt. 5:17-19)
- A description of tzedakah (righteousness) – (Matt. 5:20)
- Protection from actions of murder, anger, insult, sacrifice, reconciliation, adultery…being cognizant of what may cause you to sin (eye and hand), divorce, oaths and vows, retaliation and turning the other cheek – (Matt. 5:22-5:39)
- Going the extra mile – (Matt. 5:40-41)
- Giving – (Matt. 5:42)
- Loving your enemies – (Matt. 5:43-45)
- Greeting the stranger – (Matt. 5:46-47)
- Being complete/perfect – (Matt. 5:48)
- Acts of righteousness – (Matt. 6.1-5)
- Public and private prayer and how to pray – (Matt. 6:6-6:13 "The Lord's Prayer")
- Fasting – (Matt. 6.17-18)
- Storing up treasures – (Matt. 6:19)
- Stinginess, selfishness, greed – An "evil eye" is a Hebrew idiom for greed or selfishness – (Matt. 6:22-23)

JESUS IS JEWISH

- Only serving one Master – (Matt. 6:24)
- Don't worry – (Matt. 6:25)
- Seeking the Kingdom first – (Matt. 6.33-34)
- Measure for measure – (Matt. 7.1-2)
- Self-accountability – (Matt. 7:3)
- Be careful to whom you teach Torah – (Matt. 7:6)
- Being persistent in prayer – (Matt. 7:7-11) The
- Grand Summation – the Golden Rule – "So then, whatever you want sons of men to do to you, do the same to them, for this is the Torah and the Prophets." – (Matt. 7:12)

On occasion, other Pharisees challenged Jesus about his interpretation of the Law. Universal Christianity interprets their challenges as attacks on Jesus and anathematized the Pharisees for seeking clarity from Jesus. Yes, some, *but not all* Pharisees used questions to attempt to trap Jesus or disqualify him as a righteous Torah-observant Jew fit to lead the Jewish people.

One potential entrapment challenged Jesus on whether he could heal on the Sabbath. In Luke 13:14 we read, "The leader of the synagogue became upset that Jesus had healed her on the Sabbath, so he responded to the people, 'There are six days on which you may do work. Come and be healed on them, but not on the day of Shabbat!'" At the time, a common rabbinic opinion held that, without an immediate threat to the sick person's life, healing could wait until after the Sabbath. The sages determined the Sabbath as a day of complete rest, "so that he will be free for sacred activities in honor of his Creator."[206] Protecting the Sabbath and its sanctity even precluded work on building the new Tabernacle as established in Exodus.

The rabbis also teach exceptions to this rule. Two exceptions include saving life and the circumcision on the eighth day after birth. (Ramban) The sages agree it's better to transgress one Sabbath so a person may live and observe many Sabbaths.[207]

The synagogue leader in Luke 13 didn't confront Jesus. He reminded the crowd that the week has six days for permitted work, the seventh day is only for rest. Did this presented a perfect opportunity for Jesus to disagree and say that he came to "fulfill the law" and "abolished" the need to rest on the Sabbath, or to say that any day is permissible to designate as the "Sabbath," a view common in churches today?

If it did, Jesus didn't take it.

He spoke from a Jewish *halachic* framework and upheld the rabbinic understanding of Sabbath sanctity. Like the mercy of

JESUS IS JEWISH

saving a life or the mercy of providing water for animals to prevent suffering, mercy should include saving a person from suffering bondage. He added another reason worthy enough to "break" the Sabbath, without violating Torah. The Master responded, "You hypocrites, does not each of you on the Sabbath untie his ox or his donkey from the stall and lead him away to water him? And this woman, a daughter of Abraham as she is, whom Satan has bound for eighteen long years, should she not have been released from this bond on the Sabbath day?" (Luke 13:15-16)

Jewish law helps interpret what Jesus said. The Talmud states in b. *Shabbat* 113a that the tying and untying of knots, so long as they are not "permanent knots," is permissible. What does this mean?

Though this discussion isn't identical to Luke 13, it reflects a later development in Jewish law, which attempted to reconcile tying and untying knots to care for livestock with the *halachic* prohibition on knotting.[208]

Prohibited *melachah* (work) on the Sabbath included tying/untying knots, so how could a person water an animal if it was tied up away from water? Rabbis construed rules to allow for a violation of doing work on Sabbath for supporting the life of animals. Jesus accepted this ruling and argued in traditional rabbinic form, from "lighter to heavier." This method is *kal va'chomer*, lighter to heavier. If true that someone could violate the Sabbath to care for an animal by untying a knot for it to drink, how much more could someone violate the Sabbath to *heal a daughter of Abraham tormented by Satan for 18 years*! Torah Club writers point out, "If He considered tying or untying as actually permissible on Sabbath, His argument loses all its force."[209]

By arguing inside the halachic framework of first-century Judaism, Jesus *upheld the sanctity of the Sabbath* and at the same time used the halachic reasoning of the rabbis to argue his case. This is mercy in action encased in Jewish "law." Untying an animal to quench its thirst is "the lighter." Unbinding a woman to release her from pain and suffering is "the heavier."

The Master argued *halachah* with the Pharisees on proper observance of the Sabbath in Matthew 12 as well. The debate began after Jesus allowed his disciples to pick grain to eat on the Sabbath.

At stake was not a mere misunderstanding of Jewish legal rulings, but the office and qualifications of the Messiah. Exodus 31:14-16 reads:

> Everyone who profanes it [the Sabbath] shall surely be put to death; for whoever does any work on it, that

JESUS IS JEWISH

person shall be cut off from among his people. For six days work may be done, but on the seventh day there is a Sabbath of complete rest, holy to the LORD; whoever does any work on the Sabbath day shall surely be put to death. So the sons of Israel shall observe the Sabbath, to celebrate the Sabbath throughout their generations as a perpetual covenant.

Sabbath observance is serious. If rabbis demonstrated that Jesus violated the Sabbath, or better yet in their minds, "abolished" it, that is, misinterpreted and violated the Jewish instruction from God, he'd be disqualified as a leader and especially as the Messiah. According to Torah, no Messiah would violate the Sabbath. Any proclaimed Messiah who does violate the Sabbath is not the Messiah. Not only would the rabbis have legal grounds to discredit Jesus, but they'd have legal grounds to execute him, according to Exodus.[210]

Universal Christianity teaches that Jesus broke the Sabbath and uses these examples to build their case. On the Sabbath, Jesus healed the bleeding woman, told the lame man to carry his mat, healed another man's withered arm, and allowed his disciples to pluck grain from the wheat field to eat, *each an apparent violation* of Sabbath rest. According to this traditional Christian thinking, he broke the Sabbath.

TYRONE NICHOLS

When the Universal Church split from its Jewish lineage and adopted an anti-Semitic, Replacement-Theological paradigm, it split from its ability to divide the Word of truth rightly. Deuteronomy 13:1-5 is clear on the matter of a prophet leading God's people away from the truth. It reads:

> The entire word that I command you, that shall you observe to do; you shall not add to it and you shall not subtract from it. If there should stand up in your midst a prophet or a dreamer of a dream, and he will produce to you a sign or a wonder, and the sign or the wonder comes about, of which he spoke to you, saying "Let us follow gods of others that you did not know and we shall worship them!" – do not hearken to the words of that prophet or to that dreamer of a dream, for HASHEM [THE NAME], your God, is testing you to know whether you love HASHEM, your God, with all your heart and with all your soul. HASHEM your God shall you follow and Him shall you fear; His commandments shall you observe and to His voice shall you hearken; Him shall you serve and to Him shall you cleave.[211]

The last thing Jesus would do is violate *any* of the laws of Moses, especially the Sabbath, the sign of the covenant and the

JESUS IS JEWISH

fourth commandment. Why did he work on the Sabbath, and allow his disciples to work on the Sabbath by picking grain? *He didn't!* Rather than abolishing the Sabbath and its sanctity he upheld the Sabbath and *halachically* justified why his actions didn't violate the law *within a first-century rabbinic framework*.

Jesus *agreed* with the Pharisees that his disciples broke Sabbath law. He said they had the legal right to do so and cited two examples from Scripture to support his case.

"Have you not read what David did when he and his men were hungry—they entered the House of God and ate the Bread of the Presence, which neither he nor his men are permitted to eat, but only the priests?" (Matthew 12:3-4) Jesus agreed; David and his men did what was not lawful by eating the bread of the presence. In the same way, Jesus's disciples did what was not lawful by picking grain on the Sabbath. According to Jesus, both should be found innocent of any Sabbath defilement.

He also pointed to the priests who served on the Sabbath in the Temple. They "desecrated" the Sabbath. "Have you not read in the Torah that, on the Shabbat, the priests desecrate the Shabbat in the Temple, yet do not have iniquity?" (Matthew 12:5) The priests violated the Sabbath commands but were found innocent *because the Torah commanded them to do so*. Temple service takes priority over Sabbath observations for the priests. The sages articulated in b. *Shabbat 133a,* "Wherever you find a positive commandment and a negative commandment contradicting, if you can fulfill both of them, it is preferable; but if not, let the positive command come and supersede the negative command." The positive command of Temple service took precedence over negative ones. Jesus showed that the positive command of saving a life supplanted the negative command not to work on the Sabbath.

Jesus combined his arguments in a summary. Jesus showed that hunger takes precedence over Sabbath commands, and that Temple service takes precedence over the Sabbath rest. Principle: human need takes precedence over the Sabbath. How? If human need is greater than Temple service, and Temple service is greater than Sabbath observance, then human need is greater than the Sabbath. The sages also agree with this logic in b. *Yoma* 85b where we read, "If the service in the Temple supersedes the Sabbath, how much more should the saving of human life supersede the Sabbath laws!"

The preservation of life, *pikuach nefesh,* always takes precedence over Sabbath commandments. Torah agrees in Leviticus 18:5, "You shall therefore keep my statutes and my rules; if a person does them, he shall live by them." Life takes precedence over the commands because the law says, "…you shall live by them." The

JESUS IS JEWISH

law does not read, "…you shall die by them."

When using our Jewish paradigm, we find an authentic Messiah who upheld the Sabbath laws and "violated" them only when human need took legal precedence. Nowhere in Scripture do we find the Messiah having desecrated the Sabbath, abolished the Sabbath, or changed the laws of the Sabbath. According to Jesus, the Sabbath is God's holy day. It remains intact, and is lawfully listed as one of the Ten Commandments.

Let's continue to look at his Messianic credentials. His straightforward message is consistent with the prophets that had come before him. His gospel reads "Repent, for the Kingdom of Heaven is at hand," a familiar idea to those acquainted with the Hebrew Scriptures. Jesus proclaimed the same message with different authority; his own.

The gospels record that people stood amazed at his teaching, usually for two reasons. Jesus expounded upon the Scriptures unlike any other teacher the *am ha'aretz* (the common people) had heard. He taught with wisdom, insight, and clarity that resonated like a clarion call from a trumpet hitting pitch-perfect notes. The second reason, obvious to the first-century Jew but perhaps not to us, is that Jesus didn't teach in another rabbi's name. He taught in his own name, as one having authority.

TYRONE NICHOLS

"They were amazed at his teaching, for He was teaching them as one having authority, and not as the scribes." (Mark 1:22) In first-century Judaism, citing traditions and scriptural interpretations of previous sages lent credibility to the speaker. Most rabbis in Jesus's day began their teachings with "In the name of Rabbi so-and-so" and transmitted the early understanding of the Scripture or law, which linked one generation to the next. A typical lesson went something like, "Rabbi X, said in the name of Rabbi Y, who taught in the name of Rabbi Z, that such and such is the case." Within the rabbinic world, this form of teaching was and still is used.

For the 21st-century Gentile Christian reader to understand the importance of this idea, let's get a quick introduction to rabbinic literature and teachings. First:

> …when one has finished reading the Hebrew Bible, he will not have read anything about synagogues, rabbis, Pharisees, Sadducees, Essenes, Zealots, Herodians, etc. When one opens the Brit Chadashah (New Testament) all these things just seem to appear without introduction. Obviously, some major changes had occurred in Judaism between the close of the Old Testament and the opening of the New.[212]

What *were* those major theological changes that occurred?

JESUS IS JEWISH

Let me explain.

Ezra, upon his return from exile in Babylonian captivity, began the school of the Sopherim, or "the school of the scribes." These pre-Tannaim teachers began with Ezra and are described by the *Mishnah* as:

> the early body of teachers beginning with Ezra and ending with Simeon the Just, though sometimes it would appear to apply to later Talmudists too; The Rabbis derive the word from sofar, to count: hence the body who counted the letters of the Torah or grouped subjects by number, e.g., four chief causes to damage, thirty-nine principal modes of labor forbidden on the Sabbath (infra 30a; Sanh. 106b.)

> ...This body has been identified with the Men of the Great Synagogue...Weiss...maintains that they were separate bodies, though their objects were alike. The Sopherim were the theoretical scholars who interpreted the law; the Men of the Great Synagogue were the practical legislators.[213]

The Sopherim educated the Jewish people on laws and stipulations of Torah. The prophet Hosea said, "because of a lack of

Torah, the people perish." Ezra and his scribes took the 613 commandments God gave Moses for the Jewish people and wrote out how to follow each one. This encouraged Israel to keep the Law, avoid divine punishment, and receive divine blessings. The Sopherim built "fences" around each Torah commandment to help prevent a Jew from breaking the law. The Sopherim provided a way for people to avoid divine judgment.[214]

To decide what the "fences" would be, the Sopherim had a general principle; a Sopher could disagree with a Sopher, but they couldn't disagree with the Torah. God gave the Torah to Moses and no one disagreed with God. As the Sopherim built fences around the Torah, they might disagree with one another, but the majority opinion among them became Law.[215]

Each of these rabbinic enactments, called *halachah*, means "step" or "guidance." The Talmud defines the *halachah* as "(a) the final decision of the Rabbis, whether based on tradition or argument, on disputed rules of conduct; and (b) those sections of Rabbinic literature which deal with legal questions as opposed to the *Aggadah*. (b. *Temruah, Glossary*, p. 257).[216]

The period of the Sopherim began around 400 B.C. and ended in 30 B.C. and is known as the period from "Ezra to Hillel."

JESUS IS JEWISH

Now you have an idea about the theological arena that Jesus entered. Before we continue the narrative of Jesus, we learn about the next period of rabbinic history in the theological culture of Jesus.

From 30 B.C. to approximately 220 C.E., or from Hillel to Yehudah HaNasi (Judah the Prince), we find the second group of rabbis known as the Tannaim (teachers). "These men looked upon the work of the Sopherim and concluded that there were still too many holes in the fence. Hence, they continued the process of adding new laws and regulations to the Torah for another two-and-a-half centuries."[217] The Tannaim operated under a similar exegetical framework of "fences" around the Torah as the Sopherim except that they couldn't disagree with the Sopherim's decisions. A Tanna could disagree with another Tanna but could not disagree with a Sopher. By this time all the rules of the Sopherim became sacrosanct, equal with Scripture.[218]

"Wait a second."

I understand your raised eyebrows.

We need to understand how Judaism views the Talmud so we can properly contextualize it. Why? *Because it's the environment in which Jesus lived.* Many of his conversations can only be understood through his framework of first-century Judaism.

TYRONE NICHOLS

Let's discuss that fact that Judaism considers the oral traditions of the Fathers, codified in the Talmud, as equal with Scripture. Why is this important? Because this belief helps us understand why Jesus engaged in conversations about "washing hands" or "plucking grain on the Sabbath." He engaged in Talmudic or traditional debates with his Jewish brothers to arrive at ways to love your neighbor, to show a way to all Jews how to "do Torah" in their daily lives. These codified oral traditions assist us with how to observe the commands as outlined in Torah. Jesus endorsed the traditions of the Fathers when he participated in these halachic discussions.

"What?! No way!"

Hold that thought. Let's look at more history.

During the period of the Tannaim, they introduced a new idea which taught the "Doctrine of the Two Torot [Laws]." This doctrine said:

> God gave two bodies of commandments to Moses on Mount Sinai. The first was the Written Law. It contained the 613 commandments which Moses wrote down in the Books of Exodus, Leviticus, Numbers, and Deuteronomy. The second was the

JESUS IS JEWISH

Oral Law, called that because Moses did not write these thousands of additional rules down, but simply committed them to memory. The Oral Law, sometimes called "Oral Torah," the "Second Torah," or the "oral tradition," was also revealed to Moses on Mount Sinai, and according to the sages, it explained the written Torah. Moses, in turn, passed the Oral Law down to Joshua, who passed it down to the Judges, who passed it down to the prophets, who passed it down to the Sopherim. Each group would encourage the next to "be prudent in judgment," to "raise up many disciples," and to "make a fence for the Torah." So, they taught that the Sopherim did not originate all these new rules; they simply got them from the prophets, who got them from the judges, who got them from Joshua, who got them from Moses, who got them from God. And, indeed, from about 400 B.C. until A.D. 220, none of these rules were written down; certain Jews had them committed to memory. The New Testament mentions both Pharisees and scribes frequently as closely connected. Both were Pharisees, so what was the difference? The scribes were those Pharisees who had committed all these rules to memory, and they would be the ones who would declare what had been handed down by tradition.[219]

According to Fruchtenbaum, "the rabbis knew that forgetfulness was their most dangerous enemy. In trying to prevent the Oral Law from falling into oblivion, they elevated it, putting it on the same level of importance as the Scriptures."[220] Daniel Gruber agrees with Fruchtenbaum when he quotes R. Meir in Ab. III.9 "Every man who forgets a single word of his *Mishnah* (i.e., what he has learned), Scripture accounts it unto him as if he had forfeited his soul!"[221]

The Tannaim were followed by the Amoraim, a word that means "teacher," "expounder," or "expositor." Active from 220 C.E. until about 500 C.E., this group looked at the body of work created by the Sopherim and Tannaim and concluded too many holes in the fence remained, then added new regulations for about three more centuries. They operated under the same rubric: an Amora could disagree with an Amora, but they could not disagree with a Tanna, as by this time all the rules of the Tannaim had become revered, equal with Scripture.

Here's a subject that'll assist in understanding Jesus and his world on a level you may never have understood before. Stay with me for another page.

JESUS IS JEWISH

The Sopherim and the Tannaim produced the *Mishnah*. The *Mishnah* is the distillation of centuries of Oral Law passed down from Moses to the Sopherim.[222] The Gemara is what the Amoraim produced, which is the part of the Talmud that contains the traditions, discussions, comments, and rulings of the Amoraim on the *Mishnah*.[223] The Talmud consists of the *Mishnah* and the Gemara, and Talmud literally means "instruction" and "learning."

Another important fact to note is that two Talmuds exist and are available to us today. The larger and more widely used is the Babylonian Talmud, edited around 450 C.E. by Rabbi Ashi and Rabina. The second is the Jerusalem Talmud, better entitled *The Talmud of the Land of Israel*, edited by Rabbi Johanan in 300 C.E. In Judaism, the Talmud is immeasurable in value. According to Jewish tradition, it's to be studied daily along with the Scriptures.

I felt it essential, even crucial, for you the reader to see the stages of rabbinic development. Why?

Now you know where Jesus entered the timeline of Jewish history, Jewish thought, and Jewish debate on the laws of God. Debate arose because sages and rabbis, for centuries, sought to love God, themselves, and their neighbors by providing clear ways about how to live Torah every day.

Now you know when Jesus said, "You have heard it said...*but I tell you*..." he affirmed people in his audience who had "heard it said" from the Sopherim who spoke the Torah and the Oral Tradition from memory!

Now you can understand the amazement of people when Jesus taught in his own name. Rather than beginning each teaching as the scribes did with an opening statement of "Rabbi X said in the name of Rabbi Y," Jesus would say *"but I tell you."* His powerful form of teaching, new to the listeners of first-century Judaism, likely threw the *am ha'aretz* (the people of the land) and the religious leaders for a loop! *No other rabbi taught in his own name.*

Even in this, Jesus did not stray from the borders of Proto-Rabbinic Judaism. As the Great Tzadik, (tzadik meaning righteous one), God inspired him and he interpreted Torah rightly through His spirit. With love, Jesus corrected errors that may have been passed down from one generation to the next.

Jesus affirmed and confirmed the scribes and Pharisees as well. He knew they operated within a divinely ordained office. He said to the crowd and to his disciples, "The scholars (scribes) and the Pharisees sit in the seat of Moses, so whatever they tell you, observe and do it. Only be careful not to do as their deeds, for they say things, but they do not do them." (Matthew 23:1-3)

JESUS IS JEWISH

The "seat of Moses" refers to Exodus 18 where Moses sat to judge the people and rule on the laws of Torah. His father-in-law Jethro suggested that Moses divide the responsibility of this enormous job and appoint 70 judges, in essence creating the first operating Sanhedrin. In Matthew 23 we read Jesus's endorsement of the Jewish Sanhedrin, with its origins in Exodus. He affirmed their right to rule on the Law.[224]

For centuries from Moses' time, the Sanhedrin's job, to "bind" and to "loose" (prohibit and permit) rulings as it related to Torah, endured. This may come as a big surprise to most Christians: *Jesus endorsed the Sanhedrin as the authority over the Jewish people*, which derived its authority from Torah, which came from God.

This endorsement didn't stop Jesus from criticizing the hypocrisy of some who served on the Sanhedrin. He said, "They bind heavy loads and burdens on the shoulders of people, while they themselves are unwilling to even lift a finger." (Matthew 23:4) On the one hand, we have Jesus's outright endorsement of the institution of the Sanhedrin, and on the other, his chastisement of *some* hypocrites who ruled one way and did another.

When Jesus referred to "heavy loads and burdens," he spoke about some errant rulings of the Oral Law that made observance of

God's commands more difficult or almost impossible. This understanding widens and deepens our insight into Peter's argument before the Messianic Sanhedrin in Acts 15. He asked them why they would place a burden on the Gentiles that the Jewish people could not bear! Peter likely referred to the same yoke of Oral Law that Jesus referred to in Matthew 23.

Again, Jesus argued from *within the borders of Judaism*, not outside. Again, he did not come to abolish the Law and the Prophets, but to rightly interpret and live them. Jesus wasn't a rebel or a provocateur that championed the abolishment of Torah or the negation of Israel; rather, he championed the institutions of Judaism and the divinely inspired Torah of Moses. He pleaded with his kinsman to follow his lead and return to a pure form of *halachah* in which the heart of worship, love for God, and love for your neighbor, remained at the forefront of daily life.

In Luke 19:41-44, Jesus wept for Jerusalem. With a broken heart and a heavy burden for his people, Jesus prophesied that the same divine punishment that befell the generation of the Babylonian exile would soon befall his generation. "Amen, I say to you; all these things will surely come upon this generation. Jerusalem, Jerusalem, who kills the prophets and stones those who are sent to her! How many times I have desired to gather your sons like a hen gathers her chicks under her wings, but you were unwilling." (Matthew 23:37)

JESUS IS JEWISH

Universal Christianity interpreted this verse to mean that Jesus separated himself from the Jewish people and after his resurrection began construction of a new religion called Christianity.

Another misconception from this verse is that all of Jerusalem rejected him. That's like saying all Americans are Yankees, or all Southerners like country music. Jesus spoke of Jerusalem in a metaphor, in a general way, and likened her to chicks that needed to be gathered by their mother hen.

In Israel at this time, *myriads* (meaning "tens of thousands or a number too large to count") of Jewish people followed Jesus, a fact recorded in the Gospels and the book of Acts but eliminated for various reasons from the pages of interpretive history. (See Chapter 6.) He knew the Kingdom of Heaven came near, but the religious leaders, in particular the Sadducees in the Sanhedrin, *some* of the scribes and Pharisees, and *some* of the *am ha'aretz* (people of the land), didn't or wouldn't recognize him for who he was. Jesus couldn't usher in the Messianic Kingdom at that time, though it "was at hand." He instead prepared himself for the painful physical and devastating spiritual events that would follow. "Behold, your house is being left to you desolate." (Matthew 23:38) Like Jesus, the prophet Jeremiah told the people of Jerusalem that if they repented, they could enjoy peace and prosperity under the Davidic monarchy, but if not, the Holy Temple would be deserted: "This house will become a desolation." (Jeremiah 22:5)[225]

Can you not help but be moved by this scene? Do you see the irony of Jesus entering Jerusalem for the last time where throngs of people welcomed him singing, "Blessed is the one who comes in the name of the Lord" (Psalm 118:26), while tears streamed down his face from the agony and despondency of the moment? The prophecy of Isaiah stood on the verge of fulfillment: the suffering servant would die a martyr's death and atone for the sins of all people, including his generation, because his righteous life merited the grace of God and resurrection from the dead.

By taking a brief look at the early life of Jesus and his family, how Jesus upheld the institution of the Sabbath and the institution of the Sanhedrin, I hope I've played a role in re-robing Jesus in his authentic Jewish clothing. In his debates with the religious leaders of his day from within the context and borders of first-century Judaism, I hope I've shown that he never abandoned his people, the Torah, or the traditions of the Fathers. Rather, these deliberations were family debates and belong in the garden of Judaism.

More information is available today for anyone interested in finding out about the Jewish Jesus than at any other time in human history. Each person who calls himself or herself a disciple of Jesus

JESUS IS JEWISH

needs to weigh the evidence and rightly decide Jesus's true identity and to re-robe him in his authentic Jewishness. For more than 1800 years the Universal Church hid Jesus in the clothing of Western or Eastern Christianity, *religions that did not exist in the first or second centuries.* Repentance is incumbent upon us. We need to repent of our misguided decision to remove Jesus from his Jewish family and humbly ask forgiveness for the role we have played in maintaining his disguise.

This process is far from easy. Gentile Christianity broke and bruised the relationship with our Jewish brothers and sisters, so it's understandable if they never forgive us. As for my house and prayerfully many more houses of many more Gentiles, we will repair the broken relationship with one person, with one word, and with one deed at a time. We long for our Jewish brothers and sisters to proclaim, "Blessed is He who comes in the name of the Lord," but they first must be able to recognize him, consider him, and evaluate him as he is: a Torah-observant citizen of Israel who did not abolish the Torah, but rather upholds it in the way only the Messiah can.

With regret, I report the most significant conflict I encounter on this journey arises from some of my Christian brothers and sisters who resist Jesus's full and complete Jewish identity. It seems they fear potential impacts on their theology and way of life. I am fortunate to have found some, like me, who seek and want the truth and are willing to spend the money and time God gave them to peel back the centuries of misinformation and embrace the Jewish Jesus of Nazareth.

I believe hundreds and thousands of Gentile believers in Jesus have a passion and heart to love God and love people, fulfilling the two greatest commands of the Torah. Most of these genuine lovers of God have never been introduced to the idea that Jesus is Jewish, or they don't realize they need to see him as such, or don't have access to knowledge to learn this.

Maybe this is you? I understand. I was in your shoes before 2008. My heartfelt hope is that this book will humbly inspire you and me to foster a deeper connection with God as we progressively embrace the authentic identity of Yeshua of Nazareth.

As we draw the curtains on this exploration of Yeshua's identity, we are reminded that the robes of history are often woven with threads of misconception. For too long, the portrayal of Yeshua has been colored by cultural and theological biases that strip away the rich tapestry of his Jewish heritage—a heritage that is not merely an accessory to his identity but the very fabric from which it is cut.

Yeshua of Nazareth, a figure deeply rooted in Jewish

JESUS IS JEWISH

tradition, walked the paths of ancient Israel not as a stranger to its laws and customs but as a native son. His teachings, parables, and actions were not abstract philosophies meant to establish a new religion divorced from Judaism. Instead, they were the flowering of Jewish thought, the embodiment of Torah, and the fulfillment of the prophet's visions.

The quest to clothe Yeshua once more in his authentic Jewish garments is not a mere academic exercise; it is a journey toward truth—a truth that holds profound implications for interfaith dialogue, Christian theology, and the shared spiritual legacy of Jews and Christians alike. It challenges us to confront our preconceptions, seek understanding with humility, and forge a path of reconciliation and mutual respect.

Therefore, let us commit to a faithful study of Yeshua within the Jewish world he inhabited, embrace the fullness of his teachings, and recognize the common ground we share. May this acknowledgment be more than a restoration of historical accuracy; let it be a bridge that spans the divide between communities, enriching our collective faith and drawing us closer to the heart of the divine narrative.

As we move forward, may we carry the lessons of history with a spirit of repentance where needed and a resolve to honor the

TYRONE NICHOLS

Jewish roots of Christianity. In doing so, we pay homage to the Jewish Messiah who came not to abolish but to affirm, not to alienate but to unify, not to end the story but to invite us all into its continuing saga.

JESUS IS JEWISH

Chapter 14
Why It Matters – Dismantling Replacement Theology

If you can see the Apostle Paul as a rabbi and a disciple of Jesus who lived a life of unreproachable Torah observance, then you can recognize the fallacy of supersessionism with ease. With supersessionism removed, Israel will take her proper place of prominence and position in God's theological universe. The Universal Church stamped out this understanding; the root of this ecclesiastical error grew in the historical soil of Christianity and poisoned the fruit consumed by its laity and clergy. The disastrous result of this grievance against the Word of God cannot be overstated. The venomous root of Replacement Theology or supersessionism stands as the primary cause for our failure to recognize that Jesus is Jewish.[226]

Replacement Theology believes that the Christian Church replaced Israel as God's chosen people, and promises made to Abraham and his descendants now only apply to "true believers" in Jesus Christ. May a spark ignite in the hearts and minds of both Jews and Christians to return Israel to the center of biblical theology and may these words play a part in eliminating supersessionism.

TYRONE NICHOLS

Kendall Soulen, author of *The God of Israel and Christian Theology*, summarizes the Christian quandary succinctly. He writes regarding the Christian religion:

> The God of Israel is the firm foundation and inescapable predicament of Christian theology. Pursued without reference to the God of Israel, Christian theology is hopelessly exposed to the charge of being mere vanity, for the gospel about Jesus is credible only if predicated on a living God who "gives life to the dead and calls into existence the things that do not exist."[227]

Supersessionist Christian theologians face an impossible-to-solve logical dilemma. Either God is a covenant-keeping, promise-keeping God, or He is not. Either God is the same yesterday, today, and forever, or He isn't. If He doesn't keep His word, the Christian and Jewish faiths shatter. If He isn't the same yesterday, today and forever, all consciousness of hope vanishes as if it never existed.

A colossal misconstruction of God's promises made to Abraham in Genesis lies at the heart of the black stain in the very center of the Universal Church and its narrative toward Israelites. Although the supersessionist adherents try, no amount of exegetical wizardry can disguise the plain reading of the text. Here it is again,

JESUS IS JEWISH

"I will establish My covenant between Me and you and your descendants after you throughout their generations for an everlasting covenant, to be God to you and to your descendants after you."

Joel Richardson, the New York Times best-selling author of *When a Jew Rules the World; What the Bible Really Says About Israel and the Plan of God*, takes a gigantic swing of the proverbial axe to the root of supersessionist thought:

> ...believing that God will fulfill His promises to Abraham is to affirm the very integrity, reliability, and faithfulness of God to His word and to His promises. Simply stated, if any Christian desires to be called a child of Abraham, then believing the things that Abraham believed is a basic requirement.[228]

At the heart of the Universal Church's replacement canonical story is the misguided idea that the "spiritual Church is destined from all eternity to replace carnal Israel in God's plans."[229]

When you read the Bible inside this canonical theological paradigm, you'll believe the Scriptures started and finished as Christian-centric rather than Israel-centric. The catastrophic results of such an understanding *remove Israel from the center of God's dealings with mankind* and relegate the descendants of Abraham, at best, to the distant background of God's purposes, or at worst, to complete irrelevance.[230]

Joel Richardson quotes Albertus Pieters, a cited supersessionist, when he writes:

> The visible Christian Church being now the new covenant Israel, those whom we call "The Jews" are outsiders, cut-off branches, having no more connection with either promises or prophecies than any Gentile group. Those now called "Jews,"...have...no prophetic destiny, except a continuance of their sad and bitter state...The closed book of Israel's history will not be reopened.[231]

Richardson goes on to say: "While not every modern supersessionist is this blunt or harsh when articulating his or her views, Pieters has very accurately described the historical supersessionist position."[232]

The beginnings of supersessionist thought crystalize in the writings of an early church father named Saint Augustine, who carried on Justin Martyr's ideology and formed a spiritual scaffolding that left Israel's displacement as one of its exegetical

JESUS IS JEWISH

foundations. In the book *Future Israel: Why Christian Anti-Judaism Must Be Challenged*, author Barry Horner quotes Jeremy Cohen in his work *Living Letters of the Law: Ideas of the Jew in Medieval Christianity*. Cohen writes on Augustine:

> Augustine of Hippo bequeathed so much to western civilization that one need hardly wonder if this bequest included his ideas on Jews and Judaism. Indeed, modern students of Jewish-Christian relations typically attribute the theological foundations of the medieval church's Jewish policy to Augustine, referring as a matter of course to the legacies and principles of Augustinian Anti-Judaism.[233]

Going hand in hand with his theological position of anti-Judaism, Augustine employed an end times narrative which supported his position called "amillennialism." The amillennialist eschatological framework argued that the one-thousand-year-reign of the Messiah on earth isn't literal but spiritual. It suggested the Messiah currently sits on the throne of David in a spiritual sense, and we don't have a need to wait for Him to set up his earthly kingdom to rule and reign from Jerusalem. Dan Juster in his book *Israel, the Church and the Last Days* describes amillennialism as follows: "Amillennialism usually holds that the Israel of God is now the Body of believers, Jew and Gentile. Many amillennialists, not all, do not have a place for Israel in their scheme because they look at the true Israel as being the Body of believers, the Church."[234]

Augustine employed a non-literal (i.e., a spiritualized) hermeneutical narrative to scriptural exegesis, which enabled him to keep his canonical account of Scripture intact. That narrative resulted in an anti-Judean, pro-Christian understanding of Scripture. Augustine understood the promises to Abraham in a "spiritual" manner so that he could apply those promises to the "new Spiritual Israel" or "the true Israel," i.e., the Church. Augustinian theology wounded the Jewish people and crippled the relationship between Jews and Christians for two millennia. Barry Horner writes:

> But since the time of Augustine, the amillennial doctrine of the super-cession of national Israel by the Christian church has resulted in the vilification of the Jewish people over the centuries...[235]

Note that the biblical interpretation employed by Augustine caused a multi-millennial identification problem. Both Christians and Jews claim faith in the same God: the God of Abraham, Isaac, and Jacob. Neither assembly will deny this statement.

But the poisonous residue of Augustinian theology, where

JESUS IS JEWISH

allegorical text interpretation is acceptable, allows the Universal Church to claim God as their own only and not leave him as the God of the Jews. Please review how the Bible describes God and the titles God uses for Himself in Chapter 3.

The God of Creation and of the nations identifies Himself as the God of the Jews. Proper identification of God is clear when we use a literal, straightforward interpretation of Scripture. God is the God of Abraham, Isaac, and Jacob. The quandary for a supersessionist, Augustinian amillennial theologian, rears its ugly (or pretty, depending on your point of view) head; either God is the same yesterday, today, and forever, or He is not.

Someone might say that the New Testament, with much about Jesus and the "Church," changed this understanding of God's identity. No, it doesn't.

Look at the witness of the New Testament:

- "The God of our Fathers raised Jesus from the dead." (Acts 5:30)
- "The God of Abraham, Isaac, and Jacob, the God of our fathers, has glorified His servant Yeshua." (Act 3:13a)
- "The God of our fathers…" (Acts 22:14)

- "Men of Israel and you Gentiles who worship God, listen to me! The God of the people of Israel chose our fathers…" (Act 13:16-17)
- "I admit that I worship the God of our fathers…" (Acts 24:14)
- "He has helped his servant Israel, remembering to be merciful to Abraham and his descendants forever, even as He said to our fathers." (Luke 1:54-55)
- "The people were amazed when they saw the mute speaking, the crippled made well, the lame walking and the blind seeing. And they praised the God of Israel." (Mt. 15:31)

Daniel Gruber summarizes his position on God's identity with the following statement:

> The God of Israel looks on the heart, not the passport; but His identity is not negotiable. He is not a generic god. He is not the same as the gods and idols of the nations. "The Portion of Jacob is not like these, for he is the Maker of all things, and Israel is the tribe of His inheritance. The LORD of hosts is His name." (Jer. 10:16) The God of the Bible remains the God of Israel.[236]

JESUS IS JEWISH

Augustinian theology stole the identity of God and appropriated His relationship to the Church in place of Israel. This interpretation caused absolute destruction of the proper identification of the people of Israel, their purpose, and their proper place of prominence in the center of biblical theology.

Augustinian thought presented another problem. With whom did God "cut" His new covenant?

Augustine decided He cut it with the Church. The literal reading of this passage means that the New Covenant is "cut" *with the house of Israel and the house of Judah*. "Behold, days are coming, declares the LORD, when I will cut a new covenant with the house of Israel and with the house of Judah." (Jer. 31:31) Even now if you type the term "New Covenant" into a Google or other search on the Web, the following definition emerges at the top of the page: "The Covenant between God and the followers of Jesus Christ."[237]

Really? C'mon, REALLY?

Let's again read the New Covenant promise in context from Jeremiah 31:31-33

> "Behold, the days are coming," says the LORD, "when I will make a new covenant with the house of

Israel and with the house of Judah – not according to the covenant that I made with their fathers in the day that I took them by the hand to lead them out of the land of Egypt, My covenant which they broke, though I was a husband to them," says the LORD. "But this is the covenant that I will make with the house of Israel after those days," says the LORD: "I will put My law in their minds, and write it on their hearts; and I will be their God, and they shall be My people."

This promise, given to the houses of Israel and Judah, in which God, the God of Abraham, Isaac, and Jacob, promises to put his Law (Torah) in their minds and write it on their hearts, reveals God's amazing love. *He* will empower them to live according to the righteous standards of Torah as handed down to them by Moses, and *they will have* the relationship with God as always intended. Augustinian theology, through biblical interpretative gymnastics, removed the house of Israel and the house of Judah as one of the partners in the covenant and replaced them with the "spiritual Church."

Israel is *never* used as a synonym for the Church, and this idea cannot be found anywhere in Scripture. Barry Horner writes:

JESUS IS JEWISH

> There is no use of the term "Israel" in the NT [New Testament] that is an explicit equivalent to the Christian church. Regarding Paul's usage, Burton declared, "There is, in fact, no instance of his using Ἰσραήλ [Israel], except of the Jewish nation or a part thereof." Furthermore, there is no evidence from history that the term "Israel" was synonymously used with regard to the church before AD 160."[238]

The misperception of the Church and Israel being interchangeable stems from Augustine's teachings that the "New Spiritual Israel" replaced Jews. False. This interpretation hides the Apostle Paul's message in Romans Chapters 9-11 regarding Israel's identity. The entire book of Romans is *vigorously* Judeo-centric.

Universal Christianity claims that since the nation of Israel rejected the Messiah during his time on earth, the nation forfeited their rights to the promises of God and gave them to the "New Spiritual Israel," the Church. This idea *cannot* be found anywhere in Scripture. It's another offshoot of poisonous Augustinian theology.

Romans Chapter 11 confirms that the God of Abraham, Isaac, and Jacob remains the God of Abraham, Isaac, and Jacob. Paul's eschatology (and theology) is Jewish.[239] Paul stated in no uncertain terms that God never rejected Israel. Horner writes:

> I believe that a *prima facie* [accepted as correct until proven otherwise] reading of Romans 9–11 readily leads to this conclusion and that only a preconceived, dominant system of doctrine such as that of the Roman Catholic Church, or of entrenched Augustinianism, forces an alternative interpretation. Paul is adamant in this matter when, in reply to the question, "Has God rejected His people?" he vehemently responds, "Absolutely not! (m genoito, "perish the thought; it is unthinkable," Rom 11:1)."[240]

Mark Nanos, an acclaimed Pauline scholar, reveals the heart of the matter in his subtitle, "The Jewish Context of Paul's Letter." He summarizes the book's ethos and Paul's message, and agrees with Horner in his unequivocal statement:

> Paul's concerns are those of a Jewish missionary, and his message and framework of thinking are those of one who considers himself working within the historical expectations of Israel – the Savior of Israel has come to Zion to rebuild the tabernacle of David and to bring light to all the nations – for the One God

JESUS IS JEWISH

of Israel is the One God of the whole world.[241]

The Christian Church can and should reorient Israel to its proper place, for Israel contains God's people and is the center of God's plan for mankind. Paul, or Rabbi Shaul, used an olive branch metaphor to describe the nation of Israel. Paul's readers knew this symbolism since the olive branch is often used as a symbol for Israel. Paul explained that Gentile believers in Jesus became grafted into the olive branch of Israel through faith in Israel's Messiah. Nanos writes:

> The mystery Paul reveals is that the root still supports the branches, that is, Israel's restoration and even her pruning precede and support the gentile mission. Furthermore, even the initiation of the gentile mission, which commences with a warning to the "stumbling," is in the service of the restoration of Israel, that they might be provoked to jealousy as they see the fulfillment of the promises in Paul's apostolic ministry to the gentiles taking place before their very eyes without their participation as expected.[242]

Most of the Church's history and theology has this backwards, that is, the Church is the olive root and all believing Jews are grafted into the Church! Any study of the Church's past reveals the truth of this *backward* theological idea. You can also ask any Jew knowledgeable about Jewish history, and he or she will be quick to recount the prideful, arrogant, and shameful position the Universal Church has toward Jewish converts throughout history. *The term "Jewish convert" is an oxymoron.* Paul wouldn't have understood "a Jewish convert to Christianity." Jews always remained Jews, and Gentiles by faith were to be *grafted* into the olive branch of Israel. Nanos addresses the potential arrogance the Gentile believer may have toward his Jewish brother: "Paul thus explains that the grafting in of the gentiles does not support the root, 'but the root supports you' (v. 18), a significant metaphor that Paul expects will deepen the impact of this challenge to their temptation toward arrogance in their new status."[243]

In all of Jesus's teachings, he supported the idea that the Kingdom of God would be realized in the restoration of Israel's national independence. In all the "Old Testament," Israel is never spiritualized or marginalized to be anything other than God's partner in His everlasting covenants.

Now is the time for the Universal Church to agree with Scripture, humbly remove itself from the center of biblical theology, and promote the descendants of Abraham, Isaac, and Jacob to their rightful position as the everlasting covenant partners of the eternal

JESUS IS JEWISH

God.

How?

In the forthcoming chapter, we will explore practical steps the Church can take to realign with biblical truth. This includes fostering dialogue with Jewish communities, re-educating our congregations, and revising liturgical expressions to reflect a genuine respect for our shared spiritual heritage. By doing so, we not only correct our theological stance but also pave the way for healing and reconciliation.

Let us move forward with eyes open to the Scriptures and hearts attuned to the Spirit, ready to embrace the fullness of our Messiah's Jewish identity and the undeniable Jewish roots of our faith. In this act of restoration, we draw closer to the heartbeat of God's eternal plan, eagerly anticipating the day when all believers, Jew and Gentile alike, will unite in proclaiming, "Blessed is He who comes in the name of the Lord."

TYRONE NICHOLS

Chapter 15

Why It Matters – Course Correction

Historians date the start of the Protestant Reformation to be around 1517 when Martin Luther published his "Ninety-Five Theses." Two key concepts carried the Reformation forward. First, it called for purification of the Roman Catholic Church (hereafter, the Church), the only major western church at the time. Second, it insisted the Bible alone, not tradition, should be the sole source of spiritual authority.

The practice of selling indulgences, prevalent in the Church at the time, disturbed Luther. Purported to reduce the amount of punishment given for sins, indulgences could be purchased for yourself or for deceased souls who resided in purgatory, according to the Church. Luther believed this practice perverted penance and forgiveness. He objected to indulgences and other practices and doctrines of the Church listed in his "Ninety-Five Theses," which he reportedly nailed to the door of the Castle Church in Wittenberg, Germany. People consider his act to be the spark that ignited the Protestant Reformation. Even though he was excommunicated for his actions, Luther never desired to leave the Church. He wanted to improve it.

JESUS IS JEWISH

Lutheranism soon became the preferred religion of much of Germany, Switzerland, and areas of the Baltics. People eager to understand the Bible without the encumbrance of the hierarchy of priests, bishops, and the pope embraced Luther's ideas. His approach reduced the weight of church traditions. Both of these ideas, and others, appealed to the masses in general. Thanks to the invention of the printing press, Luther's views spread fast.

In 1541, a Swiss theologian John Calvin penned his *Institutes of the Christian Religion* while in exile from Catholic-controlled France. His Protestant beliefs made him a target of persecution, so he sheltered in Geneva, which became the hotbed for Protestant pastors. His beliefs spread to other countries, including Scotland and France, and Dutch Calvinism became a religious tsunami for the next 400 years.

Perhaps you know most of the above brief historical summary. You might *not* know is that Calvin *never* referred to God as the God of Abraham, Isaac, and Jacob in any of his voluminous works. That Calvin never refers to God in this way helps deepen our awareness of anti-Jewish theology transferred from the Universal Church (Roman Catholicism) to the newly forming subsets of Protestant denominations. Calvin's sentiments may have been influenced by Luther's distressing anti-Semitic comments late in life. Here is an example from Luther's writings:

TYRONE NICHOLS

I had made up my mind to write no more either about the Jews or against them. But since I learned that these miserable and accursed people do not cease to lure to themselves even us, that is, the Christians, I have published this little book, so that I might be found among those who opposed such poisonous activities of the Jews who warned the Christians to be on their guard against them. I would not have believed that a Christian could be duped by the Jews into taking their exile and wretchedness upon himself. However, the devil is the god of the world, and wherever God's word is absent he has an easy task, not only with the weak but also with the strong. May God help us. Amen.[244]

Only recently, in the era of post-Holocaust scholarship, theologians from inside and outside the Church seek to set the record straight: The Jesus of history and the Bible is Jewish. This modest but exceptional statement encourages truth-seekers in this world to re-examine Christian theology and their own beliefs. Messianic Judaism, though modest in size yet growing, is at the front edge of efforts to offer both the Church and Jewish communities a cohesive, consistent, and genuine portrayal of Jesus. Of course, this portrayal includes his perpetual ties to the Jewish people and his Jewish identity.

JESUS IS JEWISH

More than 1800 years of theological sediment weighs down the treasure chest of authenticity. Remember the game we used to play as kids called "dog pile?" Imagine you're the kid on the bottom with all your buddies piled on top of you. Try to get out from under their collective weight. You can't. While they grin and giggle, you can barely breathe. The rarified air of faith in Jesus with its origins in the land, people, and Scriptures of Israel is buried under a centuries-old "dog pile" of theological errancy.

I will nibble at some theological ideas that I believe should be re-examined within the Church to course-correct on a right path for the future. Before I do, I need to make a few statements.

- I do not promote the abolishment of the Church.
- I advocate for a theological adjustment to set the Church in alignment with Paul's olive tree theology.
- I believe many God-fearing pastors and laypeople have a deep and genuine love for God and love people from inside the walls of Universal Christendom.

I remember a tagline of a church I attended for some time: "Love God. Love People." Beautiful! Why? This summarizes the two most important laws in the Torah. In Matthew 22:35, an expert in the Law inquisitively asked Jesus the following question:

TYRONE NICHOLS

"Teacher (Rabbi), which commandment is greatest in the Law (Torah)?"

Before the answer, if there were ever a moment for Jesus to say something like, "The Torah isn't important, only loving people and loving God is important" or "The Torah will soon be done away with, as I am bringing a new law, which is to love one another," this would have been that moment! If there were ever a moment for Jesus to convey the message "The Torah of God is not eternal," this would have been a perfect opportunity. *Jesus instead answered the questioner's question by endorsing the Torah!* Jesus said, "Love the Lord your God with all your heart and with all your soul and with all your mind. This is the great and first commandment. And a second is like it: You shall love your neighbor as yourself. On these two commandments hang all the Law and the Prophets." Wow!

Notice the wording; Torah and the Prophets "hang" from these two commandments. The Torah and the Prophets do not dry up and wither away due to the adherence to the first two "greatest" commandments! No. They continue to be valid and "hang" from these two tenants of loving God and loving people. The first portion of the answer Jesus gave the Torah expert is a recitation of the Shema, found in Deuteronomy 6:4-6. The *Shema* prayer stands as the most important prayer in Judaism.

JESUS IS JEWISH

"Hear O Israel, the Lord our God, the Lord is One. You shall love the Lord your God with all your heart and with all your soul and with all your might." In Mark's version of this story, Jesus recited the Shema verbatim with the words, "Hear O Israel, the Lord our God, the Lord is One." (Mark 12:29)

Paul taught his assembly in Rome the same idea. He wrote in Romans 13:9b-10, referring to Leviticus 19:28, "You shall love your neighbor as yourself. Love does no harm to a neighbor; therefore, love is the fullness of the Torah." Remember, we learned earlier that the word "fulfill" does not mean fill it up to do away with it. It means to *live rightly* and to *interpret accurately* the commands of the Torah. Paul's exhortation is understood within the context of rightly living out a lifestyle based on the commands of Torah.

I urge the Church to acknowledge the everlasting Torah of God. Our Master said, "For truly I tell you, until heaven and earth pass away, not a single jot, not a stroke of the pen, will disappear from the Law until everything is accomplished." (Matt. 5:18) Christianity took the phrase "until everything is accomplished" and joined it to the Messiah's crucifixion as the act in which everything was accomplished. It steps over the next statement "everything cannot be accomplished until heaven and earth pass away." The correct reading means *not until the New Heaven and the New Earth emerge on the timeline of human history will "everything be accomplished.*" Why will the Torah pass away then? Because the presence of God will be with His creation, we will see Him and know Him, our Lord and King.

The Bible maintains a harmonious story from Genesis to the Revelation of John. The Torah has not been nullified. It's the living Word of God, passed down through hundreds of generations. Everyone who heeds its wisdom will endure to experience the New Heaven and the New Earth. When we recognize the enduring relevance of the Torah, we align our theology with the consistent theme of the entire Bible.

Many of my Christian friends become nervous at this point. The logic of these arguments makes sense and leaves them in an awkward, confused, and head-spinning place.

I experienced similar feelings of awkwardness, confusion, and bewilderment. Questions arose I'd never had before. "If the Torah is still relevant and in effect, should I be practicing Torah?" and, "Am I sinning because I'm not practicing Torah?"

Most God-fearing Christians already practice Torah; they simply don't call it that. Acts such as giving to charity, taking care of the poor, taking care of widows and orphans, doing acts of kindness, and similar deeds stand as acts of Torah. When you realize

JESUS IS JEWISH

much of Christian practice includes the commandments of the Torah, you can see it's easier than you first thought to comprehend Torah.

You may have heard, according to the rabbis, 613 commandments exist in the Torah. Not all these commandments apply to every person. Some commands apply to the High Priest, some to the Levites, some to males, some to females, some to foreigners living with them in the land, and so forth. Many laws don't apply to Gentiles living outside the land of Israel. Some laws don't apply to *Jews* living outside the land of Israel.

Gentiles living in the land after Jesus ascended to heaven, believed in Jesus and joined an assembly with Jews. Gentiles followed four requirements that honored the belief system of Judaism and smoothed interaction with their Jewish brothers and sisters. We read in Acts 15 that the Apostles required any Gentile believer in Jesus to follow these. James pointed out that, "Moses [the Torah] is taught in synagogues every Sabbath," He indicated the Gentiles who joined the movement of Jesus would learn Torah in the synagogues and from the worldview of first-century Judaism. A formal "church" did not exist for Gentiles to learn about God. By what he said, James instructed new believers to "go to the synagogue and learn about Moses and the Law."

TYRONE NICHOLS

Note that *remembering* the Sabbath is one of the Ten Commandments. I've made a point that those in the Church agree to and, in most cases, follow the other nine commandments. But the Sabbath commandment, the fourth commandment, is conflated with a misinterpretation of one of Paul's letters. He wrote that remembering one day (of rest) is as good as any other. Did he?

No.

Some also misinterpret Jesus's teachings as if he did away with the command to honor the Sabbath and keep it holy, because our 21st century cultural meaning of the word "abolished," is wrong. The word "abolish" in the Bible means to incorrectly interpret or incorrectly obey the commandment as discussed previously.

I've also made the point that if Jesus were teaching the Jews to violate the Sabbath, he'd be disqualified as the Messiah. Why? Deuteronomy 13 verse 5 reads, "The prophet or dreamer must be put to death for inciting rebellion against the Lord your God…for…trying to turn you away from the way the Lord your God commanded you to follow."

If Jesus violated even the smallest of the commands of the Torah, he'd symbolize a blemished lamb, that is, a man who committed sin. The religious authorities would find sin in him. But

JESUS IS JEWISH

they didn't, and they couldn't. Why? He never violated Torah.

Some people misinterpret the book of Galatians as if Paul abolished the Sabbath. Ironically, he wrote the letter to a Sabbath-observant community in Galatia! Did he tell the Galatians to stop doing what they were doing? No.

The text of Galatians is a polemic (verbal attack) written to combat the idea that believing Gentile Galatians needed full conversion to Judaism to enter the Kingdom of Heaven. Some Jewish believers in Jesus wrestled with Paul over whether the Gentiles who believed in the Messiah should go through full conversion. Until you have this perspective on the issue, the book of Galatians is opaque and difficult to understand.

Returning to the topic of the Sabbath, the prophets wrote about its observance. They foretold of future days in the Messianic Kingdom when all the nations would be observing the seventh day, the day of rest. Isaiah 58:12-14 reads:

> Your people will rebuild the ancient ruins; you will restore the age-old foundations; you will be called Repairer of the Breach, Restorer of Streets of Dwelling. If you turn your foot from breaking the Sabbath, from doing as you please on My holy day,

if you call the Sabbath a delight, and the LORD'S holy day honorable, if you honor it by not going your own way or seeking your own pleasure or speaking idle words, then you will delight yourself in the LORD, and I will make you ride on the heights of the land and feed you with the heritage of your father Jacob. For the mouth of the LORD has spoken.

Again, in Isaiah 66:22-24 we read:

For as the new heavens and the new earth, which I will make, shall remain before me, says the Lord, so shall your seed and your name remain. And it shall come to pass, that every new moon, and every Sabbath, shall all flesh come to worship before me, says the Lord. And they shall go forth and look upon the carcasses of the men who have transgressed against me; for their worm shall not die, nor shall their fire be quenched; and they shall be a loathing to all flesh.

And Ezekiel 44:22 says:

In any dispute, the priests are to serve as judges and decide it according to my ordinances. They are to

JESUS IS JEWISH

keep my laws and my decrees for all my appointed festivals, and they are to keep my Sabbaths holy.

In each prophecy about the Millennial Kingdom, people observe the Sabbath. Dispensational theology teaches the idea of the "Church Age." The question for us is this: do we live in the "Church Age," an era that temporarily sets aside the Sabbath? The Bible, from Genesis to Revelation, always identifies the Sabbath *as the seventh day of the week*, from Friday night to Saturday night. Wouldn't it be right to acknowledge that Sunday isn't the biblical Sabbath?

Even so, to go to church on Sunday is not a sin. As believers in the Messiah, we can worship on any day of the week. That freedom doesn't make the day we rest or the day we worship the actual Sabbath. In the early 300s, the Church institutionalized Sunday worship as the Sabbath, but did this *in error*.

One of my pastor friends told me he takes his Sabbath on Monday, a widespread practice for Christian pastors. I said, "I understand; however, your decision to rest on Monday doesn't make Monday the actual, biblical Sabbath." The seventh day is the day of God's Sabbath.

Did we lose track of which day is the "real" seventh day of

the week during the past 4,000 or more years? No. The seventh day of the week is the day of the week that the Jewish nation, whether in exile or in the land, celebrates it. Jewish religious leaders kept track of the correct day during the passing centuries. Why would they have accidentally shifted the seventh day of the week away from the actual seventh day? The LORD who created the universe knows which day of the week is the "actual" seventh day and He communicates that truth to those who obey His covenant: the Jewish nation.

Sabbath Celebration demonstrates how Replacement Theology embedded itself in Universal Christianity. With sincerity, the Church holds the belief that Sunday is the Sabbath day. As an institution, Christianity hasn't honored the command God gave to Israel about Sabbath observance in Leviticus 23. Sunday worship is a remnant of Roman Catholic belief, which began during the reign of Constantine, who declared Sunday as the day of rest.

On March 7, 321 C.E. Constantine proclaimed, "On the venerable Day of the Sun [an idea from pagan sun worship] let the magistrates and the people residing in cities rest, and let all workshops be closed."[245] The Roman papacy later confirmed this law at the Council of Laodicea in 364 C.E.

Christians shall not Judaize and be idle on Saturday

JESUS IS JEWISH

> but shall work on that day; but the Lord's Day they shall especially honour [sic], and, as being Christians, shall, if possible, do no work on that day. If, however, they are found Judaizing, [worshiping on the Sabbath, or following the Jewish Calendar, etc.] they shall be shut out from Christ.²⁴⁶ [Brackets mine]

Cardinal Gibbons freely admits in his work *Faith of Our Fathers*:

> You may read the Bible from Genesis to Revelation, and you will not find a single line authorizing the sanctification of Sunday. The Scriptures enforce the religious observance of Saturday, a day which we [the Roman Catholic Church] never sanctify…The Catholic Church…by virtue of her divine mission, changed the day from Saturday to Sunday.²⁴⁷

In the Roman Catholic record of London published in 1923, we read, "Sunday is our mark of authority… *the church is above the Bible*, and this transference of Sabbath observance is proof of that fact."²⁴⁸ [Italics mine]

The Patriarchs, the Israelites, the Prophets, Jesus, the

Apostles, the early believers, and the Diaspora believers obeyed the fourth commandment, as will those in the Millennial Kingdom.

In light of the above, the process of reevaluating Christian theology requires bravery, mental strength, and determination. I'm confident millions of Christians exist who, like me, yearn for truth and to follow Jesus as one of his disciples and will do so, regardless of challenges. The cost of this discovery can be high. Being alert to and removing traces of Replacement Theology from your beliefs can be time-consuming and a mental exercise in vigilance.

Let me offer some examples of how this pursuit may challenge your current Christian beliefs. Did you know that the Church fathers created Christmas, Easter, Lent, and the Eucharist as *alternatives* to biblical holidays? The Church invented Christmas (various theories exist as to why), Easter replaced Passover, Lent replaced the counting of the Omer between Passover and Shavuot (Pentecost), and the Eucharist, derived from the Passover Seder, became a mystical or semi-mystical Christian practice.

These traditions, prevalent in Universal Christianity, wouldn't be recognized by early Jesus followers or by Jesus himself. Should we continue to follow the traditions in Christianity set by Constantine, or should we revert to the traditions of Yeshua and his disciples?

JESUS IS JEWISH

For me, any change in personal habits or family traditions comes down to answering this question: *Whose disciple am I?* Am I a disciple of Protestant Evangelical Christianity? Lutheranism? Maybe Roman Catholicism? Perhaps a disciple of one of the 45,000 or so Christian denominations around the world? *Or am I disciple of the Jewish Messiah, Yeshua of Nazareth, Son of David, Son of Abraham, the Son of God?*

If I'm a disciple of Yeshua, then I'm a disciple of a Torah-observant, Jewish Messiah. I'm a disciple of the man who fulfilled many of the Messianic prophecies in the Hebrew Scriptures and will fulfill all of them in future. I'm a disciple of the man who upheld the Law of Moses, who rightly interpreted and rightly lived out the laws given to the people of Israel in the ceremony between God and them at Sinai. I'm a disciple of the savior whose Father said, "This is my son, in whom I am well pleased" (Matt. 3:17). He now sits at the right hand of the Father awaiting the command to return to the earth and set up His kingdom on earth from Jerusalem.

How far our religious practice has strayed from the first-century movement of Yeshua! He didn't teach against the Temple, he said it's his Father's house. He didn't teach against the Levitical sacrificial system, he participated in it. He didn't develop a Christian identity outside Judaism, he created a movement of disciples inside the borders of it. He didn't teach against the Torah; he commanded his followers to observe even the smallest of its commands that applied to them. He didn't do away with his Father's calendar as outlined in Leviticus 23, he observed the festivals his entire life and traveled to Jerusalem to participate in them. He didn't teach the abolition or "cancellation" of the Sabbath, he defended its sanctity and holiness, and participated in Sabbath observance as was his custom.

Much of Universal Christianity's theology comes with an anti-Torah, anti-Jewish, anti-Temple bias. Why?

I trust this book helps you begin to answer that question. I don't seek controversy, though my writings may stimulate it. My aim is to encourage each of us to live a life that reflects the original vision and purpose of the Master. We Gentiles are of the nations who have been called by the God of Abraham, Isaac, and Jacob to glorify and honor Him. We attach ourselves as wild olive shoots to the covenant promises of God given to the people of Israel. We're grafted into the root of Israel through faith in Yeshua the Messiah.

How do we correct our course? We reorient our worldview so that Israel is the center of biblical theology. This can happen when the Church recognizes that Israel is, *and always has been*, the people group through whom God chose to show Himself to the nations. Israel is the people group by whom God will bring forth His

JESUS IS JEWISH

kingdom through the reign of His Messiah and establish His presence on earth. Israel is the protagonist God positioned front and center in the biblical narrative, and they are the nation and people of God. In Abraham Heschel's book *An Echo of Eternity*, he writes, "God has chosen Jerusalem and endowed her with the mystery of His presence; prophets, kings, sages, priests, made her a place where God's calling was heard and accepted."[249] The Psalmist writes:

> If I forget you, O Jerusalem, let my right hand whither. Let my tongue cleave to the roof of my mouth if I do not remember you, If I do not set Jerusalem above my highest joys. (Psalm 137: 5-6)

Chapter 16
Why It Matters – Restoring Israel to Her Rightful Place

On the momentous day of July 30, 1492, approximately 200,000 Jews faced an unfathomable dilemma: convert to Christianity or be forced into exile from Spain as decreed by King Ferdinand II and Queen Isabella I. The monumental directive, known as the Expulsion of the Jews from Spain, or the Alhambra Decree, carved a deep, indelible mark on the narrative of Jewish history.

This expulsion intertwined with the notorious Spanish Inquisition, a campaign of religious scrutiny and persecution that began 14 years earlier. The Inquisition, with Father Tomas de Torquemada at its helm, had birthed out of the conviction of the Church that if Jews remained in Spain, they could influence newly converted Christians *to revert to Judaism*.

Concerned about this perceived risk of Jewish influence, Torquemada succeeded in convincing King Ferdinand and Queen Isabella to seek papal authorization for a Spanish-specific inquisition. Note that the broader Inquisition had already been in operation since the early 13th century, primarily focused on rooting

JESUS IS JEWISH

out Christian heretics. Once Pope Sixtus IV gave his assent, Torquemada promptly established his tribunals, and laid the groundwork for what would culminate in the heart-wrenching expulsion of the Jews.

The Jews fled for their lives. Reduced to carrying their belongings on their backs, they left behind everything that couldn't be loaded on a wagon or carried by a donkey or horse, if they were so lucky to own one of these. In desperation for safe passage, Jews paid exorbitant sums to Spanish sea captains. They hoped for a quick and clandestine escape to safety; instead, the ship crew dumped them overboard in the middle of the ocean. Rumors spread throughout Spain that the Jews had swallowed gold and precious stones. Whether true or not, brigands knifed Jews to death hoping to find treasures in their stomachs.[250]

To write about such things, to come face to face with such evil, caused great sorrow in me. When I examined the depths of the wickedness and depravity of man, I couldn't walk away mentally or emotionally unscathed. To me, these actions stand as unconscionable, and I reel with disgust, "How is this possible?"

Historical narrative of anti-Semitism within the Church is easy to find. For obvious reasons, church history isn't taught from the pulpit, and if taught, it's most likely from the supersessionist point of view. In my research, the sheer amount of raw data about the persistent perpetuation of Christian anti-Semitism overwhelmed me. In my examination of church history over the years, I've been dismayed and nauseated when I come across yet another instance of Christian hate toward the Jews. What I share next is an abbreviated list of an extensive, sad, and sorrowful history of Christian anti-Semitism. These few examples demonstrate the need for the Church to acknowledge the harm it caused the Jewish community.

My aim is to bring about reconciliation between them.

I've introduced you to Justin Martyr, who lived between the years 100 – 165 C.E. One of the earliest of the church fathers, he taught that Christians became the "New Israel" because the Jews received divine punishment for "murdering the Just One." Another early father, Ignatius of Antioch, taught that those who partake in the Passover join with those who killed Christ.[251] Bishop Melito (120-185 C.E.) took on this ugly theme when he preached, "The Jews murdered God." Church Father Irenaeus (130 – 202 C.E.) taught a lie; that Jews were disinherited from the grace of God.[252] St. Hilary of Poitiers in France proclaimed another lie that the Jews were a perverse people, forever accursed by God (367 C.E.).

As presented in previous chapters, documents from the Council of Nicea record the Council members' claim: that the Jews

JESUS IS JEWISH

are "odious people" and "we should have nothing in common with them." The Council's words added fuel to the development of Universal Christendom's anti-Semitism. Eusebius (275-339 C.E.) proclaimed that blessings in the Old Testament belonged to the Gentiles and curses for the Jews. He also asserted that the Church is the "New Israel."

In North Africa, Father John Chrysostom (349 – 407 C.E.), the patriarch of Constantinople known as the "bishop with the golden tongue," taught his parishioners:

> Jews are the most worthless of men – they are lecherous, greedy, rapacious – they are perfidious murderers of Christians, they worship the devil, their religion is a sickness...The Jews are the odious assassins of Christ and for killing God there is no expiation, no indulgence, no pardon. Christians may never cease vengeance. The Jews must live in servitude forever. Since God hates the Jews, it is the duty of Christians to hate them, too. He who has no limits in his love of Christ must have no limits in his battle with those who hate Him. I hate the Jews. It is incumbent on all Christians to hate the Jews.[253]

The translator of the Latin Vulgate, St. Jerome wrote an

entire treatise entitled, *Tract Against the Jews* where he accused them of being liars from birth. He calls the synagogues, "brothels and a den of vice, the Devil's refuge, a place to deprive the soul, and an abyss of every conceivable disaster and whatever else you will, you are still saying less than it deserves." He also writes, "God hates the Jews and I hate the Jews."

These men are church "fathers," founders of the Christian faith. The gravity of the above statements and how they damaged the nation of Israel is impossible to comprehend.

In Spain during the 7th century, Bishops Isadore and Julian wrote polemics against Judaism. In France during the 9th century, the *Epistles of St. Agod*, written by the Archbishop of Lyons, set out to prove that the Jews were born slaves and sold Christian babies to the Arabs. In the 13th century, Pope Innocent III asserted that Jews stood consigned to perpetual servitude because they crucified the Lord and therefore were summarily rejected by God. Thomas Aquinas agreed. In his *Letter on the Treatment of the Jews* he writes, "The Jews by reason of their crucifying the Lord are sentenced to perpetual servitude," and "Jews in all Christian provinces, and all the time, should be distinguished from other people by some clothing."[254]

In the 14th century, renowned English Poet Geoffrey

JESUS IS JEWISH

Chaucer penned the anti-Semitic *The Prioress's Tale* as part of his famous *Canterbury Tales*. This story accused the Jews of the notorious "blood libel." Some people read it, then tortured and massacred Jews. In the 16th century, famed Dutch theologian Erasmus wrote, "If it is Christian to detest the Jews, on this count we are all good Christians, and to spare."

This brings us to Martin Luther, the father of the Reformation, who began his career as a theologian defending Jews but later in life turned vehement and hostile toward them. We looked briefly at Martin Luther's statements earlier, but let's look again at his words to help us comprehend the depth of his effect on today's theology. At the end of his life, Luther published a book entitled *Concerning the Jews and Their Lies*. You can read about his anti-Semitic remarks on the Jewish Virtual Library webpage here. If the link doesn't connect you, go to www.jewishvirtuallibray.org and type in "Martin Luther."

https://www.jewishvirtuallibrary.org/martin-luther-quot-the-jews-and-their-lies-quot

He writes:

> Therefore, be on your guard against the Jews, knowing that wherever they have their synagogues,

nothing is found but a den of devils in which sheer self-glory, conceit, lies, blasphemy, and defaming of God and men are practiced most maliciously and veheming his eyes on them.²⁵⁵

You may be thinking, "Surely at some point in Christian history this type of evil rhetoric stops!" I thought so, too. It continues:

> John Calvin, who was somewhat favorable toward the Jews at times, still could not detach himself from the anti-Semitic paradigm from which Christianity formed. He writes, "I have had much conversation with many Jews: I have never seen either a drop of piety or a grain of truth or ingenuousness – nay, I have never found common sense in any Jew." He is also quoted as calling Jews "profane dogs" who "under the pretext of prophecy, stupidly devour all the riches of the earth with their unrestrained cupidity." In his infamous minor tract, Ad Quaelstiones et Objecta Juaei Cuiusdam Responsio (A Response to Questions and Objections of a Certain Jew), he wrote: "The Jews' rotten and unbending stiffneckedness deserves that they be oppressed unendingly and without measure on end

JESUS IS JEWISH

and that they die in their misery without the pity of anyone."[256]

In New Amsterdam, Peter Stuyvesant, who served as the Director General for the Dutch colony of New Netherland (this colony included parts of the states of New York, New Jersey, Pennsylvania, Maryland, Connecticut, and Delaware) in the mid-1700s, considered the Jews as hateful enemies and as blasphemers of the name of Christ. In the 1800s in Germany, Karl Marx published *Zur Judenfrage* (On the Jewish Question), an economic and cultural criticism of Jews and Judaism.

Comte de Gobineau, a French aristocrat best known for helping legitimize racism by using scientific racist theory, published his *Essay on Inequality*. He put forth a theory that human races ranked from superior to inferior, and the Nordic race topped the list at most superior. Modern anti-Semitism drew heavily from this racist thesis.

German social scientist and philosopher, Eugen Dühring, published *The Jewish Question as a Problem of Race, Customs and Culture*. In this book, he slandered the Jews as an intellectually inferior and depraved race that lacked loyalty, reverence, and any scientific or artistic creativity. He declared that the duty of Nordic people included the extermination of such a "parasitic race," as we exterminate snakes and beasts of prey.[257]

The fruits of these ideas led to one of the most horrific events in human history: the Holocaust. Not counting any soldiers killed in World War II, SIX MILLION Jews, about two-thirds of the European Jewish population and about thirty-five percent of all the non-combatant people murdered by Germans, died at the hands of Hitler. Six million is a number so large our minds can't fathom it. Hitler wrote in his book *Mein Kampf*:

> "Hence today I believe that I am acting in accordance with the Almighty Creator. By defending myself against the Jew, I am fighting for the work of the Lord."

I haven't written about the Crusades, which lasted three hundred forty-eight years (1000 – 1348), or the Black Death when Jews were accused of poisoning wells to kill Christians (1348 – 1354), or a detailed outline of the Inquisitions (1200s – 1500s), or the anti-Semitic underpinnings of the Reformation (1500 – 1599), or the Pogroms in Russia (see the *Protocols of Zion*), or the Dreyfus Affair in France. Neither have I decided to tackle the prominent leaders in the U.S. like Henry Ford or Charles Lindberg, who openly espoused anti-Semitic views.

JESUS IS JEWISH

What I have done, as briefly and succinctly as possible, is *connect the dots*. Universal Christendom's history is anti-Jewish, and its effect on world opinion cannot be denied.

While anti-Semitism mars the history of the Church, some people in its ranks stood apart and demonstrated a deep respect and love for the Jewish people and their faith. These people resisted the cultural and religious biases of their times and extended hands of friendship and understanding rather than hostility and prejudice.

For example, take Nicholas of Cusa, a 15th century German cardinal, philosopher, and theologian. He posited that Jews and Christians both anticipate the Messiah, though they understand this promise in different ways. He promoted mutual understanding and peaceful dialogue, and urged Christians to read the Hebrew Scriptures in their original language to better understand the Jewish perspective.

The 17th-century philosopher and theologian, John Locke displayed a notable departure from the anti-Semitic sentiments of his era. He argued vehemently for religious tolerance, including toward Jews. His "Letter Concerning Toleration" explicitly included Jews among those groups to be granted freedom of worship, a radical, inclusive view for his time.

TYRONE NICHOLS

In the 20th century, the influential Protestant theologian Karl Barth stood firm against the rising tide of Nazism and voiced opposition to their anti-Semitic ideology. He maintained that Jewish people remained God's chosen, despite main stream supersessionist beliefs in the Church. His refusal to support the Nazi regime or their anti-Semitic theology led to his eventual expulsion from Germany.

Throughout history, people within the Church refused to subscribe to anti-Semitic views, challenged the status quo, and helped foster a spirit of unity and respect between Jews and Christians.[258]

To its credit, in 1998, the Second Vatican Council issued the following statement to begin repair to the relationship between the Roman Catholic Church and the Jews:

> This century has witnessed an unspeakable tragedy, which can never be forgotten — the attempt by the Nazi regime to exterminate the Jewish people, with the consequent killing of millions of Jews. Women and men, old and young, children and infants, for the sole reason of their Jewish origin, were persecuted and deported. Some were killed immediately, while others were degraded, ill-treated, tortured, and utterly robbed of their human dignity, and then

JESUS IS JEWISH

murdered. Very few of those who entered the [concentration] camps survived, and those who did remained scarred for life. This was the Holocaust.

The Second Vatican Council statement summoned all Roman Catholics to reappraise their attitudes regarding Jews to promote Catholic-Jewish harmony. This change in policy and action came as a remarkable positive step toward a spirit of renewal.

I salute the importance of the Second Vatican Council and the significant steps initiated toward healing nearly two millennia of anti-Semitism. I include in my salute the awareness and actions of the many people in Universal Christendom that valiantly defended the Jewish people.

I believe that the effort of Universal Christendom to reverse Replacement Theology, eliminate anti-Semitism, and honor Jews and Judaism has much to overcome. Positive steps, such as this statement, signify a beginning of change, but the root of the issue goes deeper.

Anti-Semitism not only appeared in historical actions of Universal Christendom but is still ensconced in its theological fabric. You might argue, "Not in my church! We love Israel and provide constant support."

Simple support of Israel isn't enough to eradicate Replacement Theology, though it's commendable and a good beginning. Let's revisit some ideas from the previous chapter through a set of probing questions:

1. Do you or does your church recognize the biblical Sabbath as Friday night to Saturday night?
2. When people are baptized at your church, is there any mention at all of their new connection to the family of Israel and to the patriarchs, Abraham, Isaac, and Jacob?
3. Are any Jews attending your church classified as potential converts to Christianity and encouraged to leave their Jewish roots, culture, and traditions?
4. Do you celebrate Easter with references to Passover or the Feast of First Fruits?
5. Are you taught that Jesus was put on the execution stake on Passover? Do you know he was raised from the dead on the Feast of First Fruits?

Answering these questions in honesty might lead you to discover the origins of Christianity's rituals and holidays that distance us from the faith and traditions of our Master.

Until we examine and challenge these ingrained practices,

JESUS IS JEWISH

dig out the roots, and repent from our errors, attempts to heal the relationship between Christians and Jews will only skim the surface and likely fail. The changes we need necessitate a profound theological transition: the diligent discard of Replacement Theology and the thoughtful introduction of the truth in its stead.

Most of us in Universal Christianity don't practice a faith recognizable to first-century followers of Yeshua. What we do have in common with the first-century believer is our shared belief that Yeshua is the Messiah.

Let's look at this from another perspective. Have you ever wondered why it's so difficult for Jewish people to consider that Jesus might be their Messiah? I know I did.

The Church presents the Jewish people a non-Torah observant, non-Jewish Messiah that *we* worship. What Jewish person would acknowledge that Messiah? *That* one did away with the Torah, shunned Sabbath observance, promoted a non-Kosher diet, and re-assigned the status of the "elect" to the Christian Church!

The Jewish community perceives a figure who, according to the standards outlined in the Torah, *is ineligible to be the Messiah!* I'll repeat that. Most, if not all, of both the Jewish people and the non-Jewish people of the world see Jesus as a version of a Christianized Jew and ineligible to be the Messiah.

The perplexity of the present situation leaves me astounded and baffled. Although the Church hails Jesus as the Messiah, it disqualifies him at the same time. How? It ignores and dismisses the authenticity of the scriptures that validate his Messiahship! The Church espouses the belief that the Torah has been nullified except for nine of the Ten Commandments, is no longer relevant to Jesus's followers, adorns Jesus in foreign and un-Jewish garb, and then expects Jewish people to identify him as one of their own. What?

Added to my perplexity is the surprise and confusion Christians express when they see the Jews' unwavering refusal to consider Jesus at all, let alone as the Jewish Messiah! Can you understand this reasonable Jewish reluctance, given how un-Jewish the Universal Church believes Jesus is?

If we are sincere about repairing our relationships with our Jewish brothers and sisters, I suggest we humbly repent of the almost 2000 years of both anti-Semitic behavior and anti-Semitic theology. We are the ones who must reconcile ourselves to an *accurate portrayal of the Jewish Jesus* rather than hold to centuries of errant theology. We have a lot of work to do.

JESUS IS JEWISH

I realize the enormity of what I ask. We'd see an earth-shattering miracle if Universal Christendom re-evaluated its historical anti-Jewish narrative, and returned Israel to the center of God's story.

It would mean that our theological seminaries would change course and change content of many courses.

It would mean that we'd have to re-examine, edit, republish all of our Christian commentaries, and revise theological tenants starting from the Council of Nicaea onward.

It would mean that we'd ask the Jews for their forgiveness and entreat them to see us as brothers and sisters rather than conquerors.

It would mean for local pastors and clergymen to admit that, for however long they have preached and taught, portions or large sections of their theology will be re-evaluated, revised, and rewritten. These actions for some may be a mountain too hard to climb.

It would mean changes to our views of the ways of the LORD and how to we'd observe His laws that are applicable to Gentile disciples of Yeshua.

TYRONE NICHOLS

It would mean reassessment of Yeshua by Jews as a potential candidate for the office of Messiah within the context and framework of Torah.

It would mean the Torah of Moses repositioned not as a relic of the distant past, but as a living document with relevant information for the *here and now*.

It would mean honor and support for the Law (Torah) as Yeshua depicted it and acknowledgment it has transformational power.

David Stern in his book *Restoring the Jewishness of the Gospel* writes:

> When the Church proclaims a Gospel without its Jewishness restored, she is at best failing to proclaim, "the whole counsel of God" (Acts 20:27). At worst she may be communicating what Paul called "another Gospel" (Galatians 1:6-9). Moreover, not only Jews suffer from this off-target preaching — Gentiles suffer too. [259]

Both believing Gentile Christians and Jews suffer from Universal Christendom's choices and continued unwillingness to see Jesus as Jewish. My hope is that Universal Christendom will

JESUS IS JEWISH

unwind its knotted storyline by getting its house in order. We'd humbly engage in dialogue with our Jewish brothers and sisters about all we have in common.

I recognize that change of such magnitude will be slow. Patience, persistence, and ongoing conversations would support and sustain this journey, which will include cross-generation commitment to this marvelous and massive effort. Resistance and obstacles that stem from deeply ingrained beliefs, historical wounds, and fear of relinquishing long-held perspectives, require change and healing from both Christian and Jewish communities. We can navigate a path toward genuine reconciliation through open dialogue about these challenges and the potential difficulties.

Part of the reconciliation requires that we acknowledge the Bible is a *Jewish document*, written by Jewish men (with the possible exception of Luke) from Genesis to Revelation, and records Jewish history. The Bible's consistent theme: God chose Israel to be His people and through them all mankind can find salvation.

Dr. Stern writes, "If Christianity's roots are Jewish, if the Gospel itself is Jewish in its very essence, *why should it need to be contextualized for Jews?*" [Italics mine][260] Post-Holocaust scholars propose that these documents deserve presentation in a first-century Judaism context. This allows us to fully comprehend the gospels and the New Testament, which is perhaps better named as the Jewish Apostolic Writings.

Jesus's early followers saw the Messiah's arrival and establishment of the Kingdom as part of Jewish theology and history. They looked to the Tanakh as the authority that defined and identified all things Messianic. When Gentiles joined the movement, *the disciples understood their inclusion to be a fulfillment of Jewish prophecy.*

As we have studied, *the original paradigm was a Jewish presentation of the gospel to Gentiles.* Today, Gentile followers of Jesus believe that they need to present the gospel message to Jews in a different context, a Christian one.

Is the notion accurate that the Church became the focal point of God's theological realm? Or, as I have argued, is it that Israel has *always been* and will *continue to be* God's eternal chosen people? After all, God Himself declares to Abraham in Genesis 17:7, "I will establish my covenant between me and you, and your descendants after you, as an everlasting covenant to be God to you and your descendants after you."

Recognizing that *Jesus is Jewish* is the way we rectify past wrongs committed by Universal Christendom, foster vibrant

JESUS IS JEWISH

Jewish-Christian relationships based on our shared heritage, and restore Israel to its rightful place at the center of the biblical account. We attach ourselves to the concepts of first-century Messianic belief and return, to the best of our ability in the twenty-first century, to the original vision of "The Way."

The undeniable truth that Jesus is Jewish stands as the key to unlock the concealed identity of Jesus of Nazareth. This pursuit is not a mere academic, brain-focused one, but a transformative journey with the power to reshape our relationships with God, the Jewish people, and the world at large. Jesus, the embodiment of Jewish faith and heritage, has the answers to the deepest questions of our existence. His life, teachings, and redemptive work find complete expression and life in the rich tapestry of Jewish history and Scripture.

When we recognize Jesus as Jewish, we reclaim our authentic heartbeat of faith and embrace a profound connection with our Jewish brothers and sisters as their Gentile siblings. Let's navigate the complexities of our shared heritage, seek reconciliation, and together embark on a journey of rediscovery that will unveil the true essence of Jesus, the Jewish Messiah. Through this revelation, may his concealed identity be revealed to the world.

After all…Jesus is Jewish.

TYRONE NICHOLS

Appendix A

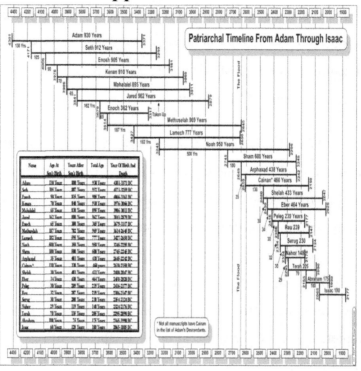

http://www.swartzentrover.com/cotor/Bible/Bible/OT/Law/Genesis/patriarchal_timeline_from_adam_through_Isaac.htm

JESUS IS JEWISH

Appendix B

The Nazarene

In Matthew 2:23 we read, "and he went and lived in a town called Nazareth. So was fulfilled what was said through the prophets, that he would be called a Nazarene." (NIV) Early believers in Jesus saw more significance than the purely geographical in the use of the word Nazarene. Scholar Richard Bauckham writes,

> It could be understood as an exegetical pun, designating Jesus the messianic "shoot" of David (Isa. 11:1: Hebrew netzer נצר) and perhaps also alluding to the term nazir/ נזיר, meaning someone "consecrated to God" (Nazirite, as in Judges 13:5, 7; 16:17). But neser/ נצר was also used in Scripture of the Messiah's people, the eschatological Israel (Isa. 60:21), while a further punning connection could be made with the root nsr/ נצר meaning "to watch, to preserve," and so with "the preserved (nesire/ נצירי or nesure/ נצורי) of Israel" whom the Messiah is to restore according to Isa 49:6 (a significant text for early Christians: Luke 2:32; Acts 13:47). The early Christians would have seen themselves as the beginning of Israel's restoration by the Messiah: the

TYRONE NICHOLS

nesire/נצירי restored by the neser/נצר.327

It is possible that Matthew purposefully referenced the "netzer-the branch" to send a coded message to his readers that, indeed, the restoration of the *kahal* of Israel had commenced. The mission of the *kahal* of Israel, for Matthew, is only comprehended in the context of prophetic fulfillment in "the branch's" mission, which can be found in Isaiah 49:6:

> Is it too light a thing that you should be my servant to raise up the tribes of Jacob and to bring back the preserved (nesire/נצירי) of Israel? I will make you as a light for the Gentiles that my salvation (Yeshua/ישוע) may reach to the end of the earth.

Thus, Matthew would have seen himself as a part of the beginning of the restoration of Israel through the mission of the Messiah and as a member of Yeshua's *ekklesia*.

JESUS IS JEWISH

Appendix C

- After the death of Abraham, God appeared to Isaac, "The Lord appeared to him and said, 'I am the God of your father Abraham. Do not be afraid, for I am with you. I will bless you and will increase the number of your descendants for the sake of My servant Abraham. (Gen. 26:24)
- God appeared to Jacob in a dream and said, "I am the LORD, the God of your father Abraham and the God of Isaac. I will give you and your descendants the land on which you are lying." (Gen. 28:13)
- As Jacob returned to face Esau, he prayed, "God of my father Abraham, God of my father Isaac, O LORD, who said to me, 'Go back to your country and your relatives and I will make you prosper..." (Gen 32:9)
- From the burning bush, God told Moses, "Say to the descendants of Israel, 'The LORD, the God of your fathers – the God of Abraham, the God of Isaac, and the God of Jacob – has sent me to you.' *This is my name forever, the name by which I am to be remembered from generation to generation.* (Italics mine.) (Ex. 3:15) (Side note - How in the world did the writers of the Christian Creeds miss this?)
- Elijah challenged the priests of Baal on Mount Carmel. "You call on the name of your god, and I will call on the Name of the

LORD. The god who answers by fire – He is God." (1 Kgs. 18:24b)

- Elijah prayed, "O LORD, God of Abraham, Isaac and Israel [remember Jacob's name was changed to Israel by God], let it be known today that you are God in Israel and that I am Your servant and have done all these things at Your command." (I Kgs. 18:36)
- Moses and Aaron told Pharaoh, "This is what the LORD, the God of Israel, says: 'Let My people go, so that they may hold a festival to Me in the desert.' Pharaoh said, "Who is the LORD, that I should obey Him and let Israel go? I do not know the LORD and I will not let Israel go!" (Ex. 5:1-2)
- "Hear, O Israel: The LORD our God, the LORD is one...For the LORD your God is God of gods and Lord of lords, the great God, mighty and awesome, who shows no partiality and accepts no bribes." (Dt.6:4; 10:17)
- Hezekiah prayed: "O LORD, God of Israel, enthroned between the cherubim, you alone are God over all the kingdoms of the earth. You have made heaven and earth...It is true, O LORD, that the Assyrian kings have laid waste these nations and their lands. They have thrown their gods into the fire and destroyed them, for they were not gods but only wood and stone, fashioned by men's hands. Now O LORD our God, deliver us from his hand,

JESUS IS JEWISH

so that all kingdoms on earth may know that You alone, O LORD, are God." (2 Kings 10:15, 17-19)

- "I am the LORD your God (whose God, Israel's God) who brought you out of Egypt, out of the land of slavery. You shall have no other gods before Me." (Ex. 20:2-3)
- Use honest scales and honest weights, an honest ephah and an honest hin. I am the LORD your God, who brought you out of Egypt...I am the LORD your God, who brought you out of Egypt to give you the land of Canaan and to be your God." (Lev. 19:36, 25:38)
- "I am the LORD your God, who brought you up out of Egypt. Open your mouth wide and I will fill it." (Ps. 81:10)
- I am the LORD your God, who brought you out of Egypt. You shall acknowledge no God but Me, no Savior except Me." (Hos. 13:4)
- "For who is God besides the LORD? And who is the Rock except our God?" (Ps. 18:31)
- "May the LORD, the God of your fathers, increase you a thousand times and bless you as He has promised!" (Dt. 1:11; cf. Dt. 4:1, 6:3, 12:1, 26:7)
- Jesus/Yeshua (Yeshua is his Hebrew name) challenged those who doubted the reality of the resurrection of the dead. He said the proof of the resurrection lies in God continuing to be "the

God of Abraham, and the God of Isaac, and the God of Jacob." (cf. Mt. 22:32; Mark 12:26; Luke 20:37)

- It is this same God, who raised Jesus/Yeshua from the dead. As his ambassadors told the council: "The God of our fathers raised Yeshua from the dead." (Acts 5:30)

- "The God of Abraham, Isaac, and Jacob, the God of our fathers, has glorified His servant, Yeshua." (Acts 3:13a)

- Ananias told Paul after praying for him to receive his sight "The God of our fathers has chosen you to know His will and to see the Righteous One and to Hear words from his mouth..." (Acts 13:16-17)

- "I admit that I worship the God of our fathers as a follower of The Way, which they call a sect. I believe everything that agrees with the Law and that is written in the Prophets." (Acts 24:14) That is Paul speaking while on trial. It is a powerful personal testimony as to where Paul stands in relation to the Law of Moses, and one that is difficult for Christians to grasp.

- "He helped His servant Israel, remembering to be merciful to Abraham and his descendants forever, even as he said to our fathers." (Luke 1:54-55)

- "Praise be to the Lord, the God of Israel, because He has come and has redeemed His people." (Luke 1:68)

JESUS IS JEWISH

- "The people were amazed when they saw the mute speaking, the crippled made well, the lame walking and the blind seeing. And they praised the God of Israel." (Mt. 15:31)

Appendix D

Shadow Side of Nicaea

"We ought not therefore to have any thing in common with the Jews, for the Savior has shown us another way. And consequently, in unanimously adopting this mold, we desire, dearest brethren, to separate ourselves from the detestable company of the Jews. How can they be in the right, they who, after the death of the Savior, have no longer been led by reason but by wild violence as their delusion may urge them? It would still be your duty not to tarnish your soul by communications with such wicked people as the Jews. It is our duty not to have anything in common with the murderers of our Lord."

- Emperor Constantine, 325 AD.

"When the question arose concerning the most holy day of Easter, it was decreed by common consent to be expedient, that this festival should be celebrated on the same day by all, in every place. For what can be more beautiful, what more venerable and becoming, than that this festival, from which we receive the hope of immortality, should be suitably observed by all in one and the same order, and by a certain rule. And truly, in the first place, it seemed to everyone a most unworthy thing that we should follow the custom

JESUS IS JEWISH

of the Jews in the celebration of this most holy solemnity, those polluted wretches! Having stained their hands with a nefarious crime, are justly blinded in their minds."

- Emperor Constantine, 325 AD

"It is fit, therefore, that rejecting the practice of this people..."

- Emperor Constantine, 325 AD

"Let us have nothing in common with the most hostile rabble of the Jews..."

- Emperor Constantine, 325 AD

"...let us withdraw ourselves, my much-honored brethren, from that most odious fellowship."

- Emperor Constantine, 325 AD

"For what can they rightly understand, who, after the tragical death of our Lord, being deluded and darkened in their minds, are carried away by an unrestrained impulse wherever their inborn madness may impel them."

- Emperor Constantine, 325 AD

"As it is necessary that this fault should be so amended that we may have nothing in common with the usage of these parricides and murderers of our Lord."

- Emperor Constantine, 325 AD

These quotes are from a letter Constantine wrote to the churches, recounting the "glorious" events of the Council of Nicaea. He officially establishes an anti-Judaic foundation for the doctrine and practice of the Church. In the strongest of terms, he declares contempt for the Jews, demands a separation from them, and decrees that this should be the official position of the Church.

Remember, Jesus is Jewish.

JESUS IS JEWISH

Bibliography

Books

Armmitage, Mark J. Aquinas's "Perspectives" on Paul: Thomas, Paul and the Problem of Torah. Pro Ecclesia 18 no. 4 Fall 2009 ppg. 393-414. 2009.

Attridge, Harold W., Dale B. Martin, and Jürgen Zangenberg, eds. Wissenschaftliche Untersuchungen Zum Neuen Testament,. Vol. 210, Religion, Ethnicity, and Identity in Ancient Galilee: a Region in Transition. Tübingen: Mohr Siebeck, ©2007. Accessed April 05, 2017. http://catdir.loc.gov/catdir/toc/fy0804/2007476048.ht ml.

Baḥya ben Asher ben Ḥlava. Midrash Rabbeinu Bachya: Torah Commentary. 2nd ed. Jerusalem: Lambda Publishers, ©2003.

Bockmuehl, Markus. *Jewish Law in Gentile Churches: Halakhah and the Beginning of Christian Public Ethics*. Grand Rapids, Mich.: Baker Academic, 2003.

Brown, Francis, S. R. Driver, and Charles A. Briggs. *The Brown-driver-briggs Hebrew and English Lexicon: with an Appendix Containing the Biblical Aramaic: Coded with the Numbering System from Strong's Exhaustive Concordance of the Bible*. Reprint ed. Peabody, MA: Hendrickson Pub, 1996.

TYRONE NICHOLS

Charlesworth, James H. Jesus Within Judaism: New Light from Exciting Archaeological Discoveries. New York: Doubleday, 1988.

Charles R.H., "The Book of Jubilees" Oxford: Clarendon Press, 1913 College *http://www.pseudepigrapha.com/jubilees/15* Scanned and Edited by Joshua Williams, Northwest.

Clorfene, Chaim; Katz, David. *The World of the Ger*. Copyright Chaim Clorfene, 2014.

Donaldson, Terrance L. Zealot and Convert: The Origin of Paul's Christ-Torah Antithesis. Catholic Biblical Quarterly 15 no 4 1989. Ppg 655 – 682.

Epp, Jay Eldon. Jewish-Gentile Continuity in Paul: Torah And/Or Faith? (Romans 9:1-5) Harvard Theological Review 79 no. 1-3 1986 Ppg. 80-90.

Fredriksen, Paula "Mandatory Retirement: Ideas in the Study of Fruchtenbaum, Dr. Arnold. Yeshua: The Life of Messiah from a Messianic Jewish Perspective-Vol. 2 by Dr. Arnold Fruchtenbaum. Edited by Christiane Jurik. San Antonio TX: Ariel   Ministries, 2017.

JESUS IS JEWISH

Gruber, Daniel. Copernicus and the Jews (the Separation of Church and Faith. Vol. 1). Hanover, NH: Elijah Publishing, 2005.

Gruber, Daniel C. The Separation of Church and Faith: Copernicus and the Jews. Elijah Publishing, Hanover, NH 2005.

Gurtner, Daniel M., Joel Willitts, and Richard A. Burridge, eds. Jesus, Matthew's Gospel and Early Christianity: Studies in Memory of Graham N. Stanton. T and T Clark Library of Biblical Studies. London: Bloomsbury T & T Clark International, 2013.

Halbertal, M. *Coexisting with the Enemy: Jews and Pagans in the Mishnah*. In G.N. Stanton and G.G. Stroumsa (eds.), Tolerance and Intolerance in Early Judaism and Christianity. New York: Cambridge University Press, 1998.

Heschel, Abraham Joshua. Israel: An Echo of Eternity. New York: Farrar, Straus and Giroux, 2013. Accessed October 9, 2015.

Horner, Barry E. Nac Studies in Bible and Theology. Vol. 3, Future Israel: Why Christian Anti-Judaism Must Be Challenged. Nashville, TN: B & H Academic, 2007.Christian Origins whose time has Come to Go" Studies in Religion 35 2006 Pg. 232.

Hoyland, Knut. Chosen to Follow: Jewish Believers through History and Today. Caspari Center for Biblical and Jewish Studies, 2013.

TYRONE NICHOLS

Jews, Modern Israel and the New Supersessionism. Place of publication not identified: Kings Evangelical Divinity, 2013.

Juster, Dan, and Keith Intrater. Israel, the Church, and the Last Days. Shippensburg, PA: Destiny Image Publishers, 2003. Accessed October 9, 2015.

Jeremias, Joachim. *Jesus' Promise to the Nations*. Philadelphia, PA: Fortress Pr, 1982.

Konradt, Matthias (2014-10-15). Israel, Church, and the Gentiles in the Gospel of Matthew (Baylor-Mohr Siebeck Studies in Early Christianity) (Page 334). Baylor University Press. Kindle Edition.

Ladd, George Eldon. The Gospel of the Kingdom: Scriptural Studies in the Kingdom of God. Grand Rapids, Mich.: Eerdmans, ©1959.

Lancaster, Daniel, *Torah Club: Shadows of the Messiah*, Vol. 6., First Fruits of Zion, 800.775.4807, www.ffoz.org.

Liddell, Henry George. An Intermediate Greek-English Lexicon: Founded Upon the Seventh Edition of Liddell and Scott's Greek-English Lexicon. Oxford England: Clarendon Press, 1991, ©1889.

JESUS IS JEWISH

Murphy, Frederick J. Early Judaism: The Exile to the Time of Jesus. Baker Academic, 2006.

Nanos, Mark D. The Mystery of Romans: The Jewish Context of Paul's Letter. Minneapolis: Fortress Press, ©1996.

Nanos, Mark D., and Magnus Zetterholm. Paul Within Judaism: Restoring the First-Century Context to the Apostle. Minneapolis: Fortress Press, 2015.

Nanos, Mark D. A Torah Observant Paul?: What difference could it make for Christian/Jewish Relations Today? May 9, 2005. © Mark D. Nanos.

Nanos, Mark D. Rethinking the "Paul and Judaism" Paradigm. May 10, 2005 © Mark D. Nanos.

Novak, David. *The Image of the Non-Jew in Judaism: The Idea of Noahide Law*. 2nd ed. Edited by Matthew Lagrone. Littman Library of Jewish Civilization. Oxford: The Littman Library of Jewish Civilization, 2011.

Prokulski, Walenty, "Conversion of St. Paul" Jesuit Theologate, Warsaw.

Richardson, Joel. When a Jew Rules the World: What the Bible Really Says About Israel in the Plan of God. New York:

WND Books, 2015. Accessed October 9, 2015.

Richardson, Joel. Mideast Beast: The Scriptural Case for an Islamic Antichrist. Washington, D.C.: WND Books, 2012.

Runesson, Anders The Question of Terminology: The Architecture of Contemporary Discussions on Paul cited from Paul Within Judaism: Restoring the First-Century Context to the Apostle.

Sacks, Jonathan. Koren Sacks Siddur: Compact Size. Place of publication not identified: Toby Press, 2013.

Saldarini, Anthony Matthew's Christian-Jewish Community, (The University of Chicago Press, Chicago, 1994) and Overman,

J. A., Matthew's Gospel and Formative Judaism, (Fortress Press, Minneapolis, 1990).

Sanders, E. P. *Jesus and Judaism*. Philadelphia: Fortress Press, 1985.

Schiffman, Lawrence H. *Who Was a Jew? Rabbinic and Halakhic Perspectives On the Jewish Christian Schism*. Hoboken, N.J.: Ktav Pub. House, 1985.

Shmuley, Boteach "Jesus was Jewish" accessed on Oct 17, 2013,

JESUS IS JEWISH

http://www.jpost.com/Opinion/Op-Ed-Contributors/Jesus- was-Jewish.

Skarsaune, Oskar, and Reidar Hvalvik. Jewish Believers in Jesus: The Early Centuries. Peabody, Mass.: Hendrickson Publishers, ©2007.\

Soulen, R Kendall. The God of Israel and Christian Theology. Minneapolis: Fortress Press, ©1996.

Young, Brad H. The Parables: Jewish Tradition and Christian Interpretation. Reprint ed. Peabody Massachusetts: Baker Academic, 2008.

The Chumash: The Torah, Haftaros and Five Megillos = [ḥamishah Ḥumshe Torah. 11th ed. Artscroll Series. Brooklyn, N.Y.: Mesorah Publications, 2000.

Rudolph, David J., and Joel Willitts. Introduction to Messianic Judaism: Its Ecclesial Context and Biblical Foundations. Grand Rapids, MI: Zondervan, 2013. Accessed October 9, 2015.

Runesson, Anders Behind the Gospel of Mathew: Radical Pharisees in Post-War Galilee Currents in Theology and Mission 37 6 (December 2010) Pg. 460-461.

Runesson, Anders Inventing Christian Identity: Paul, Ignatius, and Theodosius I. Pages 59-92 in Exploring Early Christian

TYRONE NICHOLS

Identity. Edited by Bengt Holmberg. WUNT 226. Tübingen: Mohr Siebeck, 2008.

JESUS IS JEWISH

PDF

Ballanger, Isam, "Missiological Thoughts Prompted by Genesis 10. Review and Expositor, 103, Spring 2006. PDF.

Dallmayr, Fred, "The Dignity of Difference: A Salute to Jonathan Sacks" "How to avoid the Clash of Civilizations." London and New York: Continuum Press, 2002. PDF.

Danby, Herber "Tractate Sanhedrin, Mishnah and Tosefta, The Judicial Procedure of the Jews as Codified Towards the End of the Second Century" London, Society for Promoting Christian Knowledge, New York, The Macmillan Company, 1919 PDF.

Donaldson, Terrance L. "Proselytes or 'Righteous Gentiles'? The Status of Gentiles in Eschatological Pilgrimage Patterns of Thought" College of Emanuel and St. Chad Saskatoon, Saskatchewan, Canada PDF.

Langer, Ruth "Jewish Understanding of the Religious Other." Theological Studies 64 (2003) Pp. 255-277.

Niggemann, Andrew J. "Matriarch of Israel or Misnomer? Israelite Self-Identification in Ancient Israel Law Code and the Implications for Ruth" Journey for the Study of the Old Testament. Vol. 41.3 (2017) 355-377. PDF.

TYRONE NICHOLS

Harrison, Bernard "Judaism" Hillel Foundation at the University of California Los Angeles. JSTOR, Sage Publications. PDF.

Safrai, Shmuel Jesus and the Hasidim – PDF.

Talmud – Mas. Avodah Zarah. PDF.

White, Benjamin "The Eschatological Conversion of 'All the Nations' in Matthew 28.19-20: (Mis)reading Matthew through Paul" Journal for the Study of the New Testament, 2014 vol. 36(4) 353-832. PDF.

Yu Suee Yan, "The Alien in Deuteronomy" Bible Translator Vol. 60, No. 2, April 2009 PDF.

JESUS IS JEWISH

DVD

First Fruits of Zion. HaYesod, The Foundation [10 DVD-ROMS] (Marshfield, MO) 2009.

TYRONE NICHOLS

End Notes

Unless otherwise noted, all biblical quotations are taken from various versions, including the English Standard Version (ESV), New International Version (NIV), King James Version (KJV), and Tree of Life Version (TLV).

[1] Calvin, John. *Institutes of the Christian Religion*. Edited by John T. Mitchell, vol. II, Westminster John Knox Press, 2011, pp. 246-255.

[2] The typical evangelical salvation prayer goes something like, "Dear Lord, I acknowledge that I am a sinner, and I am in need of forgiveness and a savior. You promised in your word that if I acknowledge that you raised Jesus from the dead and accept him into my heart as Lord and Savior I will be saved. So, I now declare with my mouth that Jesus has been raised from the dead and that He is alive and well. I accept Him as my personal Lord and savior. I accept my salvation from sin right now. I am now saved.
Jesus is my Lord; Jesus is my savior. Thank you, God, for forgiving me, and cleansing me from my sinfulness and giving me eternal life. - Amen.

[3] Billy Graham Evangelistic Association. "Does God Forgive the Sins We Will Commit in the Future, or Just Those from Our Past?". 25 Sept. 2017, https://billygraham.org/answer/does-god-forgive-the-sins-we-will-commit-in-the-future-or-just-those-from-our-past/.

[4] Kuhn, Thomas S. *The Structure of Scientific Revolutions*. 3rd ed., University of Chicago Press, 1996

[5] "Some People Still Don't Know That Jesus Was Jewish." *Algemeiner*, 10 Oct. 2017, https://www.algemeiner.com/2017/10/10/some-people-still-dont-know-that-jesus-was-jewish/. Accessed 15 Oct. 2017.

JESUS IS JEWISH

[6] *Dictionary.com*. Dictionary.com, LLC https://www.dictionary.com. Accessed Nov 21, 2017

[7] "Cognitive Dissonance Basics." *Psychology Today*, Sussex Publishers, Accessed Nov 21, 2017

[8] This idea is titled Replacement Theology, or supersessionism. We will dive into this idea in later chapters.

[9] Anachronism – a thing belonging or appropriate to a period other than that in which it exists; Abstraction – something that exists only as an idea." *Google*, Accessed December 1, 2017, www.google.com.

[10] Fredriksen, Paula "Mandatory Retirement: Ideas in the Study of Christian Origins whose time has Come to Go" Studies in Religion 35 2006, Pg. 232

[11] "Binding and Loosing: What Did Jesus Mean?" *CRI (Christian Research Institute)*, November 15, 2017, https://www.equip.org/perspectives/binding-and-loosing-what-did-jesus-mean/.

[12] "What Do the Words Bind and Loose Mean in Matthew 16:19?" *Catholic Answers*, Jan, 7, 2018, https://www.catholic.com/qa/what-do-the-words-bind-and-loose-mean-in-matthew-1619.

[13] Lancaster, Daniel, First Fruits of Zion, Torah Club, Volume 4 pg. 655

[14] Read the book of Acts to watch Peter in real time exercise this agency.

[15] Runesson, Anders. "Inventing Christian Identity: Paul, Ignatius, and Theodosius I." *Exploring Early Christian Identity*. Edited by Bengt Holmberg, WUNT 226, Mohr Siebeck, 2008, pp. 59-92.

[16] The book of Hosea is a living metaphor for God's relationship with Israel.

[17] Soulen, R Kendall. *The God of Israel and Christian Theology*. Fortress Press, 1996, p. 13.

[18] Kinbar, Carl, D. Litt. Et Phil. "BIBD – 5320 Tanakh: The Beginnings of Judaism and the Jewish people." Audio notes from class, 2016.

[19] Soulen, R Kendall. *The God of Israel and Christian Theology*. Fortress Press, 1996, p. ix.

[20] Ibid., pp. 31-32.

[21] Kinbar, Carl, D. Litt. Et Phil. "BIBD – 5320 Tanakh: The Beginnings of Judaism and the Jewish People." Audio notes from class, 2016.

[22] Ibid.

[23] Ibid.

[24] Soulen, R Kendall. *The God of Israel and Christian Theology*. Fortress Press, 1996, p. 33.

[25] Gruber, Daniel. *Separation of Church and Faith. Vol. Volume One, Copernicus and the Jews*. Elijah Publishing, 2005, p. 206.

JESUS IS JEWISH

[26] Ibid., pg. 210

[27] Sacks, Jonathan. *Koren Sacks Siddur: Compact Size*. Toby Press, 2013, p. 36.

[28] Herion, Gary A., and George E. Mendenhall. "Covenant." *The Anchor Yale Bible Dictionary*. Doubleday, 1996, p. 1179.

[29] Berkhof, Louis. *Systematic Theology*, B. Erdmans Publishing, 1996, p. 262.

[30] First Fruits of Zion, *Hayesod The Foundation*, Lesson Three, pg. 3.6

[31] Genesis 21:27

[32] Genesis 12:1-4

[33] Genesis 14:18

[34] John 14:15

[35] Genesis 17:10-13

[36] Their exists within Judaism no other narrative from Scripture so often read, recited, and prayed over as Genesis 22. During the daily prayer services, after the initial morning blessings and before the recitation of the laws of sacrifice, the devoutly observant Jew recites the story of the binding of Isaac. Thus, the observant Jewish world reads and prays over the narrative of Genesis 22 every single day of the year. The binding of Isaac is also the principal synagogue reading for the second day of the Rosh Hashanah. Judaism calls the story of Genesis 22 the Akeidah (עקדה) – "binding." Lancaster, Daniel. "Parashat Vayera." *Torah Club: Shadows of the Messiah*. First Fruits of Zion, www.ffoz.org, p. 51.

TYRONE NICHOLS

[37] There is Jewish mystical understanding that speaks to this passage allegorically, likening Jacob as the nation of Israel. Thus, the angels of God literally ascend and descend on Israel, and God stands above Israel. In the same way, Israel can be likened unto a ladder between heaven and earth. Through Israel comes the revelation of the Scriptures, the prophets, and the Messiah – the quintessential Israelite – the perfect Jacob – the perfect ladder between heaven and earth over which God Stands. Lancaster, Daniel. "Parashat Vayetze." *Torah Club: Shadows of the Messiah*. First Fruits of Zion, www.ffoz.org, p. 97.

[38] Genesis 19:4-9

[39] Exodus 20

[40] Exodus 24:9-11

[41] Exodus 31:16-17

[42] *Hayesod: The Foundation*. Lesson 3, First Fruits of Zion, p. 3.30.

[43] Sacks, Jonathan. *Koren Sacks Siddur: Compact Size*. Toby Press, 2013, p. 36.

[44] Knut Hoyland writes about a topic which two scholars, Israel J. Yuval and Peter Schafer, have entitled *The Ways that Never Parted.* We read, "Unlike the traditional paradigm, where the flow of ideas was seen as a one-way street from Jewish to Christian, their paradigm opens the possibility of an intense two-way flow, with Christians taking over and developing pre-Christian Jewish ideas and rabbis in their turn responding to these Christian developments, thereby modifying their own ideas in the process. In fact, these scholars claim that the relationship with Christianity was of fundamental significance for the self-definition of rabbinic Judaism right from the early second century CE onward. Hoyland, Knut. *Chosen to Follow: Jewish Believers through History and Today*. Caspari Center

JESUS IS JEWISH

for Biblical and Jewish Studies. Kindle Edition, Kindle Location 855.

[45] Hoyland, Knut. *Chosen to Follow: Jewish Believers through History and Today*. Kindle Edition, Kindle Location 1123.

[46] BibleHub." http://biblehub.com/greek/3461.html.

[47] First, in his own hometown they were unwilling to accept his teachings. Second, in the region of Gerasene, they asked Jesus to leave because "they were overcome with fear" (Luke 8:37) after he cast out the legion of demons from a hoard of pigs which in turn made a bee line straight over the cliff and drowned in the water. John records for us a third time in which Jesus's teaching was not received. He writes, "And among the crowds there was much whispering about him. Some said, 'He's a good man;' but others said, 'No he is deceiving the masses.'" Finally, the fourth instance of the rejection of Jesus's teachings came from the theopolitical rulers.

[48] Matthew the tax collector (Mt. 9.9), many other tax collectors and "sinners" (Mark 2:15), Zacchaeus the chief tax collector (Luke 10:3), two blind men (Mt. 9:31), Bartimaeus and another blind man (Mark 10:47), the blind and the lame who came to him at the Temple because they believed Yeshua could heal them (Mt. 21:14), a woman who had been bleeding for 12 years who was healed just by touching (Mt. 9:20), a royal official in Cana of Galilee who frantically sought after Yeshua to heal his son, (John 4:54), Jairus, who was a ruler of the congregation who pleaded with Yeshua to heal his daughter (Luke 8:41-42), and a member of the Sanhedrin named Nicodemus who approached him under cover of darkness as the spokesman for himself and others within the Sanhedrin who believed his teachings (John 3:2). All of these people were JEWS.

[49] John 11:48, John 12:19

[50] Gruber, Daniel C. *The Separation of Church and Faith: Copernicus and the Jews*. Elijah Publishing, 2005, p. 92

[51] Smith, Calvin, *The Jews, Modern Israel and the New Supersessionism*. New Revised and Expanded Edition. King's Divinity Press. Kindle Locations 942-943

[52] Bazzar: A Middle Eastern term for market.

[53] Gruber, Daniel C. *The Separation of Church and Faith: Copernicus and the Jews*. Elijah Publishing, 2005, p. 94

[54] Josephus. *Antiquities of the Jews*. XX, 9, 2-4.

[55] Matthew 28:1-8

[56] The resurrection accounts in the gospels, and as presented by Paul in his letter to the Corinthians, seem to be at odds with one another, because the stories don't match. However, this seeming discrepancy actually gives the story a particular reality. Each encounter is told from the perspective of the eyewitness. This bears witness to the retelling as they were experienced and remembered by real people. Ask any officer of the law whose job it is to investigate a crime scene and they will tell you that no two stories are ever the same. Each eyewitness sees the account from his own perspective. The fact that the Gospels tell a slightly different version of the same story, gives the accounts more credibility, not less. *Daniel Lancaster, FFOZ*

[57] "Whatever Happened to the Twelve Apostles?" Christianity.com, https://www.christianity.com/church/church-history/timeline/1 300/whatever-happened-to-the-twelve-apostles-11629558.html.

[58] Joel 3:1-5 (2:28-32)

JESUS IS JEWISH

[59] Psalm 16:8-11

[60] Acts 2:29-31

[61] Acts 2:36

[62] Acts 3:12a-13

[63] Acts 7:51-53

[64] Acts 7:54-59

[65] Bjoraker, William, PhD. "The Parting of the Ways Between Judaism and Christianity: Temple and Torah." PDF file. Page 8.

[66] Acts 14:28

[67] Acts 15:5

[68] Acts 15:6-11

[69] Acts 15:16 – 18, referencing Amos 9:11-12

[70] Acts 15: 11-22

[71] Lichtenstein, Yechiel Tzvi. *Commentary on the New Testament: The Acts of the Apostles*. Unpublished, Vine of David, 2010. Originally published in Hebrew as *Beiur LeSiphrei Brit HaChadashah*. Professor G. Dahlman, 1987.

[72] Ephesians 3:6

[73] *Jewish Believers in Jesus: The Early Centuries.* Hendrickson Publishers, 2007, p. 48.

[74] The term bi-ekklesia is not to be confused with bi-lateral ecclesiology. When I use the term bi-ekklesia I am trying to communicate the idea that the assembly of Yeshua should consist of believing Jews faithful to Torah Observance and believing Gentiles who are learning the ways of Torah as commanded and taught by Yeshua, the living Torah. It is my assessment that a bi-ekklesia is what the Apostles and Paul had in mind when they considered what synagogue worship and congregations should look like. An ekklesia where humility and brotherly love permeate the atmosphere of the congregation. One in which the Jew is free to follow his obligations as a faithful covenantal partner as stipulated at Sinai, and the Gentile who at a minimum observes the righteous Gentile laws, and over time is instructed in Torah as taught by the Master - Yeshua.

[75] Assemani, Stefano. Acta Sanctorium Martyrum Orientalium at Occidentalium. Vol. 1, Rome, 1748, p. 105.

[76] Nicene Creed. (325/381)

[77] Acts 26:28 (ESV)

[78] I Peter 4:16 (ESV)

[79] Nanos, Mark D. *The Mystery of Romans: The Jewish Context of Paul's Letters.* Kindle Edition, Kindle Locations 606-608.

[80] bid., Kindle Locations 650-652.

[81] Juster, Dan. *Jewish Roots: Understanding Your Jewish Faith.* Revised Edition, Destiny Image Messianic, p. 133..

JESUS IS JEWISH

[82] Ibid., p. 134.

[83] Aharoni, Yohannan, and Michael Avi-Yonah. *The MacMillan Bible Atlas.* Revised, Macmillan Publishing Company, 1977, p. 157. Cited in Seif, Dr. Jeffrey L. *To The Ends Of The Earth: How the First Jewish Followers of Yeshua Transformed the Ancient World.* Messianic Jewish Communications, Kindle Locations 2464-2465.

[84] Seif, Dr. Jeffrey L. *To The Ends Of The Earth: How the First Jewish Followers of Yeshua Transformed the Ancient World.* Messianic Jewish Communications, Kindle Locations 471-472.

[85] Ibid., Kindle Locations 485-488.

[86] Ibid., Kindle Locations 503-505.

[87] Ibid., Kindle locations 532-533. Messianic Jewish presence and leadership in Jerusalem in his Ecc. Hist. 4, 5: 2. There, he is explicit in noting their presence until the invasion of Adrian/ Hadrian to quell the Bar Kochba Revolt, from 132– 135 C.E.— the debacle that forced their displacement, with all others: 'Down to the invasion of the Jews under Adrian, there were fifteen successions of bishops in the church, all of which they say were Hebrews... at the time the whole church under them consisted of faithful Hebrews, who continued from the time of the apostles until the siege that then took place.

[88] Ibid., Kindle Location 545.

[89] Ibid., Kindle Locations 567-569.

[90] Zetterholm, Magnus. *The Formation of Christianity in Antioch: A Social-*

Scientific Approach to the Separation between Judaism and Christianity. p. 37. Cited in Seif, Dr. Jeffrey L. *To The Ends Of The Earth: How the First Jewish Followers of Yeshua Transformed the Ancient World*. Messianic Jewish Communications, Kindle Locations 2545-2546.

[91] "The Sanhedrin." *Jewish Virtual Library*. http://www.jewishvirtuallibrary.org/the-sanhedrin.

[92] Boyarin, Daniel. *Border Lines: The Partition of Judaeo-Christianity (Divinations: Rereading Late Ancient Religion)*. University of Pennsylvania Press, p. 45.

[93] Ibid., p. 62.

[94] See Appendix C for an in depth look at the anti-Semitic nature of the Dialogue with Trypho.

[95] "Birkat Ha-Minim." *Jewish Virtual Library*. http://www.jewishvirtuallibrary.org/the-sanhedrin.

[96] Palestinian Siddur from the Cairo Genizah

[97] White, Michael L. *From Jesus to Christianity: How Four Generations of Visionaries & Storytellers Created the New Testament and Christian Faith*. HarperCollins Publishers, 2005, p. 405.

[98] Ehrman, Bart D. *Lost Christianities: The Battles for Scripture and the Faiths We Never Knew*. Oxford University Press, 2005, p. 94.

[99] Rubenstein, Richard E. *When Jesus Became God: The Epic Fight over Christ's Divinity in the Last Days of Rome*. Houghton Mifflin Harcourt, p. 8.

JESUS IS JEWISH

[100] Ibid., p. 66

[101] Ibid., p. 82.

[102] Ibid., p. 206

[103] See also Gregory of Nyssa, "On the Holy Trinity" and "On 'Not Three Gods,'" in Schaff and Wace, eds., Nicene and Post-Nicene Fathers, second series, vol. 5, Gregory of Nyssa, Dogmatic Treatises, Etc. (Peabody, Mass.: Hendrickson Publishers, 1994), 326–336.

[104] Rubenstein, Richard E. *When Jesus Became God: The Epic Fight over Christ's Divinity in the Last Days of Rome.* Houghton Mifflin Harcourt, p. 8.

[105] Ibid., p. 92

[106] Runesson, Anders. "Saving the Lost Sheep of the House of Israel: Purity, Forgiveness and Synagogues in the Gospel of Mathew." *Melilah Manchester Journal of Jewish Studies*, vol. 11, 2014, pp. 8-24.

[107] Gruber, Daniel C. *The Separation of Church and Faith: Copernicus and the Jews.* Elijah Publishing, 2005, p. 55.

[108] Konradt, Matthias. *Israel, Church, and the Gentiles in the Gospel of Matthew (Baylor-Mohr Siebeck Studies in Early Christianity)*. Baylor University Press, 2014, pp. 333-334. "In the Greek speaking world, ἐκκλησία (ekklesia) refers to the regularly convened "plenary assembly of full citizens of the πόλις who were legally responsible and fit for military service." The LXX translators use ἐκκλησία – alongside συναγωγή - to translate קהל (kahal), which means simply "assembly, gathered crowd of people" <u>and is specified by its context</u> (underline mine), further,

ἐκκλησία (or קהל) is not in itself a positive term but can also be used to refer to a gathering of evildoers, although there is a general tendency to use ἐκκλησία positively <u>in reference to Israel</u>. With this usage, ἐκκλησία occurs not only in military or other political contexts but also in reference to liturgical or cultic assemblies, sometimes in the plural. Josh 9.2 e– f LXX and Neh. 8.2 are specifically about the reading of the law before the ἐκκλησία. Philo also uses ἐκκλησία in the context of the giving or the reading of the law (Decal. 32.45, Post. 143; see also Mut. 204, Virt. 108). Following Berger, a structural analogy can be detected here with the ἐκκλησία in the Hellenistic polis – unlike that of the classical period – since, in the monarchical system, the assembly of the people became a place where laws were no longer negotiated, royal decrees were simply read out and the role of the people was reduced to the acclamation. The use of ἐκκλησία is not reserved for the assembly of the whole people but can also be used for individual groups.

[109] *An Intermediate Greek-English Lexicon [founded upon the Seventh Edition of Liddell and Scott's Greek-English Lexicon]*. Oxford Univ. Press, 1999, "sunagoge", p. 766.

[110] Ibid., "ekklesia", p. 239.

[111] Gruber, Daniel C. *The Separation of Church and Faith: Copernicus and the Jews*. Elijah Publishing, 2005, p. 56.

[112] Levine, Lee I. *The Ancient Synagogue: The First Thousand Years*. Yale University Press, 2005, www.jstor.org/stable/j.ctt1njkdh.

[113] Mat. 4:23, 6:2, 6:5, 9:35, 10:17, 12:9, 13:54, 23:6, 23:34.

[114] Gruber, Daniel C. *The Separation of Church and Faith: Copernicus and the Jews*. Elijah Publishing, 2005, p. 61.

JESUS IS JEWISH

[115] Turner, David. Matthew (Baker Exegetical Commentary on the New Testament). Baker Publishing Group, 2008, Kindle Locations 511-513.

[116] The terms Jewish-Christian or Christian-Jew need to be re-examined. They don't properly communicate a thoroughly Jewish paradigm. Jesus is Jewish. While alive, neither he nor his disciples would have thought in terms of anything Christian. The concept of Christianity did not exist at the time.

[117] Saldarini, Anthony. *Matthew's Christian-Jewish Community*. The University of Chicago Press, 1994. Overman, J. A. *Matthew's Gospel and Formative Judaism*. Fortress Press, 1990.

[118] The role of the city gate as the focal point for communal activity is well attested in biblical and nonbiblical literature. It served as a marketplace (2 Kings 7:1) and as a setting where a ruler would hold court and where prophets would speak (1 Kings 22:10; Jeremiah 38:7). As the gate was a popular meeting place for public gatherings, a variety of communal activities was conducted there. For example, Hezekiah "appointed battle officers over the people; then, gathering them to him in the square of the city-gate, he rallied them" (2 Chron. 32:6). Those who came regularly to the gate were the populace at large (see Ruth 3:11) as well as the towns' elders and leaders. The transaction between Abraham and Ephron the Hittite took place at the city-gate (Gen. 23:10, 18). Announcement of a settlement at the gate afforded it maximum publicity as well as the assent of the entire community. Moreover, prophetic activity often took place here so as to reach the greatest number of people (Isa 29:21; Amos 5:10) Lee I. Levine. "The Nature and Origin of the Palestinian Synagogue Reconsidered." *Journal of Biblical Literature*, Vol. 115, No. 3, Autumn, 1996, pp. 432-433.

[119] Lee I. Levine. "The Nature and Origin of the Palestinian Synagogue Reconsidered." *Journal of Biblical Literature*, Vol. 115, No. 3, Autumn, 1996, pp. 425 – 448.

[120] Levine, Lee I. *The Ancient Synagogue: The First Thousand Years*. Yale University

Press, 2005, p. 39. www.jstor.org/stable/j.ctt1njkdh.

[121] Runesson, Anders. "Saving the Lost Sheep of the House of Israel: Purity, Forgiveness and Synagogues in the Gospel of Mathew." *Melilah Manchester Journal of Jewish Studies*, vol. 11, 2014, p. 14.

[122] Gruber, Daniel C. *The Separation of Church and Faith: Copernicus and the Jews* Elijah Publishing, 2005 p. 62

[123] See Appendix B

[124] Ask.Com. "How Did Saint Paul Become a Christian?" 1 Nov. 2013, http://www.ask.com/question/how-did-saint-paul-become-a-christian.

[125] Acts 21:10 – 12

[126] Acts 21:17-20

[127] Acts 21:20

[128] Acts 21:21

[129] Acts 21:24

[130] Acts 21:27

[131] Acts 21:28-29

[132] Acts 21:30

JESUS IS JEWISH

[133] Acts 21:32

[134] Acts 21:33-36

[135] Acts 22:3

[136] Acts 22:1-22

[137] Acts 22:22

[138] Acts 22:23-24

[139] FFOZ Torah Club. *Chronicles of the Apostles*. Vol. 6, p. 709. Quoting Le Cornu and Shulam. *A Commentary on the Jewish Roots of Acts: Acts 16-28*. p. 1236.

[140] Acts 23:6

[141] Acts 23:7-8

[142] Acts 23:9

[143] Acts 24:2-6

[144] Acts 24:10-13

[145] Acts 24:14-16

[146] Acts 24:17-18

[147] Acts 24:18-21

[148] Acts 24:26-27

[149] Acts 25:6-8

[150] Acts 25:10-11

[151] Acts 25:12b

[152] Acts 25:18

[153] First Fruits of Zion. Torah Club Volume 6. p. 743. Quoting Witherington. The Acts of the Apostles: A Socio-Rhetorical Commentary. p. 738-739. Western Text reading based on the Harclean margin of the Syriac.

[154] Acts 26:2-3

[155] Acts 26:4-8

[156] Acts 26:9-11

[157] Acts 26:19-23

[158] Acts 26:25-29

[159] Acts 26:30-32

[160] Acts 28: 23-25

[161] Nanos, Mark D. *The Mystery of Romans: The Jewish Context of Paul's Letters*. Kindle Edition, Kindle Locations 83-85.

JESUS IS JEWISH

[162] Paul FAQs. Beliefnet, www.beliefnet.com/faiths/christianity/2004/04/paul-faqs.aspx. Accessed 31 Oct. 2017.

[163] First Fruits of Zion. *Hayesod, The Foundation*. [10 DVD-ROMS], Marshfield, MO, 2009. Lesson Seven "Our Mail-His letters".

[164] Daniel Lancaster, author of First Fruits of Zion's Torah Club, and lead Pastor of Beth Emmanuel Messianic Synagogue in Hudson Wisconsin has written extensively on the Jewishness of Paul, and I owe him a tremendous amount of thanks for the work he has done. The foundations for much of my understanding of Paul, have been transformed due to his writing.

[165] II Peter 3:16

[166] Dunn, James. "The New Perspective on Paul." *University of Manchester eScholar*, N.p., https://www.escholar.manchester.ac.uk/api/datastream?publicationPid=uk-ac-man-scw:1m1686&datastreamId=POST-PEER-REVIEW-PUBLISHERS-DOCUMENT.PDF.

[167] At times, Paul will use the phrase 'circumcision' as shorthand for 'works of the law.' Meaning that when he speaks of circumcision, he is using it as an identity marker for one who is or has become legally Jewish. A full-fledged 'son of Abraham.'

[168] Beth Immanuel Messianic Synagogue." Romans Audio Series. www.bethimmanuel.org/audio-series/romans.

[169] James 2:17

[170] James 2:22-24

[171] Romans 3:1-4

[172] Lancaster, Daniel. Holy Epistle to the Galatians: Sermons on a Messianic Jewish Approach. First Fruits of Zion, 2011, p. 232.

[173] Ibid., p. 234

[174] Colossians 2:13-17

[175] Rabbi Akiba's illustration of God as a shopkeeper, m. Avot 3:20." Quoted by Peter T. O'Brien in *World Biblical Commentary*. First Fruits of Zion, Hayesod, p. 7.15.

[176] FFOZ Torah Club Chronicles of the Messiah - Vayikra." *First Fruits of Zion*, p. 624.

[177] Buchler, A. Rabbi. "The Law of Purification in Mark XII. 1-23." *The Expository Time*, vol. 21, no. 1, 1909, p. 35. Quoted in *FFOZ Torah Club Chronicles of the Messiah - Vayikra*, p. 635.

[178] Bivin, David. "Mark 7:19: Did Jesus Make 'Unclean' Food 'Clean'?" *FFOZ Torah Club Chronicles of the Messiah - Vayikra*, First Fruits of Zion, p. 636.

[179] Commentary on the New Testament, on Matthew 5:11. Lichtenstein continues, "Peter had a better understanding of his words here, knowing that it is not permitted (Heaven forbid!) to eat forbidden things. That is why he said in Acts 10:14 "I have never eaten anything contaminated!" etc. The [Gentiles] only perceived opposition to the religion of Mosheh in the words of Yeshua...because they hated Y'isra'el and their religion from ancient times." Lichtenstein also states, "[The laws of clean and unclean in Leviticus] refer to ritual contamination of the human nefesh in general. Nefesh is meant in the sense of the phrase nefesh

chayah, a 'living creature.' Vayikra 5:2 speaks of a 'nefesh' that touches anything contaminated, thus indicating that it is the human nefesh that is contaminated. But actually, according to the Torah of Mosheh, only the physical body is contaminated by the eating of contaminated things. This is why the immersion in water is effectual, according to the Torah. Lichtenstein, Isaac, Commentary on the New Testament, on Matthew 5:11. In *FFOZ The Torah Club, Volume 4 Chronicles of the Messiah - Vayikra*, First Fruits of Zion, p. 636.

[180] Kashrut laws are the dietary laws outlined in Leviticus.

[181] Nanos, Mark D. *The Mystery of Romans: The Jewish Context of Paul's Letters*. Kindle Edition, Kindle Locations 895-896.

[182] Ibid., Kindle Locations 937-942

[183] Ibid., Kindle Locations 983-985

[184] Ibid., Kindle Locations 989-992

[185] *Hayesod: The Foundation*. Lesson 7, First Fruits of Zion, p. 7.17

[186] Ibid., Pg. 7.17

[187] "Romans 14:14." *BibleHub*, [Access date], http://biblehub.com/text/romans/14-14.htm.

[188] Fruchtenbaum, Arnold Dr. *Yeshua: the Life of Messiah from a Messianic Jewish Perspective-Vol. 2*. Ed. Christiane Jurik. San Antonio, TX: Ariel Ministries, 2017, p. 3.

[189] Young, Brad H. *Jesus the Jewish Theologian*. Reissue ed., Peabody, MA: Baker Academic, 1993.

¹⁹⁰ Charlesworth, James H. *Jesus Within Judaism: New Light from Exciting Archaeological Discoveries*. New York: Doubleday, 1988, p. 172.

¹⁹¹ Murphy, Frederick J. *Early Judaism: the Exile to the Time of Jesus*. Baker Academic, 2006, p. 405.

¹⁹² The references in rabbinic literature to Galilean sages teaching in their academies (literally, houses of study) and in the open air in Galilee, exhorting the people to higher moral standards, stressing observance of Torah, and seeking to strengthen ties to Jerusalem and the Temple, are many times more frequent than the references to such activities by their counterparts in Judea. Wherever life in Galilee is compared to that in Judea, whether explicitly or not, it is clear that Galilee came before Judea in terms of Torah, Jewish life, and the entire complex of Jewish culture. Shmuel Safrai, "Jesus and the Hasidim," *Jerusalem Perspective* 42/43/44 (1994): 3-22 [https://www.jerusalemperspective.com/2685/]

¹⁹³ Torah Club, *Chronicles of the Messiah,* First Fruits of Zion – *Volume 6 – Chayei Sarah pg. 111*

¹⁹⁴ Torah Club, *Chronicles of the Messiah,* First Fruits of Zion – *Volume 6* – pg. 111

¹⁹⁵ Torah Club *Chronicles of the Messiah,* First Fruits of Zion – *Volume 6 – pg. 111*

¹⁹⁶ In Luke 5:17-39 We read of four men who were so determined to get their paralyzed friend to see Jesus that they cut a hole in the roof of the house he was teaching in and lowered him through the opening. The crowds were so thick they couldn't get in through the front door, so they got creative and came in from above.

¹⁹⁷ Young, Brad. *The Parables, Jewish Tradition and Christian*

JESUS IS JEWISH

Interpretation. Hendrickson Publishers, 1988.

[198] *Eisegesis* –The practice of interpreting a text by reading into it one's own ideas.

[199] Schaff, Philip. *Nicene and Post-Nicene Fathers*, Second Series. Christian Classics Ethereal Library, https://www.ccel.org/ccel/schaff/npnf102.iii.html.

[200] Shmuel Safrai, "Jesus and the Hasidim," *Jerusalem Perspective* 42/43/44 (1994): 3-22 [https://www.jerusalemperspective.com/2685/]

[201] Torah Club, *Chronicles of the Messiah,* First Fruits of Zion – *Volume 4* – p. *489*

[202] Willits, Joel *Week three podcast* – Matthew in his Jewish Context – BIBL 5315, The King's University

[203] Many Christians would make a distinction between the Ten Commandments and the rest of the Torah. This error was prevalent among the Christians even in ancient times, as we see from the account in b. *Berachot* 12a, which says that [the Jewish people] used to recite the Ten Commandments every day in the Temple, and even tried to do so in the entire region. They stopped doing this on account of the sectarians, who imagined that even Jews, in doing so, were confusing that the Ten Commandments were more important that the rest of the Torah. But truly, according to the Torah, it is all the word of HaShem, and one should in no way divide them up. It appears that the Christians…believed that Yeshua and his talmadim accepted the Ten Commandments and cast aside the rest of them. Keeping the Sabbath, which is one of the Ten Commandments, created a difficulty; they took care of this at Rome by reinterpreting it as the first day of the week-the day of Messiah's resurrection-making it the Sabbath day, of course. But these are empty words. (Lichtenstein, *Commentary on the New Testament,* on Matthew 5:18) (Torah Club, *Chronicles of the Messiah,* First Fruits of Zion – *Volume 4* – *Beshalach* pp. 412)

[204] Falk, Harvey. *Jesus the Pharisee*. Wipf and Stock Publishers, 2002, p. 19. Also, consider Rashbatz on the passage: "And so said one in his name in their book that the destruction of the entire heavens and earth are easier than for one tag to fall from the Torah." Rashbatz, *Keshet Umagen*.

[205] Torah Club, *Chronicles of the Messiah*, First Fruits of Zion – Volume 4 – Beshalach p. 391

[206] Scherman, Nosson. *The Chumash: the Torah, Haftaros and Five Megillos = [ḥamishah Ḥumshe Torah: 'im Targum Onḳelos, Pe. Rashi, Haftarot Ve-Ḥamesh Megilot]*, 11th ed. Mesorah Pubns Ltd, 2000, p. 491.

[207] Ibid., p. 491

[208] Torah Club *Chronicles of the Messiah*, First Fruits of Zion – Volume 4 – Behar – p. 858

[209] Ibid., p. 845

[211] After reading this passage, is it any wonder why most Jews don't recognize Yeshua for who he is? According to them, he is exactly this person the verse is talking about – and who can blame them? Gentile Christianity has presented him as a Sabbath breaker and a lawbreaker. According to Gentile Christianity he has abolished the law and it no longer applies to anyone, including the Jew because he has fulfilled it all. He is a false Messiah! Why? He breaks the law! The true Messiah would never do that, and yet, that is exactly the person that Gentile Christianity worships – the law-breaking Messiah.

[212] Fruchtenbaum, Arnold. *Yeshua: The Life of Messiah from a Messianic Jewish Perspective-Vol. 1*. Ariel Ministries, 2017, p. 82.

JESUS IS JEWISH

[213] Ibid., Pg. 83.

For additional information on the Sopherim, see: B. *Sanhedrin* 53a-b; p. 360, n. 7; b. *orlah* III.9; Moore, *Judaism in the First Centuries of the Christian Era*, 1:309-315; Avi-Yonah and Baras, *The World History of the Jewish People,* First Series, vol. 8, pp. 54-57; Mulder, *Mikra,* pp. 24-26. B *Kiddushin,* Glossary, p. 433, p. 79.

[214] Ibid., p. 84

[215] Ibid., p. 85

For further details, see: Yitzhak D. Gilat, R. *Eliezer Ben Hyrcanus,* a *Scholar Outcast* (Ramat-Gan, Israel; Bar-Ilan University Press, 1984), pp. 470-491; Alon, *The Jews in Their Land in the Talmudic Age,* pp. 3111-315; David Weiss Halvni, *Peshat and Derash: Plain and Applied Meaning in Rabbinic Exegesis* (New York: Oxford University Press, 1991), pp. 112-119, 209-211, nn. 32-44; Schurer, *A History of the Jewish People in the Time of Jesus Christ,* Second Division, 1:334-337; E.P. Sanders, *Jewish Law from Jesus to the Mishnah*: Five Studies (London: SCM Press; and Philadelphia, PA: Trinity Press International, 1990), pp. 87-80; aln F. Segal, *Rebecca's Children: Judaism and Christianity in the Roman World* (Cambridge, MA and London: Harvard University Press, 1986), pp. 134-135.

[216] Ibid., p. 86

[217] Ibid., p. 93

[218] Ibid., p. 93

[219] Ibid., p. 95. S

See also Young, *Meet the Rabbis,* p. 231; Jacob Neusner, *Transformations in Ancient Judaism: Textual Evidence for Creative Responses to Crisis* (Peabody, MA: Hendrickson, 2004), p. 86; y.*Besah* 5:2; y. *Yebamot* 7:3; y. *Ketubot* 10:2, 11:7; y.

Gittin 5:9; b. *Menahoth* 99b; 102b; *Hullin* 96a-b; 98a; 104a; b. *Aboth* III, 8; b. *Ta'anith* 17b; b. *Yebamoth* 21a; 90a 91a; 109b; 113b; b. *Kiddushin* 29b-30a; Strack and Sternberger, *Introduction to the Talmud and Midrash*, pp. 126-129; Neusner, *Judaism in the Matrix of Christianity*, pp. 116-119.

[220] Ibid., p.102

[221] Gruber, Daniel, *Rabbi Akiba's Messiah and the Origin of Rabbinic Judaism* (Hanover, NH: Elijah Publishing, 1999), p. 142.

[222] Fruchtenbaum, Arnold. *Yeshua: The Life of Messiah from a Messianic Jewish Perspective-Vol. 1.* Ariel Ministries, 2017, p. 104.
Also See Fiensy, *Jesus the Galilean,* pp. 147-148

[223] Ibid., p. 105.
Also See Braude and Kapstein, *Pesikta de-Rab Kahana* p. 502.

[224] Torah Club, *Chronicles of the Messiah*, First Fruits of Zion –*Volume 4* – Pg. 1090. In Yechiel Tzvi Lichtenstein's *Commentary on the New Testament: The Holy Gospel According to Mattai* we read, "His meaning is not, as some interpret, that they took [their position on the Sanhedrin] upon themselves unjustly to sit there; for if that were the case, the word "therefore" in the next verse would not be right: "Therefore do everything they say to you, observe and do." ...he means that they did rightly sit there; for even in the Torah (Deuteronomy 33:10), it says of the priests that "they teach your judgments to Jacob and your Torah to Israel," etc. Thus also (Deuteronomy 17:9): "You shall go to the priests and the Levites...and at their word, every dispute and every assault shall be [settled]" (Deuteronomy 21:5).

[225] Ibid., p. 1106

[226] Supersessionism or Replacement Theology holds that the Christian Church

JESUS IS JEWISH

has replaced or superseded the nation of Israel as the divine/elect people of God. From a Supersessionist viewpoint, the very fact that Israel continues to flail against Christianity is proof that the Jews are outside of the fold of God's people.

[227] Soulen, R Kendall. The God of Israel and Christian Theology. Fortress Press, 1996, p. ix.

[228] Richardson, Joel. *When A Jew Rules the World: What the Bible Really Says About Israel in the Plan of God.* Midpoint Trade Books, 2015, Kindle Edition, Location 410.

[229] Soulen, R Kendall. *The God of Israel and Christian Theology.* Fortress Press, 1996, p. 19.

[230] Ibid., p. 29 According to the traditional Christian standard canonical model, Israel, and the church both depend exclusively upon Christ for their soteriological significance. But Israel corresponds to Christ in a merely prefigurative and carnal way, whereas the church corresponds to Jesus Christ in a definitive and spiritual way. Hence Christ's advent brings about the obsolescence of carnal Israel and inaugurates the age of the spiritual church. The written Law of Moses is replaced by the spiritual law of Christ, circumcision by baptism, natural descent by faith as criterion of membership in the people of God, and so forth. As a result, carnal Israel becomes obsolete.

[231] Richardson, Joel. *When A Jew Rules the World: What the Bible Really Says About Israel in the Plan of God.* Midpoint Trade Books, 2015, Kindle Edition, Locations 229-242.

[232] Ibid., Kindle Location, pp. 229-242

[233] Horner, Barry E. *Future Israel: Why Christian Anti-Judaism Must Be Challenged: 3 (New American Commentary Studies in Bible and Theology).*

B&H Publishing, 2007, Kindle Edition, p. 5.

[234] Juster, Dan, and Keith Intrater. *Israel, the Church, and the Last Days*. Destiny Image, 2011, Kindle Edition, p. 66.

[235] Horner, Barry E. *Future Israel: Why Christian Anti-Judaism Must Be Challenged: 3 (New American Commentary Studies in Bible and Theology)*. B&H Publishing, 2007, Kindle Edition, p. 149.

[236] Ibid., p. 212

[237] https://www.google.com/webhp?sourceid=chrome- Accessed March 25, 2018

[238] Horner, Barry E. *Future Israel: Why Christian Anti-Judaism Must Be Challenged: 3*. New American Commentary Studies in Bible and Theology, B&H Publishing, 2007, Kindle Edition, p. 265.

[239] Rudolph, David J., and Joel Willitts. *Introduction to Messianic Judaism: Its Ecclesial Context and Biblical Foundations*. Zondervan, 2013, Kindle Edition, Locations 5447-5448.

[240] Horner, Barry E. *Future Israel: Why Christian Anti-Judaism Must Be Challenged: 3*. New American Commentary Studies in Bible and Theology, B&H Publishing, 2007, Kindle Edition, p. 255.

[241] Nanos, Mark D. *The Mystery of Romans: The Jewish Context of Paul's Letters*. Frontier Press, 1996, Kindle Edition, Locations 275-277.

[242] Ibid., Kindle Locations 2649-2652

[243] Ibid., Kindle Locations 2281-2282

JESUS IS JEWISH

[244] "Martin Luther 'The Jews and Their Lies'." *Jewish Virtual Library*, https://www.jewishvirtuallibrary.org/martin-luther-quot-the-jews-and-their-lies-quot Accessed July 15, 2018

One example: I had made up my mind to write no more either about the Jews or against them. But since I learned that these miserable and accursed people do not cease to lure to themselves even us, that is, the Christians, I have published this little book, so that I might be found among those who opposed such poisonous activities of the Jews who warned the Christians to be on their guard against them. I would not have believed that a Christian could be duped by the Jews into taking their exile and wretchedness upon himself. However, the devil is the god of the world, and wherever God's word is absent he has an easy task, not only with the weak but also with the strong. May God help us. Amen.

[245] Codex Justinianus 3.12.3.*History of the Christian Church,* translated by Philip Schaff, 5th ed., vol. 3, New York, 1902, p. 380, note 1.

[246] Hefele, Charles J. *A History of the Councils of the Church, Vol. 2*. Edinburgh, 1876, p. 252. [Online] Available at: https://media.sabda.org/alkitab-8/LIBRARY/HEF_HCC2.PDF. Accessed November 22, 2018

[247] *Faith of Our Fathers*. Ninety-third carefully revised and enlarged ed., p. 97. John Murphy Company Publishers, 1917 [Online] Available at: http://www.loyalbooks.com/download/pdf/Faith-of-Our-Fathers.pdf.

[248] Catholic Record of London, Ontario." *Catholic Record*, 1 Sept. 1923, https://archive.org/details/catholic-record-full.

[249] Heschel, Abraham Joshua. *Israel: An Echo of Eternity*. Farrar, Straus and Giroux, 1969. Kindle Edition, locations 130-131.

[250] "The Spanish Expulsion 1492." *Jewish Virtual Library.* https://www.jewishvirtuallibrary.org/the-spanish-expulsion-1492.

[251] Gager, John G. *The Origins of Anti-Semitism.* Oxford University Press, 1983, pp. 127-129.

[252] LeadershipU. "The Jews as the Christians Saw Them." *www.leaderu.com*, May 28, 2017, www.leaderu.com/ftissues/ft9705/articles/wilken.html.

[253] St. John Chrysostom, the archbishop of Constantinople, 398-407 CE.

[254] Morgan, Howard *So Deeply Scarred,* Kingdom Ministries, 2019, p. 57

[255] Martin Luther: 'The Jews & Their Lies'." *Jewish Virtual Library.* https://www.jewishvirtuallibrary.org/martin-luther-quot-the-jews-and-their-lies-quot

[256] Morgan, Howard. *So Deeply Scarred.* Kingdom Ministries, 2019, p. 57

[258] We Remember. *CIU - Christians in Universities.* https://www.ciunow.org/insights/we-remember/.

[259] Stern, David H., Ph.D. *Restoring The Jewishness of the Gospel: A Message for Christians Condensed from Messianic Judaism.* Messianic Jewish Publishers, 2009, INgrooves, Kindle Edition, locations 146-149.

[260] Ibid., Kindle Location 278

Made in the USA
Las Vegas, NV
22 April 2024

88991690R00203